AD Biogra
Stargell W ✍ P9-CCS-377

Peterson, Richard F. Pops : the Willie Stargell
story   9001077826

DISCARDED BY
MEAD PUBLIC LIBRARY

POPS

The Willie Stargell Story

POPS

The Willie Stargell Story

Richard "Pete" Peterson

TRIUMPH
BOOKS

Copyright © 2013 by Richard Peterson

No part of this publication may be reproduced, stored in a retrieval system, or transmitted, in any form by any means, electronic, mechanical, photocopying, or otherwise, without the prior written permission of the publisher, Triumph Books LLC, 814 North Franklin Street, Chicago, Illinois, 60610.

Library of Congress Cataloging-in-Publication Data
Peterson, Richard F.
  Pops : the Willie Stargell story / Richard Peterson.
     pages cm
  Includes bibliographical references.
  ISBN 978-1-60078-800-0
1. Stargell, Willie, 1941- 2. Baseball players—United States—Biography. I. Title.
  GV865.S76P48 2013
  796.357092—dc23
  [B]   2013002393

This book is available in quantity at special discounts for your group or organization. For further information, contact:
    Triumph Books LLC
    814 N. Franklin Street
    Chicago, Illinois 60610
    (312) 337-0747
    Fax (312) 280-5470

Printed in the United States of America

ISBN 978-1-60078-800-0

Design by Sue Knopf

Photos courtesy of the Pittsburgh Pirates unless otherwise noted

9001077826

For the Peterson Family

Contents

Foreword

On what would have been one of the greatest days in Willie Stargell's life, he was unable to participate. His serious illness prevented him from attending the unveiling of a 12-foot bronze statue of his likeness at PNC Park on April 8, 2001—and the next day he passed away—which happened to be Opening Day at the new ballpark.

I remember Willie for his power, great arm, and good speed. You just knew he'd be a good one. In spring training in Fort Myers there were two fields—one for minor leaguers and one for the major leaguers. All the major leaguers would go over to the fence and watch him hit on the other field. The sound of the ball off his bat was completely different than anyone else on the team. He was something special.

It was not easy for Willie. He experienced segregated living conditions and racial threats in the early days but his determination to make it to the big leagues helped to keep his focus and he ended up with many Pirate records, and the ultimate honor—membership in the Baseball Hall of Fame.

Despite being hampered with major knee surgeries during his career, he never quit and never complained. The first 8½ seasons of his career were played at Forbes Field, which was at the time the major league's most spacious ballpark. Moving to Three Rivers Stadium in 1970 provided him the opportunity to add to his career totals. I believe one of the enjoyable things to watch was when he came to bat, intimidating pitchers even before they delivered the ball by pin-wheeling the bat in rhythm with their delivery.

Willie's first sight of Pittsburgh was in September 1962. Upon exiting the tunnel into downtown, he's said he felt that Pittsburgh was reaching out to welcome him. The nickname "Pops" was given to him when he was the leader of "the Family." He led by example and wore the mantle of leadership, which he assumed reluctantly after Clemente's death.

Stargell was a proud man whose entire career was with the Pittsburgh Pirates. His final appearance on the field in Pittsburgh was at the end of the 2000 season, the final game at Three Rivers Stadium, where he was joined by many of his former teammates.

Willie said that I taught him the value of patience and consistency and because of that he was able to survive baseball. It was a pleasure to play with and be associated with Willie, a fellow Hall of Famer. He was a good guy from the beginning and didn't change through the years, except that he talked a lot more in later years than he did in 1959.

I know you will enjoy reading about his career and life in baseball in this book.

—Bill Mazeroski

Introduction

I've been a Pittsburgh Pirates fan for 65 years. I grew up a Pirates fan and I'll die a Pirates fan. When I saw my first game at Forbes Field in 1948, I fell in love with slugger Ralph Kiner. Pirate fans didn't have many reasons to cheer in those days, but we did have one of the greatest home run hitters in baseball history. Fans often stayed to the bitter end of yet another Pirates loss, just to see Kiner bat one more time.

In 1960, the year I turned 21, Pirate fans fell in love with a new hero when Bill Mazeroski, with one swing of the bat, transformed the Pirates from perennial losers to World Series champions. Mazeroski was the perfect hero for a city with a working-class mentality and deep ethnic roots. Winning the World Series was like a fairy tale come true for Pirate fans, and Mazeroski was our Polish Prince Charming.

In 1971, I was a Pirates fan in exile. When the great Roberto Clemente thrilled the nation in the 1971 World Series, I was teaching at Southern Illinois University. It was a moment of great pride for Clemente, who felt that he'd never won the respect of the baseball world, including the fans of his own team. A little more than a year later, Clemente died in a plane crash while delivering aid to earthquake victims in Nicaragua. Those of us who found it difficult to embrace Clemente now felt that his tragic death had enriched and elevated our lives.

In 1979, the year of Pops Stargell and the "We Are Family" Pirates, my wife Anita and I were busy raising our own family. I was able to watch

Stargell's heroics on television, but, after more than a decade removed from my hometown, I didn't really feel as close to Stargell as I did to Kiner, Mazeroski, and Clemente. The Pirates' come-from-behind World Series victory was thrilling, but shouting with joy in my living room in Makanda, Illinois, with three baffled little kids looking at their crazy father wasn't the same as dancing in the streets with thousands of Pittsburgh fans.

When Don Gulbrandsen of Triumph Books asked me to write a book on Willie Stargell and the Pittsburgh Pirates, I was honored and more than happy to do it. Don's invitation was a gold-and-black opportunity to go back in time and relive one of the most glorious periods in Pirates history. It was also, however, a second chance to get to know Willie Stargell. Over the years, he'd become a legendary figure in Pittsburgh and one of the most beloved figures in the city's sports history.

I agreed to do the book, but decided that I'd concentrate on Willie Stargell's life in baseball rather than write a biography. Willie Stargell lived to play baseball and was most at home in the Pirates clubhouse. He was "Pops" to an extended baseball family that included his teammates and devoted Pirate fans. One of the heroes of the 1971 World Series, Pirates pitcher Steve Blass once said that there were no small hugs from Willie Stargell. During his career, Stargell managed to encompass an entire city in his embrace.

The Stargell that I encountered in my research and interviews was truly a baseball hero. He had great natural talent, but he had to overcome childhood hardships, racial hatred in his early playing days, and career-threatening injuries to reach baseball greatness. There was also, of course, the other Willie Stargell, who was a towering and inspirational presence in the clubhouse and a warm-hearted and fun-loving friend, as well as a leader capable of carrying his team to great victories and a humanitarian dedicated to fighting sickle cell anemia.

Tony Bartirome, who grew up in Pittsburgh, was a slick-fielding first baseman in his playing days with the Pirates. His friendship with Willie Stargell began in 1959, when he taught a raw rookie the rudimentary skills of playing first base. In 1967, when Bartirome became the Pirates' trainer, he spent many hours, season after season, helping Stargell overcome the physical pain from his damaged knees so he could play the next day.

Tony Bartirome was the first of Stargell's friends and teammates that I interviewed for this book. At the end of our conversation, he said that he'd give me a million dollars if I found someone who didn't like Willie Stargell. After listening to so many people who knew Pops over the span of his life in baseball, I'd like Tony to know that his money is safe.

CHAPTER 1

Why Won't Time Stand Still?

Shortly after midnight on Monday, April 9, 2001, with the historic opening of PNC Park just several hours away, Willie Stargell, Pittsburgh's beloved "Pops," died at the age of 61. In the Pirates clubhouse, just before the start of the Opening Day ceremonies, All-Star catcher Jason Kendall remembered the night before. "It was thundering really, really hard last night, and then all of a sudden it stopped.... I guess it was right around then...it's really strange now. Three Rivers gone. New season. You just know Pops is watching us."

Just two days earlier, the Pirates had dedicated a 12-foot statue of Willie Stargell at the left-field entrance to PNC Park. When Nellie Briles, Stargell's teammate on the 1971 World Series championship team and president of the Pirates Alumni Association, and Chuck Tanner, manager of the 1979 World Series champions, with the help of Pirates owner Kevin McClatchy and general manager Cam Bonifay, unveiled the statue, those in attendance saw, in bronze and larger than life, what had struck fear in National League pitchers for nearly two decades: a powerful and coiled Stargell, bat drawn back, waiting defiantly for the pitcher to deliver the baseball.

Sprinkled on the statue's circular flat base, as if they had fallen from the statue, were images of "Stargell's Stars," those embroidered felt gold stars that Pops had passed out to his teammates to wear on their baseball caps when they had done something to help the team win a game. The base was encircled by an engraved quotation of Stargell's first impression of Pittsburgh when the Pirates called him up with Bob Veale in late 1962: "Last night, coming in from the airport, we came through the tunnel and the city opened up its arms and I felt at home."

Once the statue was unveiled, Chuck Tanner stepped forward, reached up, and rubbed his hand over Stargell's batting grip. Pointing to the way the little finger of the statue's lower hand overlapped the knob of the bat, he said, "That's incredible. That's how he held the bat right there." Moved almost to tears, Tanner told those at the ceremony, "Time goes so fast…. Why won't time stand still so we can still watch Willie play?"

. . .

The historic Opening Day at PNC Park for the 2001 season should have been a welcomed relief and joyous occasion for the thousands of long-suffering fans streaming over the Roberto Clemente Bridge to the Pirates' new home. After a painful defeat in the 1992 playoffs and the loss of the reigning National League MVP Barry Bonds and former Cy Young Award–winner Doug Drabek to free agency, the Pirates, for the second time since the 1980s, were in a downward spiral of losing seasons, declining attendance, and mounting debt. Going into 2001, the Pirates had struggled through eight consecutive losing seasons.

The earlier downward spiral had begun in the early 1980s, just a few years after the "We Are Family" Pirates won the 1979 World Series. By the end of the 1985 season, the franchise's fortunes had deteriorated to the point that *The Sporting News* ran a story called "The Pirate Problem," just as the Pirates were about to finish in last place and end the season with a dismal attendance of 735,900. The article blamed the decline on everything from the Rust Belt depression and the city's racial divisions to drug scandals and fan perceptions, provoked by mounting drug allegations and millionaire salaries, that the Pirate players were spoiled rotten. The front-page photograph in *The Sporting News* of empty seats at Three Rivers Stadium appeared under the banner, "Empty Seats, Empty Hopes."

Pittsburgh's baseball franchise, on the verge of moving to another city, was rescued in late 1985 from becoming the New Orleans Pirates when the Pittsburgh Associates ownership, a loosely organized group of local business and civic leaders, purchased the ballclub from the Galbreath family, owners of the Pirates since 1946. The new ownership group, thanks to the strong efforts of Mayor Richard Caliguiri, received concessions and loans from the city to keep the franchise afloat.

By the end of the 1980s, with an influx of new talent, the Pirates became successful on the field again, if not financially. From 1990 to 1992, the team collected three division titles, two National League Manager of the Year Awards for Jim Leyland, a Cy Young Award for Doug Drabek, and two MVP titles for Barry Bonds. The franchise, however, continued to lose money and started losing key players to free agency. By the end of the 1995 season, after the team finished nearly 30 games under .500 and attendance dropped for the first time since 1985 to under a million, the Pittsburgh Associates, facing a mounting debt of over $22 million, put the franchise up for sale.

After 109 years, Pittsburgh was on the verge of losing, for the second time in a span of 10 years, the fabled franchise of Honus Wagner, Pie Traynor, Bill Mazeroski, Roberto Clemente, and Willie Stargell, until Sacramento-based Kevin McClatchy formed a limited partnership on February 14, 1996, and became the owner of the Pittsburgh Pirates. Once McClatchy took over, however, he made it clear that the only thing that could keep the Pirates franchise in Pittsburgh was a new ballpark.

McClatchy faced immediate criticism from the press, questioning his baseball and business experience and, above all, his commitment to keeping the Pirates in Pittsburgh; but one of his first moves showed both a shrewd business sense and an understanding of Pittsburgh's baseball tradition. He convinced an estranged Willie Stargell to return to the Pittsburgh Pirates organization after an 11-year exile.

McClatchy, regarded as an outsider when he took over the Pirates, told reporters, "When you got a Willie Stargell out there, you hear from a lot of people. A lot of people said I should talk to Willie.... It sounded like a good idea. We spent some time on the phone." That phone call led to McClatchy making a job offer to Stargell more than a decade after he left the Pirates to join the Atlanta Braves. "Pittsburgh is Willie's home, and he should be at home with the Pirates."

When Stargell first received McClatchy's phone call, he admitted that he had mixed feelings, "I felt good, yet I felt kind of strange. I hadn't entertained it. I had almost forgotten about the idea of coming back." But, in February 1997, after telling the Pirates that he "would love to come back, but only in a meaningful position," Stargell returned to the Pirates as an assistant to general manager Cam Bonifay. Remembering the first time he saw the Pittsburgh skyline back in 1962 and felt at home, he said, "They say sooner or later good things will take place. I realize now that it's not how long it has taken, but that it is here. It couldn't have come at a more perfect time."

• • •

Before Willie Stargell retired as a player at the end of the 1982 season, he wanted his picture taken with each member of the Pirate family. He then wrote a personal message on each photo. In his dedication to the outspoken Jim Rooker, one of the heroes of the 1979 World Series, he wrote, "You have always stood for what is right, what is real. I admire the man in you. I'm glad I know you. Willie." In his dedication to Sally O'Leary, the Pirates' assistant director of media relations at the time, Stargell wrote, "Sally—Don't think for one moment because you're not seen that much that we don't realize how much you meant to all of us. I just want to say, God bless people like yourself. A real joy over the years for me. Willie."

Stargell's elegant farewell and departure from the Pirates family, however, was short-lived. During spring training of the following year, Stargell returned to the Pirates "to perform various duties" as an assistant to executive vice president Harding "Pete" Peterson. Stargell admitted at the news conference that the one thing he wanted "more than anything else" was to stay in the Pirates organization. After kiddingly saying that "they want me to bat leadoff and steal 80 bases," he told reporters that he hoped to spent most of his time helping younger players, "Just more or less be a friend to kids in the minor leagues."

Stargell, however, missed the camaraderie of being a player. At spring training in Bradenton in 1984, he walked into the clubhouse, looked around, and shouted, "Where's the music? You've got to have music. This isn't the Pirates clubhouse." A year later, in June 1985, the Pirates, coming off their first last-place finish since Stargell's retirement and desperate for a morale boost, asked the popular Stargell to give up his work in the minor leagues and return to the Pirates clubhouse as one of Chuck Tanner's coaches. At the time, the Pirates were 18–37, the worst record in major league baseball, and were averaging 10,100 fans at their home games. But Stargell was eager to help and hoped he could bring "some fun" again to Pirates baseball, "and that's what the game is all about."

When Stargell first took the field at Three Rivers as the Pirates' first base coach, he received a standing ovation from the fans. The move was the only bright spot in a disastrous season in which the Pirates eventually lost 104 games (third worst in franchise history at the time). With attendance dropping to the lowest full-season figure in nearly 20 years, the Galbreath family, owners of the Pirates for nearly 40 years, decided they wanted out.

One of the first casualties of the Galbreath decision was Chuck Tanner, who'd been the manager of the Pirates since 1977 and led them to a World Series championship in 1979. As the 1985 season came to an end and the Pittsburgh Associates took over ownership of the franchise from the Galbreath family, Tanner told his coaching staff, which included Stargell and two other veterans of Pirate championship teams, Bob Skinner and Grant Jackson, that the new owners wanted a fresh start, so he wouldn't be asked back to manage the Pirates next season.

It was a dark moment for Pirate fans, who remembered how Tanner, who'd grown up in New Castle, just 45 miles from Pittsburgh, continued to manage the Pirates in the 1979 World Series after his mother died the morning before Game 5. With the Pirates trailing 3–1 in the Series, Tanner told his players, "My mother is a great Pirates fan. She knows we're in trouble, so she went upstairs to get some help." For Stargell, who believed that Tanner's courage in staying with the team was the inspiration for the Pirates comeback victory in the World Series, the decision to fire Tanner was unfathomable and unforgivable.

When Stargell accepted the offer to become a Pirates coach, he saw it as the first step toward becoming a manager. As a player, he said he'd never manage, but after two years of working part-time in the Pirates minor league system with young players, he decided that if he waited a few more years "I would not have to worry about managing the guys I played with and not have to contend with managing friends." He even agreed to manage a team in Puerto Rico during the winter in preparation for managing in the major leagues.

But, if Stargell held any hope that the new Pirate ownership would turn to him to lead the Pirates, it was quickly dashed when Jim Leyland, a third-base coach with the Chicago White Sox under manager Tony LaRussa, was named the team's new manager. When the Atlanta Braves organization subsequently signed Tanner to a contract to manage its ballclub for the 1986 season, Stargell, still hoping to become a big-league manager, gladly accepted an offer from Tanner to join him as a Braves coach. It was the first time Stargell would not be a part of the Pirates organization since signing his first professional contract in 1958.

• • •

In 1988, after Stargell, now wearing a Braves uniform, was elected to the Baseball Hall of Fame, he rejected an offer from the Pirates to hold a Willie Stargell night in his honor. Stories began circulating in the local press that Stargell had asked for financial compensation, ranging from an expensive car to a share of gate receipts, but Stargell made it clear that he still remembered his last days with the Pirates: "The last dealing I had with these Pirates, the new Pirates, the last thing they said to me was 'You're fired.' I haven't heard a word from the new Pirates since and now they want to honor me."

A few weeks later, when the Braves came to bat in the first inning of their next series with the Pirates at Three Rivers Stadium, there were fans who, remembering Stargell's rejection of a night in his honor and believing the recent stories about him, booed the Pirate legend as he stood in the third-base coaching box. Chuck Tanner was so upset with the mistreatment of one of the greatest heroes in Pirates history that he told reporters after the game, "I wanted to go out there at that moment and pat that guy on the back 10 times. You don't boo Willie Stargell.... I felt so bad for the guy."

Shortly after the incident, Braves general manager Bobby Cox, unhappy with the team's 12–27 start in 1988, decided to fire Chuck Tanner, but the Braves eventually offered Willie Stargell a job as a roving batting instructor in the Braves organization. Tanner went on to work in the front office for the Milwaukee Brewers and Cleveland Indians, before returning to the Pirates in 2007 as a senior advisor. Stargell, who never received an offer to manage, despite the strong recommendation of Tanner, remained with the Braves until he received the call from Kevin McClatchy that brought him back to the Pirates family.

When he was inducted into the Baseball Hall of Fame on July 31, 1988, Stargell made no mention of the booing incident. After thanking his family, friends, teammates, coaches, and managers, he turned to the issue of honor and told the crowd that the "greatest honor" of his baseball career came when he first arrived in Pittsburgh.

• • •

Besides the booing incident, Stargell had suffered another indignity while he was wearing a Braves uniform. Before the start of a game at Three Rivers, an arrogant Barry Bonds approached Stargell and yelled, "Get out of here, old man!... They forgot about you in Pittsburgh. I'm what it's all about now." Failing to see any humor in Bonds' taunting, Stargell told him, "Boy, you'd better get some more lines on the back of your baseball card before you can talk to me like that."

The irony of the confrontation was that by the time Bonds added a few more lines to his baseball card, including two National League MVP awards in 1990 and 1992, he'd become one of the most unpopular players ever to wear a Pirates uniform. Just before the Pirates home opener in 1992, after a much publicized confrontation between Bonds and manager Jim Leyland during spring training, *Pittsburgh Post-Gazette* columnist Bob Smizik wrote a column pleading with Pittsburgh fans, who'd booed Willie Stargell just four years earlier, not to boo Barry Bonds.

In the 2001 season, Bonds, with an inflated body to match his inflated ego and now in the Giants uniform worn by his father, Bobby, and his godfather, Willie Mays, became the home run king of the steroid era by shattering Mark McGwire's single-season record. Mourning Pirate fans attending the historic home opener at PNC Park at the beginning of the 2001 season, however, had a far different slugger in their hearts and minds as they made their way to the ballpark. Not only was their Pops Stargell the greatest home run hitter in Pirates history, he'd had so much raw power that often his home runs, without a boost from steroids, were so prodigious in flight and distance they became the stuff of baseball legend. Hall of Fame–pitcher Don Sutton once said Stargell "doesn't just hit pitchers, he takes away their dignity."

• • •

The powerful Stargell began his career with the Pirates while they were still playing at cavernous Forbes Field. In his nine seasons at Forbes Field, Stargell hit seven of the 18 home runs that cleared the right-field roof, a feat first accomplished in 1935 by Babe Ruth (it was the last home run of Ruth's career) and later by another Yankee slugger, Mickey Mantle, in an exhibition game. He also hit a towering homer over the massive scoreboard in left field, an amazing accomplishment for a left-handed batter.

Stargell played nearly half of his career at Forbes Field, a ballpark so unfriendly to home run hitters that in 1947, Hank Greenberg, one of the greatest right-handed power hitters in baseball history, refused to play for the Pirates until they shortened the distance in left field. The Pirates accommodated Greenberg by fencing off a bullpen area in left field that became known as Greenberg Gardens.

Shortening the distance in left field from 365 to 335 feet wasn't much of an aid for Greenberg in his one season with the Pirates, but it helped slugger Ralph Kiner who "was ready to throw in the towel" the first time he saw Forbes Field; but with the help of the Greenberg Gardens, Kiner actually tied or led the National League in home runs for seven consecutive seasons. When Branch Rickey traded Kiner in the middle of the 1953 season, the Pirates immediately dismantled Greenberg Gardens, but the

National League, pointing out that there was a rule against altering the dimensions of a ballpark in the middle of a season, made them put it back up the next day and wait until the season was over.

The first time Stargell stepped into the batting cage at Forbes Field after he was called up near the end of the 1962 season, he looked out at a daunting task for a left-handed hitter whose power was to the outfield gaps. The left- and right-center-field alleys were over 400 feet away, and the ballpark's deepest recess, slightly to the left of dead-center field, was 457 feet from home plate. Center field was so deep that the ground crew rolled the batting cage out to the 457 mark, and it rarely interfered with a game.

If Stargell was a pull hitter he might have taken some comfort in peering out at Forbes Field's right-field dimensions, but only until he looked up. When Pirates owner Barney Dreyfuss first built the ballpark back in 1909, right field, at 376 feet, was actually longer than left field. When he added the right-field grandstand in 1925, he had to shorten right field to 300 feet down the line; but Dreyfuss, no fan of the long ball, put up a 30-foot wire screen on top of the right-field wall. So any home run hit by Stargell to right field had to be lofted over a combined wall-and-fence barrier of over 40 feet.

Considering the vast dimensions and heightened barriers at Forbes Field, it's not surprising that Stargell's first hit in the major leagues was a triple not a homer, though it came close to being an inside-the-park home run. On September 20, 1962, in a game at Forbes Field against the Cincinnati Reds, Stargell hit a long drive past Reds center fielder Vada Pinson that rolled into the deepest part of the ballpark. When Stargell reached third base, Pirates coach Frank Oceak, wanting the rookie to have his first big-league home run, sent him home, but Stargell was easily thrown out at the plate.

Stargell went on to hit more home runs at Forbes Field than any other left-handed hitter in Pirates history, though, even with bad knees and a chronic weight problem, he was also routinely among the Pirates leaders in triples during his early years at Forbes Field. He'd end his career tied with his childhood idol Stan Musial with 475 home runs, but had he played in a home run–friendly ballpark, like Wrigley Field, he'd have likely hit well over 500 home runs, easily surpassing the lifetime totals of legends like Mel Ott, Ernie Banks, Mickey Mantle, and Ted Williams, and perhaps even challenging Willie Mays' mark of 660 home runs.

• • •

Willie Stargell first learned of the Pirates organization's plan to build a statue in his honor while he was in a North Carolina hospital in the summer of 1999, nearly 20 years after he dazzled the baseball world in the National League playoffs and the World Series, and less than two years before his death from a stroke. Once one of the most powerful and feared hitters in baseball, the diabetic Stargell was now suffering from heart problems and kidney failure, the result of a long history of high blood pressure.

When Kevin McClatchy visited Stargell in the hospital to tell him about the statue, he brought pictures of the Pirates hero with him. Stargell was thrilled by the news and, after going carefully through the pictures, picked out the one the Pirates would use for the statue. McClatchy remembered, "I can still hear him saying, 'I want them showing me hitting the stuffing out of the ball.'"

Though seriously ill, Stargell managed to return to Pittsburgh in late September 2000 for the Pirates final three games at Three Rivers Stadium. He wept at the Friday afternoon news conference on September 29, when the Pirates made the official announcement about plans for the Stargell statue, but, despite his failing health, he still had his impish sense of humor. Gazing at a model of his statue, he said, "Oh man. I was happy just playing here. Now you've got me where I'm going to be scaring little kids for years to come."

But he was clearly overwhelmed by the honor and several times invoked the memory of his teammate, Roberto Clemente, whose statue would be moved from Three Rivers Stadium to PNC Park, in time for the unveiling of Stargell's statue. He then added a comment about the pride of wearing a Pirates uniform that would become a part of the Stargell legend. He said that even after a game he handled his now sweaty and dirty uniform with respect. "I was so proud that not once did I throw my uniform on the floor. That's how particular I was."

When he was introduced at the pregame ceremony on Friday night, Stargell received a standing ovation from the 40,128 fans in attendance. *Pittsburgh Post-Gazette* columnist Ron Cook wrote, "It's a wonder the old stadium didn't implode then, the ovation was so thunderous." Steve Blass, one of the heroes of the 1971 World Series and now a broadcaster for the Pirates, was the emcee for the pregame ceremonies honoring Stargell that night. When the Pirates handed him a script, Blass asked if he could add a personal note. In 1973, Blass, at the most successful point in his pitching career, had inexplicably lost the ability to control the baseball (a condition that became known as Steve Blass disease). That night he told the crowd, "I'd just like to say that when I was going through my problems late in my career, no one stood taller for me than Willie Stargell.... Willie, I'll never forget that." When Blass and Stargell embraced at home plate, Blass recalled, "What a hug.... Of course, there were no small hugs from Willie Stargell."

On Sunday, October 1, 2000, the Pirates played their final game at Three Rivers Stadium and lost to the Chicago Cubs 10–9, before 55,351 fans. It was the largest regular season crowd in Three Rivers history. While the loss may have been disappointing to Pirate fans, it wasn't totally unexpected. The Pirates ended the 2000 season with a record of 69–93. But the fans who came to Three Rivers that day were there to honor the glorious 1970s and the memories of Pirate players and teams that had been champions in 1971 and 1979.

Before the game, Dock Ellis, who pitched the first game at Three Rivers in 1970, threw out the ceremonial first pitch to Manny Sanguillen. Sister Sledge, whose song "We Are Family" was adopted by the 1979 world champion Pirates team, sang "The Star-Spangled Banner." During the seventh-inning stretch, Steve Blass, with more enthusiasm than talent, belted out "Take Me Out to the Ball Game." After the game, more than two dozen former Pirates poured in through an opening in the center-field fence under a cascade of confetti and were introduced to a roaring crowd. The former Pirates included relief-ace Kent Tekulve, who threw the last pitch in the seventh-and-deciding-game victory in the 1979 World Series, and now was ready to throw the ceremonial last pitch at Three Rivers to a waiting Jason Kendall.

But just before Tekulve delivered the baseball, Art McKennan, the legendary Pirates public address announcer, whose career began at Forbes Field back in 1948, boomed out the introduction of Willie Stargell. It was a thrilling moment for Pirates fans as the player who'd hit the first Pirate home run and the most home runs at Three Rivers came slowly out of the dugout. Decked in the gold-and-black regalia of the 1979 championship team, Stargell needed help to make it to the pitching mound, but once there, he was warmly embraced by so many of his teammates from the 1971 and 1979 World Series teams, including Manny Sanguillen, John Candelaria, Nellie Briles, Grant Jackson, and his old manager Chuck Tanner.

It had to be heartbreaking for Pirate fans and his old teammates to watch their beloved Pops, his once powerful body now frail and dying, deliver the last pitch at a doomed Three Rivers, but they were grateful for one last chance to hold him in a collective and individual embrace. A beaming Stargell, who once had one of the strongest throwing arms in baseball, comparable to that of Roberto Clemente, could barely bounce the ball to a waiting and concerned Jason Kendall; but the act was uplifting for cheering fans and friends who knew that Willie Stargell, the Pirate who had provided so many clutch hits and dramatic moments for them in the past, had found the courage and the strength to come to Pittsburgh to unite them and thrill them one last time.

• • •

April 9, 2001, is an unforgettable day in Pirates history, and a day of deep and mixed emotions for Pirate fans. Paul Meyer, who was covering the Pirates for the *Post-Gazette* at that time, remembered, over a decade later, how he was driving to PNC Park to help with the coverage of the ballpark's opening when he heard on his car's radio that Stargell had died. As he was walking to the ballpark, he was struck by the beautiful sunny weather, perfect for a home opener, and how strange it was that Stargell had died on the eve of such a momentous event.

Steve Blass, who just months ago had embraced Stargell on the playing field of Three Rivers Stadium, remembered first learning about Roberto Clemente's death at 4:00 AM and going straight "to Willie's house." Now, three decades later, learning of Stargell's death, he wasn't "sure where to go this morning." Tim Foli, Stargell's teammate in 1979 and now a coach for the Cincinnati Reds, the Pirates' Opening Day opponent, remembered Stargell's big hits, "but it was his presence that was so powerful. He made everyone feel important."

The *Post-Gazette*'s Gene Collier had been assigned the task of writing Stargell's obituary months earlier when a cut on his finger "had triggered a progressive, inexorable shutdown of Stargell's system." Collier was finishing a pregame radio interview in Firewaters, a bar across the street from PNC Park, when he heard that Stargell had died. When he wandered out into the street and looked in the direction of Stargell's statue, Collier saw Kevin McClatchy standing next to the statue and, with great difficulty, delivering the Pirates' public statement on Stargell's death: "Willie battled.... He was pretty sick, but he battled, and Willie Stargell made it to Opening Day."

As the fans began arriving at PNC Park, they brought flowers to place at the base of Stargell's statue and signs to leave at the statue or carry into the ballpark. One sign read "Win One for Pops," while another, in remembrance of the 1979 "We Are Family" World Series champions, declared, "It's a sad day—there's been a death in the family." Someone placed a placard at the base of Stargell's left foot that paid tribute to the way Pirates broadcaster Bob Prince called a Stargell home run: "We kiss you goodbye." Other fans simply stood with bowed heads at the statue and wept before finally and sadly entering the ballpark.

Inside PNC Park, just minutes before the beginning of the Pirates' home opener against the Cincinnati Reds, an overflow crowd witnessed a four-minute video tribute to Stargell that ranged from the historic to the playful. Pirate fans saw the heroic Stargell once again driving a ball over a leaping Ken Singleton for the two-run homer that gave the Pirates the lead and the margin of victory in Game 7 of the 1979 World Series, but they also watched an impish Stargell who, while inexplicably trying to steal second base, signaled to the umpire for a time out when the ball arrived well ahead of him.

After a moment of silence, the crowd began shouting and applauding, while Pirates players—wearing a No. 8 on their caps in tribute to Stargell—and Reds players stood with bowed heads along the foul lines. Alan Robinson of the Associated Press noted that "Reds coach Ken Griffey, who opposed Stargell in innumerable important Reds-Pirates games in the 1970s, could be seen wiping a tear from his eye. Cincinnati first baseman Sean Casey, a Pittsburgh native who estimates he saw 15 to 20 games a year in Three Rivers as a youth, also seemed visibly moved."

After the roar finally died down, Kevin McClatchy, wearing a Pirates jersey with Stargell's No. 8 on its back, threw out the ceremonial first pitch. In a prepared statement, the owner who fought so hard for the new ballpark and brought Stargell back home to Pittsburgh, said, "We find it ironic that one of the greatest days for the franchise, the opening of PNC Park, is also one of the saddest." Baseball commissioner Bud Selig, in attendance at the game, added, "Willie's on-field accomplishments are legendary. What's more important is that he was such a decent human being."

Once the ceremony was over, the Pirates and the Reds played the first game in the history of PNC Park. The Reds won that day, just as they'd defeated the Pirates in the first game ever played at Three Rivers Stadium. The Reds' Sean Casey, who grew up in nearby Upper St. Clair, fittingly hit the first home run at PNC Park, but it was the player who hit the first Pirate home run at Three Rivers, the player who passed out gold stars to his Pirate teammates for their accomplishments, who was the brightest star at PNC Park that afternoon.

• • •

On Saturday, April 14, 2001, family and friends gathered at St. Paul's Episcopal Church in Wilmington, North Carolina, to pay their last respects to Willie Stargell. Among those in attendance were Hall of Famers Hank Aaron and Joe Morgan, as well as many of Stargell's old teammates, including Steve Blass, Nellie Briles, Dock Ellis, Al Oliver, and Manny Sanguillen from the 1971 world championship team, and Dave Parker, John Candelaria, Jim

Bibby, and manager Chuck Tanner from the 1979 world champions. Bob Veale, who drove Stargell to Pittsburgh in his beat-up Studebaker when they were called up from Columbus in 1962 and remained a close friend, was also there. In their lapels, many of them wore a gold star with an "S" in the center.

Manny Sanguillen, who was devastated by the death of Roberto Clemente, and now had to endure the loss of another close friend, showed up in a Stargell No. 8 baseball shirt. He was so grief-stricken that he could barely talk to reporters, but he did manage to tell them, "We were all like little kids around Willie. He was the big kid. He talked, and we listened. I learned so much from him." After the service was over, he joined Dave Parker, Dock Ellis, and Willie Stargell Jr. as pallbearers. He was also photographed escorting Stargell's daughter Kelli to a funeral car.

The service, which lasted 95 minutes, emphasized Stargell's humanity rather than his achievements on the field. National Baseball Hall of Fame president Dale Petroskey said that, "If there was a Hall of Fame for humanitarians, he would be a Hall of Famer in that one, too…. Come to think of it, I'm sure he made that Hall of Fame earlier this week." Recalling Stargell's passing just hours before the opening of PNC Park, Petroskey disagreed with those who said the timing was unfortunate. "Everyone who cared about the Pittsburgh Pirates was in the ballpark or was tuned in on radio or television. Willie was in everyone's thoughts. They celebrated more than his career that day. They celebrated his well-lived life. And after they did a video tribute to him on the scoreboard, the ovation felt like it was never going to end."

Joe Morgan, both a longtime friend going back to their early ball-playing days in California's Bay Area, and one of Stargell's chief adversaries when the Pirates and Cincinnati's Big Red Machine were battling for National League supremacy, echoed the feelings of so many of Stargell's former teammates and rivals, when he told mourners, "Willie Stargell was my hero…. He's the reason I wore No. 8." He remembered, when they first met in Oakland after the 1960 baseball season, that Stargell, at that time a minor leaguer with the Pirates, encouraged Morgan, just coming out of

15

high school, to follow his dream even though most scouts thought he was too small to play major league baseball.

It was the first of many times in Stargell's career when he became a father figure to younger players, including the outspoken Dock Ellis, who loved him as a father and visited Stargell several times during his illness, and Dave Parker, who idolized him as a player and a role model. After the service was over, Parker, who once described Stargell as a "man's man" and claimed you could hear the whooshing sound made by Stargell's pinwheeling bat, remembered the Stargell who took him under his wing: "He took good care of me." Ellis, in an earlier tribute, had described Stargell as a "friend to one who had no friends, a constant reminder that once a Pirate always a Pirate."

Another of those younger teammates, Al Oliver, was the only Pirate to speak at the service. An ordained deacon like his father and grandfather, Oliver had stayed in touch with Stargell through his illness and recalled that, even though his voice kept getting weaker and weaker, Stargell never complained and remained positive to the end. He reminded his teammates of the valuable lesson Pops expressed in the clubhouse through both his words and conduct: "Pittsburgh was something special. So was Willie Stargell. On behalf of all of his teammates, we feel very honored to have played with such a great player.... Our society was full of hatred, but he taught us about love.... He proved that people of different races and backgrounds can come together for one common purpose. In our case, that was winning."

But it was Joe Morgan, delivering his final words in tears, who spoke the most eloquently about the respect and adoration that Stargell earned both on and off the field: "Willie Stargell is still my hero. He is loved like we would all like to be loved. As I leave here now, I would just like to say to him, 'Rest in peace, my friend.'" At the end of the service, his widow, Margaret Weller Stargell, took roses out of a bouquet resting on top of the casket to give to Stargell's children. Stargell's body was then taken for burial to a quiet spot on a hill overlooking a small inlet, not far from the ocean.

• • •

A few days later there was one more service held for Willie Stargell, this time at St. Mary of Mercy Church in Pittsburgh, where an overflow crowd of nearly 1,000 mourners came, in the words of Bishop Donald Wuerl of the Pittsburgh Catholic Diocese, to "remember and celebrate" Stargell's life. While the loss of Stargell was painful, Bishop Wuerl reminded those in attendance that they were present to relive "the memories and highlights of a life that touched us all.... He was more than an extraordinary player. He was a good person."

Standing in front of the altar, where a simple black-and-white photo of a beaming Willie Stargell was on display beside flowers in the shape of a cross, speaker after speaker, including Kevin McClatchy, Steve Blass, Al Oliver, and Chuck Tanner, expressed their feelings for Stargell. McClatchy called Stargell "truly one of the most loved sports heroes in the city's history." Blass reminded those in attendance that Stargell always told his teammates that the best way to play the game was "to listen to the umpire. He says, 'Play ball' not 'Work ball.'" Al Oliver simply talked about Stargell's grace on and off the field: "Willie Stargell was a winner in every aspect of the word."

But the most touching words of the day came from Chuck Tanner. Calling Stargell "the greatest player" he'd ever known, Tanner said Stargell "had dancing feet. He had the heart of a lion. He had the arm of a cannon. He was fun and he was funny. He was the strongest of men, the greatest of heroes." Looking up at the heavens as he had looked up at Stargell's statue several days earlier, Tanner closed by saying, "I'm hoping to manage you again some day."

CHAPTER 2

I Felt at Home

There are four statues of Pirate greats at PNC Park, and each honors the hero of a seventh-and-deciding-game victory in the World Series. The careers of the four Pittsburgh sports legends span nearly 10 decades of Pirates baseball played on ballfields ranging from the flood-prone Exposition Park, where Honus Wagner played his first games in Pittsburgh, to the pastoral Forbes Field and the donut-shaped Three Rivers Stadium, where Bill Mazeroski, Roberto Clemente, and Willie Stargell thrilled Pirate fans.

The Pirates dedicated the first statue on April 30, 1955, just two weeks after Roberto Clemente made his major league debut at Forbes Field. The statue honored Honus Wagner, the hero of the 1909 World Series and one of the first baseball legends, along with Ty Cobb and Babe Ruth, to be inducted into the Baseball Hall of Fame. The statue stood in Schenley Park, just beyond Forbes Field's left-field wall, until it was moved in time for the opening of Three Rivers Stadium on July 16, 1970.

A few days before the Pirates hosted the 1994 All-Star Game at Three Rivers, Roberto Clemente, who'd turned the 1971 World Series into his own personal showcase, joined Honus Wagner when the Pirates dedicated a statue to Clemente, a little more than two decades after his tragic death in a New Year's Eve plane crash while trying to fly emergency supplies to the victims of an earthquake in Nicaragua. The Wagner and Clemente statues remained at Three Rivers Stadium until they were moved to PNC

Park in time for the unveiling, on April 7, 2001, of the statue honoring Willie Stargell, the hero of the 1979 World Series, just a few days before the ballpark's historic opening.

On September 5, 2010, the Pirates added a fourth statue to their baseball pantheon when Bill Mazeroski joined Wagner and his former teammates, Clemente and Stargell, at PNC Park. One of the greatest fielding second baseman in baseball history, Mazeroski won the 1960 World Series against the New York Yankees with a dramatic home run in the bottom of the ninth in the seventh and deciding game. In a *Pittsburgh Post-Gazette* poll, readers voted Mazeroski's home run as the most dramatic moment in the city's sports history, even surpassing Steeler Franco Harris' "Immaculate Reception" in a 1972 playoff game against the Oakland Raiders.

Taken together, the four statues, while honoring the Pirates' greatest heroes, also stand as symbols of a Pittsburgh forged in the flames and smoke of its steel mills, proud of its ethnic, working-class neighborhoods, but often divided, not just by its flowing rivers, but its racial prejudices and divisions. Two of the statues, those of Wagner and Mazeroski, represent the Pittsburgh of immigrant families and their hard work, determination, and hope for a better life for their children. Two others, those of Clemente and Stargell, however, are reminders that Pittsburgh, the city of many bridges, has struggled in its modern history to accept racial minorities and needed its sports heroes to inspire the building of bridges for integration and unity as well as for commerce and industry.

• • •

The legendary Honus Wagner was Pittsburgh's first sports hero and, in many ways, he was perfect for the Smoky City at the beginning of the 20th century. Born of German immigrant parents, Wagner, at the age of 12, joined his father and three older brothers in the coal mines of Carnegie, Pennsylvania, located just to the south of Pittsburgh. He also worked briefly in a steel mill before his remarkable baseball skills gave him the opportunity to play professional baseball.

Part of Wagner's appeal to Pittsburgh's working-class fan base was his immigrant background, but, for all his skills, he also had a body that seemed better suited for working in coal mines and steel mills than for playing baseball. Baseball Hall of Fame sportswriter Fred Lieb, who saw Wagner play, described him as "a bulging squat giant with a wide, thick chest, and legs so bowed one could have rolled a barrel through them. Weighing around 190 pounds, he had big awkward-looking feet, and great gangling gorilla-like arms. The arms hung loosely around him from his wide shoulders and from the ends dangled great hams of hands."

Yet the clumsy-looking Wagner played the game with a fierce determination and toughness reflective of both the hard life of his early years and the working-class character of his hometown. His most memorable moment came in the 1909 World Series against the Detroit Tigers when Ty Cobb, leading off first base, yelled, "Hey, Kraut Head, I'm comin' down on the next pitch." When Cobb took off for second base, Wagner caught the throw from catcher George Gibson and jammed the baseball into Cobb's face: "I guess I wasn't too easy about it, 'cause it took three stitches to close up his lip."

In 1933, after Fred Lieb wrote that Honus Wagner, now approaching 60, was nearly destitute, the Pirates hired Wagner as a coach. Another future Hall of Famer, Paul Waner, who played for the Pirates at the time, remembered the thrill of watching the legendary and revered Pirate play shortstop during batting practice: "When he did that, a hush would come over the whole ballpark, and every player on both teams would just stand there like a bunch of kids, and watch every move he made. I'll never forget it."

Wagner remained with the Pirates organization until 1952 when poor health forced him to step down. He died on December 6, 1955, just several months after attending the unveiling of his statue.

• • •

In the introductory notes to his Pulitzer Prize–winning *Fences*, a play that uses baseball as a backdrop for the struggles of African Americans in the 1950s, August Wilson wrote about the immigrant waves that came to Pittsburgh in the late 19th and early 20th century and the way the city embraced and nourished them and offered opportunities to each immigrant "limited only by his talent, his guile, and his willingness and capacity for hard

21

work." But Wilson, a Pittsburgh native, also wrote that "the descendants of African slaves were offered no such welcome or participation." While they also came to Pittsburgh "strong, eager, and searching," the city "rejected them and they fled and settled along the river and under bridges in shallow ramshackle houses made of sticks and tar-paper."

Wilson modeled Troy Maxson, his main character in *Fences*, on Negro League–legend Josh Gibson, a hitter so powerful he became known as the "black Babe Ruth." He set his play in 1957, 10 years after Jackie Robinson crossed baseball's color line. Once Robinson put on a Dodgers uniform, major league teams began the slow process of integrating their rosters. For older Negro League players like Maxson, however, and his real-life counterpart, Gibson, who played in Pittsburgh for the Homestead Grays and the Pittsburgh Crawfords, integration had come too late.

In Wilson's play, Maxson, after spending a career in the Negro Leagues hitting a baseball over fences, is now building a fence around his property in Pittsburgh's segregated Hill District, where Wilson grew up. Bitter at not having the opportunity to play major league baseball, he sees the fence as a way of protecting his family against a hostile world, run by whites, that crushed his dream and still haunts his spirit. Maxson, at one point, after being told the Pirates had won five games in a row, angrily replies that he has no time for the Pirates: "Got an all-white team. Got that boy... that Puerto Rican boy...Clemente. The boy could be something if they give him half a chance...A colored boy got to be twice as good before he get on the team."

• • •

Maxson's harsh judgment in 1957 of major league baseball as still "all-white" and hostile to black ballplayers may seem to ignore Jackie Robinson's dramatic breakthrough 10 years earlier, but the integration of baseball moved at a very slow and reluctant pace in the late 1940s and well into the 1950s. Going into the 1953 season only six of the 16 major league teams had at least one black player on their rosters. Some owners claimed they were willing to sign a black player if they could find one as talented and "clean-living" as Jackie Robinson, while others, like Fred Saigh of the Cardinals, complained that St. Louis was really a Southern city with a white fan base that would never tolerate a black player.

It wasn't until 1954, the same year of the Supreme Court's *Brown v. Board of Education* decision, that baseball finally began moving toward complete integration. Five more teams added black players to their rosters, including the St. Louis Cardinals, under the new ownership of beer baron August Busch. The four remaining holdouts included the defending World Series champion New York Yankees and the Boston Red Sox. In 1959, the Red Sox became the last team to integrate its roster, 12 years after Jackie Robinson played his first game.

The most unusual twist in 1954 involved the integration of the Pittsburgh Pirates. The Pirates general manager in 1954 was the baseball pioneer Branch Rickey, who after making baseball history by signing Jackie Robinson to a Brooklyn Dodgers contract, had been ousted by Dodger ownership at the end of the 1950 season. In 1954, Rickey became the first general manager in baseball history to integrate two major league teams when he brought African American Curt Roberts up from the minors to the Pirates' major league team. Rickey thought he'd found another Jackie Robinson in Roberts, a slick-fielding, clutch-hitting, base-stealing second baseman. When he signed Roberts to a contract, however, Rickey warned him that when he crossed the color line in Pittsburgh he would encounter the same abuse Robinson faced from white fans and teammates.

While the signing of Roberts excited Pittsburgh's black community, he faced racial taunts from the stands and isolation in the clubhouse. His wife Christine remembered, "If he was treated good by his teammates, if he had been close to anyone, I would have seen some of them in my house.... But there were never any white players invited to my house in Pittsburgh. That tells me Curtis wasn't treated very well." Unlike Jackie Robinson, who used racism as motivation on the ballfield, Roberts struggled emotionally and played poorly in his first year with the Pirates. A year later, after he appeared in only six games, the Pirates shipped him to the minor leagues. He returned to play 31 games for Pittsburgh in 1956 but spent the rest of his career in the minor leagues.

• • •

Curt Roberts was still in the starting lineup when the Pirates opened their 1955 season in Brooklyn, but he was on the bench when Roberto Clemente made his major league debut three days later on April 17, 1955, at Forbes Field against the Dodgers. The reports coming out of spring training claimed that the 20-year-old Clemente was a natural, one of the most gifted athletes to put on a Pirates uniform. He was so electrifying that Al Abrams, the longtime sports columnist for the *Pittsburgh Post-Gazette*, wrote, "Every time we looked up there was Roberto showing his flashing heels and gleaming white teeth to the loud screams of the bleacher fans."

Pittsburgh fans and sportswriters may have been thrilled by the rookie's spring training performance, but Abrams' description of Clemente's "gleaming white teeth" suggested they were aware of more than his extraordinary baseball skills. A native of Puerto Rico, Clemente believed that the same fans and writers who recognized his talent from the very beginning of his career also took note of his dark skin and his Hispanic heritage.

While Clemente did have trouble speaking English, Pittsburgh sportswriters made his way of speaking sound ignorant and stupid. When Les Biederman of the *Pittsburgh Press* asked Clemente if he had a girlfriend, Biederman gave his Pittsburgh readers this example of Clemente's "broken English"—"No me no married yet. Not even girl. I still young. Plenty of time. I make big ligues first. One theeng I like 'merica, new autos. Buy myself new auto. Whee!"

During his early years, the flashy and temperamental Clemente was often portrayed in the press as a "Puerto Rican hot dog," too "hot-headed" and full of himself; but when he had a great season in 1960 and the Pirates won the World Series he thought he'd finally earned the respect of the public and the press. When, however, he received little support from sportswriters for the National League MVP Award—won by his teammate Dick Groat—he felt race, not talent, had determined the outcome. An angry and bitter Clemente went on to play baseball in the decade of the 1960s as if it were a form of punishment for those who had insulted his pride and spirit.

When Clemente, at the age of 37, dazzled the baseball world with his brilliant performance in the 1971 World Series, he felt he had finally, at the twilight of his career, proven his greatness: "Now people in the whole world know how I play." Facing many of the same reporters who had slighted him for years and had now come to praise him, he turned instead to the television cameras, and speaking in Spanish, addressed his parents, "*En el dia mas grande de mi vida, les pido sas bendiciones*" ("On this, the proudest day of my life, I ask for your blessing.")

When Clemente died in a plane crash less than two years later while on a mercy mission, the condolences and blessings for the hero of the 1971 World Series came from everywhere, including the White House and the Baseball Hall of Fame. There were so many mournful farewells in Pittsburgh, but the most telling was on a neon sign perched on a hillside looming high over Pittsburgh that read, "Adios Amigo Roberto," a fitting, if ironic, tribute to the player once mocked for his "broken English."

• • •

When a contingent of Pirates, including Willie Stargell, arrived in Puerto Rico several days after Clemente's death, they took a chartered bus to Clemente's home. Their guide that day was Luis Rodriguez-Mayoral, a close friend of the Clemente family who would develop a reputation as a Latin American baseball historian, scout, and broadcaster. He remembered that when the bus struggled going up a steep hill leading to the Clemente house, Stargell, who had remained silent throughout the trip, suddenly spoke out: "'Man, if this bus can't make it the least we can do is walk.' Right then and there, Willie became the leader of the Pirates."

On July 8, 1994, the Pirates held a ceremony for the unveiling of a 12-foot bronze statue in honor of Clemente at Three Rivers Stadium. The statue, funded for the most part by public donations, showed Clemente about to drop his bat, while gazing out at the flight of one of his 3,000 hits. At the statue's feet, encased in glass, were three bases filled with dirt from Santurce Field in Puerto Rico, Forbes Field, and Three Rivers Stadium, where Clemente achieved his greatest glory.

25

Among the members of the Pirates family in attendance at the dedication were Willie Stargell, who'd become the dominant figure in the Pirates' clubhouse after Clemente's tragic death, and Manny Sanguillen, Clemente's closest friend among his Pirate teammates. Stargell told the crowd, "Roberto now has a statue exactly where it belongs, where he gave his heart and soul." Sanguillen added, "I want to wake up and see him here as if he was never gone."

The Clemente family was also in attendance at the dedication, and it was his two sons who spoke most eloquently and touchingly about what was in the hearts and souls of those who now realized what a blessing it had been to watch Clemente play baseball. Instead of addressing the crowd, an emotional Roberto Clemente Jr. spoke to the spirit of his father. "Some people say the good die young, but some people live forever, and Dad, you're one of them." Clemente's son Luis added, "I know he's looking down today.... and is very proud."

· · ·

The careers of Roberto Clemente and Willie Stargell span the entire Civil Rights Movement, but their approach to the political and racial turmoil of that time was as different as their personalities. Clemente, with his fierce pride, was closer in disposition and conduct to Jackie Robinson. The more successful he became, the more Clemente felt the need and responsibility to speak out for black athletes, both African American and Latin American.

In the 1960s, Clemente also became a role model for the Pirates' younger black players, ranging from Willie Stargell and Manny Sanguillen to Al Oliver and Dock Ellis. When Martin Luther King was assassinated in 1968, Clemente played a pivotal role in the Pirates' refusal to play its season opener in Houston and the team's eloquent public pronouncement that the Pirates, who had 11 black players, more than any other team in the major leagues, were acting out of respect for "what Dr. King has done for mankind." Baseball responded to the Pirates' action by delaying the opening of the 1968 season until after Martin Luther King's funeral.

Stargell, with his engaging and infectious personality, was closer, in his approach to racial issues, to Willie Mays, who charmed rather than defied the public and the press. He'd spent his teenage years in the 1950s growing up in Alameda, California, just across the bay from Oakland, where he lived in the projects with his mother, stepfather, and half sister, and attended the racially-mixed Encinal High School. He didn't experience any racial threats or confrontations in the projects or at school, but, in an interview in the early 1970s, he recalled, "I was exposed to everything any black kid gets to see. Pimps and con men, dope pushers, and gamblers. I could easily have taken the wrong road, but I always wanted to be a baseball player."

The irony of Stargell seeing baseball as the road out of the projects was that his first real encounter with racial hatred came once he signed a baseball contract in 1958 with the Pittsburgh Pirates. In 1959, his first year playing professional baseball, he was assigned by the Pirates to their Class D farm club in San Angelo, Texas. After the team struggled with poor attendance, it moved in midseason to Roswell, New Mexico, where it finished out the season.

The San Angelo/Roswell team played in a league made up of small cities and towns in midwestern Texas and southeastern New Mexico. It wasn't the deep South where so many black players, like Hank Aaron and Billy Williams, played minor league baseball in the 1950s on their way to the major leagues, but it was a part of the country where segregation was still the norm. It was an area that Stargell described in his autobiography as made up of "dust, ghost towns, pueblos, plazas, and a deep racial hatred toward Negroes."

Stargell had to deal with experiences that were common well into the 1960s for black minor league ballplayers. He was segregated from his white teammates except when they were together on the ballfield. He boarded with black families at home and on the road stayed at motels in the black section of town. When he was on the road, he either ate, out of sight, in the kitchens of diners or, if he wasn't allowed in the diner, had to wait on the bus until a white teammate brought food out to him.

But the worst of Stargell's experiences with racism in his first year in the minor leagues also became the most defining moment of his baseball career. It would test his courage and his commitment to playing baseball and his attitude and approach to racial issues and relationships for the rest of his life.

Walking to the ballpark for an afternoon game in Plainview, Texas, Stargell was suddenly confronted by a white man carrying a shotgun in his hands. In his autobiography, he vividly describes the encounter: "He didn't fool too long with me. He stated his purpose up front. 'Nigger,' he told me, 'if you play that game tonight, I'll blow your brains out.'" Stargell was terrified by the incident but he played baseball that night. Three years later he would step to the plate in a Pittsburgh Pirates uniform for his first at-bat in the major leagues.

Thirty years later, just after being named the Most Valuable Player in the 1979 World Series, he'd go back to that first year in the minor leagues and a time when he felt his "life was on the line." In an interview with Eliot Asinof, author of the acclaimed *Eight Men Out*, he remembered, "What hit me then was my surprise at the prejudice." When Asinof, who had encountered prejudice in the minor leagues as a Jewish ballplayer, said, "It can make a man bitter," Stargell responded. "You have to come to a decision as to who you are and what you intend to do with your life.... I knew I had to make the big decision—either play ball or go back home. But I wanted to play ball so badly, I said to myself I wasn't going to let nothing interfere. Nobody had the right to stop me from trying.... I just wanted to play ball."

• • •

In 1955, Roberto Clemente's rookie season, the Pittsburgh Pirates had just begun the integration of their roster. In December of that year, the Civil Rights Movement, led by Martin Luther King, took one of its biggest steps in Montgomery, Alabama, when Rosa Parks refused to give up her seat on a bus to a white man. When Willie Stargell began his rookie season in 1963, after a brief call-up toward the end of the 1962 season, the Pirates had several black players on its roster, including Earl Francis, their starting pitcher on Opening Day. In late August of that year, Dr. King stood in front of a crowd of over 200,000 participants in the March on Washington rally and delivered his "I Have a Dream" speech.

The increasing integration of the Pirates that coincided with America's advancing Civil Rights Movement included, thanks to Pirates super-scout Howard Haak, both African American and Hispanic ballplayers. Haak, who was deeply involved in scouting Roberto Clemente for Branch Rickey, scoured Latin America and the Caribbean for the Pirates during the 1950s and 1960s and discovered a number of future World Series teammates of Stargell, including Manny Sanguillen, Omar Moreno, and Rennie Stennett. Sanguillen spoke for scores of Hispanic ballplayers signed by Haak when he said, "We thank God for him."

By the late 1960s, the Pirates had more black players on their roster than any other team in the major leagues. During the 1967 season they came close to making baseball history when they fielded an all-black starting lineup with the exception of pitcher Dennis Ribant. The Pirates manager that year was Harry Walker, the brother of Dixie Walker, who 20 years earlier had asked the Dodgers to trade him because he didn't want to be on the same team with Jackie Robinson. The Dodgers accommodated Walker by trading him to the Pittsburgh Pirates in 1948.

• • •

A racially divided Pittsburgh hardly seemed like a city suited for breaking down color barriers, but, thanks to its major university sports teams, it had already witnessed two historic racial breakthroughs in the '50s. In 1950, Duquesne basketball star Chuck Cooper became the first African American drafted by an NBA team when the Boston Celtics selected him in the second round and as the 12th overall pick in the draft. Six years later, when Pitt took the field against Georgia Tech in the 1956 Sugar Bowl, Pitt's outstanding defensive back Bobby Grier became the first African American to play in the Sugar Bowl.

Four years after the Pirates came close to fielding an all-black lineup, they joined Duquesne and Pitt in achieving a racial milestone in sports history. On September 1, 1971, manager Danny Murtaugh, just before a night game with the Philadelphia Phillies, filled out a lineup card with the names of nine black ballplayers. It was a major landmark in baseball, but it was hardly noticed in Pittsburgh because a pressman's strike had shut down the city's major newspapers on May 15 and wouldn't be settled until September 19.

Black players filled nearly half of the Pirate roster spots in 1971, so the all-black lineup also drew little attention from the players who were making history that night. Al Oliver, who started at first base, said he wasn't aware of the historic event because the Pirates usually had several black players in the starting lineup. Around the third or fourth inning, however, Oliver said that second baseman Dave Cash yelled over, "'Hey, Scoop, we got all brothers out here.' You know I thought about it, and I said, 'We sure do!'"

The Pirates went on to win the World Series in 1971, the franchise's first since 1960. When the Pirates took the field against the Yankees in the seventh and deciding game of the 1960 World Series, Roberto Clemente was the only black player in the starting lineup. The only other black players who appeared for the Pirates in the 1960 World Series were Gene Baker and Joe Christopher. The veteran Baker, who, with Ernie Banks, integrated the Chicago Cubs in 1953, was used by Murtaugh as a pinch hitter in three of the seven games. Christopher appeared as a pinch runner in three games.

In the 1971 World Series, when the Pirates took the field for the seventh and deciding game against the Orioles, they had 10 black ballplayers on their roster and seven in the starting lineup. Only pitcher Steve Blass and first baseman Bob Robertson were white. When Pulitzer Prize–winning author David Halberstam searched for the year that was the turning point in racial relationships for baseball and the country he selected 1964. In his critically acclaimed *October 1964*, he celebrated the World Series champion St. Louis Cardinals for overcoming their early resistance to Jackie Robinson and becoming a fully integrated ballclub at a time when America was undergoing its civil rights revolution. In 1971, the World Series champion Pirates, without any notice from historians, achieved another landmark in baseball, by doubling the 1964 Cardinals in the number of black players on their World Series roster.

• • •

In 1971, Willie Stargell had the greatest season of his career. After coming into spring training in great physical shape, he set a major league record with

11 home runs in April. His performance was so impressive that he attracted attention from sportswriters from around the country. Dick Young, writing for the *New York Daily News*, described Stargell as "this year's man of April, this year's man to run humpty-six games ahead of Ruth's schedule, and two asterisks ahead of Roger Maris." When asked the reason for his success, Stargell replied, "No new stance, no new bats, just this new figure."

Hitting in the friendlier confines of Three Rivers Stadium, Stargell continued to challenge the home run records of Ruth and Maris until his chronic knee problems flared up in July. Playing in pain, he still managed to hit a league-high and personal-best 48 home runs and drive in 125 runs while leading the Pirates to the division title, though he struggled in the playoffs and the World Series. After the Pirates won the World Series, Stargell, believing that the player who helped his team the most deserved the honor, fully expected to be named the National League's Most Valuable Player.

The announcement that the Cardinals' Joe Torre had won the National League MVP Award came when Stargell was in the hospital recuperating from knee surgery. Like Clemente in 1960, Stargell was stunned by the announcement. "It was like a ton of bricks hitting me. I was disappointed and let down." When Clemente went through the same situation in 1960, he believed that the color of his skin and his heritage had cost him the honor. Stargell preferred to think otherwise, at least in public. "Though the postseason is not supposed to be considered when choosing a player for the league's MVP, I'm sure my poor showing in the playoffs and World Series cost me the award."

When Clemente didn't win the National League MVP award in 1960, he went on to play inspired baseball for the rest of the decade. He also publicly criticized the press for stereotyping black athletes, both African American and Latin American, and became a team leader in the Pirates clubhouse. In 1966, he became the first Latin American to win the National League MVP Award and *The Sporting News* Player of the Year. He also became involved in raising money for charities, and in 1970, when the Pirates honored him with a special night, he asked that the event also be used to raise money for Pittsburgh's Children's Hospital. After his triumph in the 1971 World Series, he announced plans to build a Sports City in Puerto Rico for children.

When Stargell didn't win the National League MVP Award in 1971, he, like Clemente, went on to play some of the best baseball of his career. He hit more home runs in the 1970s than any other player in the major leagues. After Clemente's death, he also, reluctantly, became the leader in the Pirates clubhouse and became a father figure for younger Pirates. During that period Stargell also became more active in Pittsburgh during the off-season in working with minorities, something he'd begun as early as the late 1960s when he did volunteer work with the Job and Youth Corps, in conjunction with the Pittsburgh's War on Poverty movement. He told Les Biederman, in a 1968 interview for *The Sporting News*, that he'd spent some time talking to teenagers living in the Hill District. "I asked them why they'd drop out of school and they said they couldn't go to classes without breakfast. Their parents had no money to give them for lunch, either.... The only clothes they had were on their backs.... I'd like to spend some time with them and show them how to get more out of life. I feel I owe it to them."

• • •

Stargell's reason in 1968 for wanting to work with black teenagers in Pittsburgh's Hill District most likely went back to the rioting that occurred there after the assassination of Martin Luther King. After King's death, the Hill, one of the most impoverished areas in the city and with a black population of over 95 percent, exploded with fire bombings and looting. After two days of rioting, the *Pittsburgh Post-Gazette* reported that nearly 1,000 arrests had been made and several people had suffered gunshot wounds. Pennsylvania governor Raymond Shafer closed the state's liquor stores and ordered the National Guard to Pittsburgh. Mayor Joseph Barr imposed a curfew on the city and ordered residents—to little immediate effect—to stay in their homes after dusk.

The rioting had no direct effect on the Pirates. After the brief postponement for King's funeral on April 9, they opened their season on April 10 in Houston. It did, however, threaten the Civic Arena, which was built in the Lower Hill at the base of Pittsburgh's Golden Triangle downtown area in the early 1960s after hundreds of black families were evicted from their homes. Two weeks after the rioting, it was where the ABA's Pittsburgh Pipers, a team with four black starters, including the controversial Connie Hawkins, hosted the first game of the league's playoff finals on their way to the ABA championship. In "An Unforgettable Team That Pittsburgh Forgot," Chris Elsey noted that, oddly, when only 2,665 showed up at the arena for the game, Pittsburgh sportswriters ignored the after-effect of the riots on attendance: "Instead journalists lashed out at readers for shunning the Pipers."

The most visible sign of Stargell's growing commitment to the residents of the Hill District came two years after the rioting, when he invested in former Pittsburgh Steeler Brady Key's All-Pro Chicken franchise and opened a restaurant just before the beginning of the 1970 season that became popularly known as "Chicken on the Hill, With Will." To promote the restaurant, Stargell offered free chicken to anyone in the restaurant waiting for an order when he hit a home run.

The flamboyant Pirate broadcaster Bob Prince loved the idea, and when Stargell came to the plate would yell out, "Spread some chicken on the Hill, Will." On one occasion, in a critical game, with the score tied in the ninth, Prince blurted out, as Stargell walked to the plate, "We need some chicken here and send the Gunner the bill." When Stargell connected, people, assuming that Prince was paying for anyone even near the restaurant, came pouring in for their free chicken. The bill for all the free chicken handed out that night, which Stargell delighted in giving to Prince, was for $400.

◆ ◆ ◆

After the 1970 season was over, Stargell was part of a group that made a USO-sponsored tour to visit the troops in Vietnam. The group included Pirates broadcaster Bob Prince, teammate Mudcat Grant, and Baltimore Orioles Eddie Watt and Merv Rettenmund. He was devastated by what he saw during the trip, especially when he visited the hospitals and talked to so many soldiers who had lost their limbs or were suffering from severe burns all over their bodies. He also became keenly aware of the struggles of the

Vietnamese people. Mudcat Grant remembered waking up at 5:30 AM and seeing Stargell standing at their hotel window, staring out at "the women of Saigon, outlined in the moonlight, huddled on the streets, trying to sleep, their small children pressed between them, protected from the night cold." Stargell told Grant, "Makes you think, doesn't it.... I'll never complain again."

Stargell's determination to help the black community in Pittsburgh had taken a personal and dramatic turn even before he left for Vietnam. During the 1970 season, he discovered that his oldest daughter, Wendy, after a series of tests to determine why she was having fainting spells, was diagnosed with the sickle-cell anemia trait. The vulnerable condition of his daughter, combined with the horrors he had witnessed on his tour of Vietnam, convinced him it was time to reach out beyond the struggles of minorities in Pittsburgh.

When Dock Ellis, after suffering fainting spells during the 1971 season, announced that he, too, had the sickle cell trait, the Pirates' team physician, Joseph Finegold, told the press that it was a non-fatal condition "which has some of the symptoms of sickle-cell anemia." In *Dock Ellis in the Country of Baseball*, Donald Hall described sickle cell anemia itself as "a fatal disease, which occurs almost exclusively among black people. If you have sickle-cell anemia, you may not hope for a long life." Hall also pointed out the importance of education in preventing the disease: "Sickle cell anemia is a recessive trait. It is easy enough to identify people who have the trait by examining their blood. If two trait-carriers reproduce, chances are they will reproduce doomed children."

While concerned about the vulnerability of his child to a disease that sportswriter Dick Young once called "the leukemia of blacks" because it was most commonly found in African Americans, Stargell launched a campaign that in the 1970s would most define his efforts to help the black community. In 1971, he started the Black Athletes Foundation for Sickle Cell Research to raise money for research and treatment, but also to publicize the disease and educate members of the black community to the importance of being tested for the sickle cell trait.

Stargell, along with 32 athletes, including Connie Hawkins and two of Pittsburgh's most outspoken sports figures, Dock Ellis and ABA star

John Brisker, donated $1,000 each to begin the campaign, then recruited prominent black musicians to help with their message. One of the organization's first events in Pittsburgh was a fair held to test blacks for the sickle cell trait. It also set up tents at various sporting venues to test for the sickle cell trait. When Congress began its debate on appropriating funds for finding a cure for sickle cell anemia, black ballplayers, including Stargell and Ellis, testified and then signed autographs for the congressional committee members.

• • •

In an interview Stargell gave to *Ebony* magazine just after the 1971 World Series, he reiterated what he told Les Biederman in early 1968: "Black ballplayers should be responsible to the black community.... They should be visible to the kids in the ghetto." During the turbulent 1970s, Stargell, appointed team captain when Mazeroski retired after the 1972 season, became a dominating presence in the Pirate clubhouse and on the field. He was also increasingly active and visible in organizing sickle cell anemia charitable events, including a celebrity bowling tournament featuring many of Pittsburgh's brightest sports stars. His Willie Stargell Bowling Tournament for sickle cell anemia started out in 1972 as a modest affair held at North Versailles Bowl, but, largely due to the popularity of Stargell, it quickly blossomed into a major celebrity and charity event. In the 1970s, Pittsburgh sports fans could watch or bowl with Steeler and Pirate Super Bowl and World Series heroes as well as some of baseball's brightest stars, like Joe Morgan and Reggie Jackson. Even Satchel Paige showed up at one tournament to sign autographs.

At the end of the 1973 season, Stargell lost out to Pete Rose for the National League MVP Award, but, at the beginning of the 1974 season, he received the Roberto Clemente award, presented to the player "who best exemplifies the game of baseball on and off the field" for his work in combating sickle cell anemia. When Stargell received the award from Commissioner Bowie Kuhn, he said, "Of all the awards, this ranks No. 1 with me because it identifies with Clemente who always tried to help people."

At the end of the 1974 season, he received the Lou Gehrig Award given to "the major league player best exemplifying the ability and character of Gehrig" by the Phi Delta Theta fraternity at Columbia University, where Gehrig played his college baseball and was a member of the fraternity. In 1977, he was honored in Los Angeles with the Brian Piccolo Award for Humanitarian Services, awarded by the National Council of YMCAs. Stargell told Pittsburgh sportswriter Pat Livingston he was particularly pleased with the award because he could take his mother, who was living in Oakland, to the ceremony: "My mother never saw me get an award. All the awards I ever got were on the East Coast. She's the one who's really excited about this."

• • •

In 1979, after leading the "We Are Family" Pirates to a World Series victory, Stargell finally received the baseball award that had eluded him since 1971, but, after another controversial vote, he had to share the National League MVP honor with Keith Hernandez of the St. Louis Cardinals. Stargell easily outdistanced Hernandez in first place votes on the 24 ballots submitted by baseball writers, garnering 10 to only four for Hernandez. Four of the writers, however, in an act described by Hall of Fame writer Joseph Durso as "a mystery," didn't include Stargell on their ballots, even for 10th place.

Stargell learned of his selection while he was appearing at a luncheon in Dallas, Texas, held in support of his sickle cell anemia initiative. Lowell Reidenbaugh, the senior editor for *The Sporting News*, wrote that Stargell was "the epitome of grace and amiability" when he found out he had to share the honor because four sportswriters had left him off their ballots. Ignoring the political or racial implications, Stargell told the press, "I'm just happy for myself and happy for Hernandez. I know what type of player he is." Reidenbaugh reminded his readers that, given Stargell's role in leading the Pirates to the world championship, "Willie was a runaway winner" for *The Sporting News* Man of the Year honor. When *The Sporting News* editors met to make their selection, Stargell's name "was the first, last, and only named proposed."

Stargell received yet another top award when he was named the co-winner of the *Sports Illustrated* Man of the Year, an honor he happily shared with Pittsburgh Steeler Super Bowl MVP Terry Bradshaw. The cover of *Sports Illustrated*, with its photograph of a jubilant Stargell and Bradshaw, probably hangs in a frame in more beer joints in Pittsburgh than any other Pittsburgh sports photograph, with the exception of Mazeroski circling the bases after hitting his World Series–winning home run in 1960. The *SI* cover article by Ron Fimrite celebrated the role of Pops in bringing fans and the team together: "It was Stargell who continually reminded the fans that the Pirates were something special, a collection of individuals from disparate backgrounds and cultures who worked together out of respect and even love for one another. And like a benevolent schoolmaster he passed out gold stars to Pirates who performed above and beyond the call. The stars became badges of honor. The Pirates, he argued, were what the United Nations intended to be. It worked. The fans believed."

Stargell was also elected the 1979 Male Athlete of the Year by the Associated Press, easily outdistancing welterweight champion Sugar Ray Leonard. In Pittsburgh, he was the recipient of the Dapper Dan Man of the Year award, his second since sharing the Dapper Dan in 1971 with Danny Murtaugh and Roberto Clemente. At the banquet, manager Chuck Tanner described Stargell as "the most valuable person." At the banquet, Stargell avoided answering questions about his retirement from baseball, but he did hint that when his career was over, he'd consider becoming a manager under the right conditions.

What may have prompted Stargell's comment was the Cleveland Indians' firing of Frank Robinson during the 1977 season and the White Sox decision, after the 1978 season, not to bring back interim manager Larry Doby. Robinson, one of Stargell's adversaries in the 1971 World Series, had made baseball history in 1975—nearly 30 years after Jackie Robinson played his first game with the Dodgers—when he became the first African American to manage in the major leagues. The newly fired Doby was the first African American to play in the American League when he joined Bill Veeck's Cleveland Indians during the 1947 season.

• • •

Because of Stargell's leadership role in the campaign against sickle cell anemia, he garnered a number of honors as he contemplated his retirement, including an honorary doctorate from St. Francis of Loretto on April 15, 1980, for his humanitarian efforts. Stargell, who wore cowboy boots under his robe, said, "When I first heard of the award I could think of 42 reasons not to come. But when I heard it was going to be for what I did outside of baseball, I accepted. It's an honor because of what I've done for the community."

When the Pirates scheduled a "Willie Stargell Day" in July 1980 to honor Pops, he asked fans to bring a donation of food to help families of unemployed steel workers who'd lost their jobs during Pittsburgh's Rust Belt depression. In return, the 43,194 fans who came to the game received a felt "Stargell Star" like the ones he passed out to his teammates during the 1979 championship season. Among the gifts Stargell garnered that day was a $10,000 donation from the Pirates organization to the Willie Stargell Foundation, an outgrowth of his Black Athletes Foundation.

But perhaps the greatest honor Stargell received came shortly after his retirement when the Eastman School of Music at the University of Rochester invited him to join its touring 109-piece philharmonic in the world premiere of *New Morning for the World* by Pulitzer Prize–winning composer Joseph Schwantner. When asked to narrate a text taken from the writings and speeches of Martin Luther King Jr., Stargell responded, "I've always admired and respected Dr. King, and I can't think of a greater honor than to be asked to be a part of this."

The Schwantner composition had its premiere on January 15, 1983, Dr. King's birthday, at the Kennedy Center in Washington. It was also performed at the Academy of Music in Philadelphia, Carnegie Hall in New York, and Pittsburgh's Heinz Hall, before the tour ended on January 19 at the Eastman Center in Rochester, New York.

After the premiere of *New Morning for the World*, Jane Leavy, who would later write critically acclaimed biographies of Sandy Koufax and Mickey Mantle, wrote an article for the *Washington Post* that singled out and praised Stargell's performance. Noting that too often baseball's brightest stars squander the goodwill and affection of their adoring fans, Leavy wrote, "Then along comes Willie Stargell in white tie and tails, standing before a 109-piece orchestra and speaking the words of Martin Luther King on the 54th anniversary of the latter's birth."

At the end of the performance, Stargell's 20-year-old daughter, Precious, gave him a huge hug both in relief and celebration. Afterward, three stage hands, who wore Pirate caps for the occasion, received Stargell Stars for their caps. Stargell also gave gold stars to the conductor and each member of the orchestra. As for Stargell's own feelings, he believed that, like Martin Luther King, he began his life with a dream, and in delivering Dr. King's words, he reached "the top of the mountain."

* * *

For a city that prides itself on its immigrant, working-class heritage and cheers pierogi races at PNC Park, Bill Mazeroski is the perfect hero. Born in nearby Wheeling, West Virginia, into a coal miner's family, he grew up playing baseball in the small town of Tiltonsville in southeastern Ohio, before signing a contract with the Pittsburgh Pirates at the age of 17.

When the 19-year-old rookie joined the Pirates in 1956, Roberto Clemente was 21 and in his second year with the team. The two future members of the Hall of Fame would remain teammates until 1972, when Mazeroski retired at the end of the season and Clemente died tragically a few months later. Mazeroski and Clemente were in the prime of their careers when Willie Stargell joined the Pirates as a 22-year-old rookie near the end of the 1962 season. They were nearing the end of their careers in 1971 when Stargell, now in his prime, had the best season of his career and led the Pirates to the playoffs and World Series.

For years, Mazeroski's tattered glove was on display under glass at Cooperstown with a citation describing him as the greatest second baseman of his generation. It took nearly 30 years, however, before the veteran's committee, in 2001, selected him for the Baseball Hall of Fame, where he finally joined his teammates Roberto Clemente and Willie Stargell. At the induction ceremony, he gave baseball fans an emotional moment to rival his dramatic home run in the 1960 World Series. A minute or two into what he had described as "12 pages of speech," he was so overcome with emotion that he told the overflow crowd, "You can kiss these 12 pages down the drain. I want to thank all of my family and friends for making the long trek up here to hear this crap. That's it. That's enough."

Mazeroski joined Clemente and Stargell once again when a bronze statue immortalizing his joyful romp around the bases after his dramatic home run in the 1960 World Series was unveiled near PNC Park's right-field entrance on September 5, 2010, Mazeroski's 74th birthday. This time his former teammates, Pittsburgh fans, and his family didn't have that far to travel. Four of those teammates from the 1960 World Series, Bill Virdon, Roy Face, Dick Groat, and Bob Friend, joined Mazeroski's sons, Darren and David, and his grandson, Billy, in unveiling the statue, while Mazeroski and his wife, Milene, looked on from the speaker's platform.

When Mazeroski, described by Steve Blass as "a man of few words," spoke after the unveiling, he told everyone there that he didn't feel worthy of the statue. "Geez, how could anyone dream of something like this? All I dreamed of was being a major league player. I didn't need all of this." It was a dream he'd shared with Honus Wagner, Roberto Clemente, and Willie Stargell, whether they played their first baseball in the shadow of a steel mill, plantation, project, or coal mine.

Missing from the unveiling of the Mazeroski statue were his teammates Roberto Clemente and Willie Stargell, but they had been very much a part of his career. In 1971, Mazeroski told Pittsburgh sportswriter Phil Musick that he and Roberto Clemente were teammates "longer than bacon and eggs," and that he'd watched Clemente "grow up and mature." Mazeroski also noted that while Clemente sometimes upset people with his controversial comments, he admired Clemente's honesty and outspokenness. "You never have to guess where you stand with Clemente."

When Stargell joined the Pirates, he quickly learned that Roberto Clemente and Bill Mazeroski were team leaders both in their play on the field and their presence in the clubhouse. Over the early years of his career, they became his "most influential teachers." From Clemente, who later became one of his closest friends, he learned to be "proud of his profession." From Mazeroski he learned the value of "patience and consistency."

But perhaps the most important lesson Stargell learned from Clemente and Mazeroski came from observing their common decency. Clemente and Mazeroski may have lived their dream and become the stuff of dreams for generations of Pirate fans, but it was their ability to touch the humanity of those who admired them that transformed them into legends.

Near the end of the first decade of the 20th century, Honus Wagner gave working-class Pittsburgh a feeling of pride. A little more than 50 years later, Mazeroski brought a sense of joy to the city. A decade later, Roberto Clemente united Pittsburgh with his compassion and sacrifice. At the beginning of the 21st century, Willie Stargell reminded the city of the value of family. Their statues at PNC Park now stand as reminders of the way the four Pirate heroes, coming from such diverse and opposed backgrounds, brought Pittsburgh's communities, black and white, together in moments of triumph and tragedy through their greatness as ballplayers and their common humanity.

CHAPTER 3

A Tall, Skinny Kid

Wilver Dornell Stargell (his first name a combination of his father's first name, William, and his mother's middle name, Vernell) was born on March 7, 1940, in the small town of Earlsboro, Oklahoma. Earlsboro was founded in 1891 and named after James Earls, a local African American barber who served as an orderly for a Confederate general in the Civil War. Earlsboro began as a railroad town on the Choctaw Coal and Railroad line running from Seminole Nation into Oklahoma Territory, but, because it was located inside the "wet" Oklahoma Territory and next to the "dry" Indian Territory, it quickly became a saloon town.

Its population, after reaching about 500 residents, dropped to a few hundred during Prohibition, but the town was rescued and revived by an oil boom in 1926. Its population increased to a few thousand until the wells ran dry in 1932, and the boom turned into a bust. That didn't, however, stop the notorious gangster Pretty Boy Floyd from robbing the town's bank. Of Earlsboro's history, the *Daily Oklahoman* once wrote, it's "the town that whiskey built and oil broke."

In his autobiography, Stargell said he'd like to claim he "was the most famous athlete to emerge from Oklahoma," but he'd "be lying" because the great Jim Thorpe was born in Indian Territory on a former reservation near Earlsboro. The irony of Stargell's observation is that, while Stargell owed his fame to a long and successful career in baseball, Thorpe fell into disgrace because he played two summers of minor league ball when he was in college.

Less than a year after Thorpe won gold medals at the 1912 Stockholm Olympics in the pentathlon and decathlon and was celebrated as the best athlete in the world, the International Olympic Committee discovered that he'd played professional baseball prior to the Stockholm games. An All-American football player, Thorpe explained that it was common for college athletes to play professional baseball during the summer to earn a few dollars, but, unlike Thorpe, they used an assumed name to protect their amateur standing. But the IOC rejected Thorpe's appeal, declared him ineligible, removed his Olympic records, and, after he returned his gold medals, gave them to the second-place silver medalists.

• • •

In his autobiography, Stargell also claimed that "the best-remembered Oklahoman" to play for the Pirates in his "lifetime" was second baseman Johnny Ray, *The Sporting News* Rookie of the Year in 1982 and one of Stargell's favorite teammates in his last season before his retirement. Stargell, however, overlooked two Oklahoma brothers, both in the Baseball Hall of Fame, who had long careers with the Pirates and were still playing in Pittsburgh when Stargell was born in 1940.

Paul and Lloyd Waner, the Pirates' famed "Big and Little Poison," were born on a farm outside Harrah, Oklahoma, a small town near Oklahoma City. Older brother Paul once boasted, "You can spell that backward and forward." Paul also went to college at Ada, and, of course, also pointed out, "And you can spell that backward and forward, too."

Paul Waner was signed by a baseball scout who had never seen him play. The scout, who worked for the minor league San Francisco Seals in the pre-Rickey days when minor league teams were independent and not a part of a major league farm system, had gone on a bender while he was returning to the West Coast by train. When he arrived in San Francisco, the team wanted to know what had taken him so long. Remembering that a railroad conductor had told him about a college ballplayer at Ada who was dating his daughter, the scout lied and told them he'd discovered a baseball talent while passing through Oklahoma. To cover his "tracks" the scout wrote to Paul and asked for statistical information because he'd never seen him play and didn't even know if he was a right-handed or left-handed hitter.

The rest, of course, is the stuff of Pirates history. Paul signed a contract to play with the San Francisco Seals, and a few years later the Pirates purchased his minor league contract. He played his first season for the Pirates in 1926, and, after he recommended his younger brother Lloyd to the Pirates, they played together in the same outfield in the 1927 World Series against Babe Ruth's New York Yankees. By the time their careers were over, Paul and Lloyd had played 14 seasons side by side in the Pirates outfield. Paul, who became the seventh player in baseball history to reach 3,000 hits, was elected to the Baseball Hall of Fame in 1952. His younger brother Lloyd, who set a major league record in his rookie season for singles, was selected for the Hall of Fame by the Veterans Committee in 1967.

• • •

Willie Stargell, like Paul Waner, also traveled from Oklahoma to the Oakland Bay Area on his way to Pittsburgh and Cooperstown, but under entirely different circumstances and for entirely different reasons. Paul and Lloyd Waner's father, while a successful farmer, was also a former professional ballplayer. He actually turned down an offer from the legendary Cap Anson, arguably the greatest player/manager in the early history of baseball, to play for the Chicago White Stockings because he didn't want to leave the farm. He encouraged Paul and Lloyd to play baseball, but he also made them promise to set aside money from their signing bonuses so that, if their baseball careers didn't work out, they could go back to college and get a good education.

Willie Stargell's father left his wife shortly after she became pregnant. Stargell wouldn't meet his father until he signed a professional contract with the Pittsburgh Pirates and was playing minor league baseball in their farm system. After divorcing her first husband, Stargell's mother remarried and followed her second husband to Alameda, California, where he'd been a dock worker. After divorcing her second husband in 1945, she met and married Percy Russell, a former sailor and civil service truck driver.

At the age of six, Stargell's life, as narrated in his autobiography, reads like a nightmarish tale out of the Brothers Grimm. Though his mother had little contact with her family, her older sister, Lucy, now living in Orlando, Florida, came to Alameda and offered to take young Willie back to Orlando with her, at least for a year, to ease the family's financial burdens. That Lucy didn't make the offer out of the goodness of her heart is clear by Stargell's description of his aunt: "Lucy, large-boned, bowlegged and with a pinch of snuff tucked loosely inside her lower lip, carried herself awkwardly, almost like a retired cowboy. She had a strict disposition, which showed in the scowl on her face. A smile would have been an unnatural act for Lucy; she was as hard as nails."

Stargell's description of his Aunt Lucy as an Oklahoma ogress fits what he claimed happened to him once he arrived in Orlando. His aunt, who didn't believe in sparing the rod and spoiling the child, forced him to perform heavy chores, while underfeeding him. What began as a one-year stay became a six-year sentence of hard labor, whippings, and malnourishment, until his mother finally came to Orlando to bring her son back to Alameda.

About to enter his teen years, Stargell had the opportunity, once he was back in the care of his mother and step-father in Alameda, to recover his health and play baseball for the first time in his life. The kids of families living in the Alameda projects had little money for entertainment, but there were project baseball teams representing the city's various subdivisions to keep them out of trouble. The competition was fierce, though the teams had no uniforms, few volunteer coaches, and little in the way of baseball equipment.

Stargell played his first organized baseball for Encinal in a 16-and-over league made up of several teams from the Alameda projects. While his Encinal team often faced threats and fistfights when they played on the dirt-covered, rock-and-glass-laced fields in other subdivisions, Stargell believed that project baseball was exactly what he needed and wanted at such a vulnerable time in his life: "We didn't have the color, glamour, or organization of teams in wealthier neighborhoods, but we did have spirit. Baseball was our only true pastime. White boys from richer families were given alternatives such as the Boy Scouts, family vacations, and field trips. We relied solely on baseball for entertainment. Baseball was all we had."

Robert Earl Davis, who played on Stargell's Encinal projects team and would also become his teammate at Encinal High School, remembered that, even as a young teenager, Stargell had already decided to become a major league ballplayer. With his long thin arms and quick wrists, he could drive a baseball so far that he often seemed like "a man among boys," even though he was still underdeveloped physically and uncoordinated in his play. According to Davis, Stargell didn't connect that often, but, when he did, he hit balls that challenged, and sometimes cleared, the 341 mark in right field at Encinal's ramshackle ballpark. Davis also remembered that Stargell, while competitive, was a quiet kid who stayed out of trouble. Even at a young age, Stargell "was always a gentleman, and you can underline that twice."

• • •

When Stargell started playing for the Encinal High School baseball team, he'd already developed a sense of pride and competitiveness on project fields that would serve him well on his way to the major leagues. He also joined a team that had two other players destined to play in the major leagues. A gangly and underweight teenager, Stargell, who, according to Davis was "too injury prone," wasn't even the best player on his high school team or the one that drew baseball scouts to their games.

The star on Encinal's baseball team and the best athlete in the school was Tommy Harper. After graduating from Encinal and attending Santa Rosa Junior College and San Francisco State, Harper signed a contract with the Cincinnati Reds in 1960 and began his major league career in 1962, the same year that Stargell made his debut with the Pirates. Possessed with great speed, he led the American League in stolen bases twice. He had his best season with the American League Milwaukee Brewers in 1970, played in the 1970 All-Star Game, and finished sixth in the AL Most Valuable Player voting. His only postseason appearance came in 1975 with the Oakland Athletics, when he batted as a pinch hitter in a playoff game against the Boston Red Sox and drew a base on balls.

Though not as skilled as Tommy Harper, Curt Motton was the other future major leaguer on Stargell's Encinal baseball team. Motton, like Harper, also enrolled at Santa Rosa Junior College after high school, but, instead, went on to play ball at the University of California at Berkeley. He signed a contract with the Chicago Cubs in 1961, but didn't make his major league debut until 1967 with the Baltimore Orioles. He never played regularly with the Orioles, but he did appear in the 1969 World Series and was on the Orioles bench in the 1971 World Series, though he never made an appearance against the Pirates.

Stargell, like Harper and Motton, was an all-around athlete who played basketball and football, as well as baseball. His decision, at the urging of Tommy Harper, to play football, however, would haunt him for his entire athletic career. Harper, Encinal's star quarterback, wanted the tall, ranging Stargell to play wide receiver, but, in practice, Stargell, while reaching for a pass, had his legs cut out from under him and severely damaged his knee. He recovered well enough to play baseball in his senior year, but his knee would become a recurring problem for him.

Hampered by his knee, Stargell played mostly first base for the Encinal baseball team. He described himself as "a free swinger with a lot of power" in his high school days and once told Charley Feeney of the *Pittsburgh Post-Gazette* that "he weighed only 150 pounds with a 5'10" frame" at that time. Even though his football injury restricted him to first base, he had a strong throwing arm that would draw favorable comparisons to Clemente's when Stargell arrived at his first Pirates spring training camp.

Baseball scouts during the mid-1950s had to be very careful in approaching young high school prospects because of the strict bonus rule that had gone into effect in 1953. Any player who signed a contract for more than $4,000 had to be kept on a major league roster for two years. If a team sent a bonus baby to the minor leagues, he became eligible in the baseball draft after the season was over.

The most notorious example of a bonus baby left unprotected and subsequently drafted by another team came when the Brooklyn Dodgers, instead of keeping Roberto Clemente on their major league roster for the 1954 season, had sent him to their AAA minor league club in Montreal.

The Dodgers, who already had several black players on their team, denied that they'd sent Clemente to Montreal because of an unwritten quota system that restricted the number of black players on big-league rosters, but, whatever the reason, the Pirates had the first pick in the winter draft, and they selected Clemente.

The Pirates, under general manager Branch Rickey, were one of the most aggressive teams in signing bonus babies, but most of their signings turned out to be disasters. Rickey, who developed the first farm system when he was with the Cardinals and integrated baseball when he was with the Dodgers, decided to build a championship team in Pittsburgh with inexperienced teenagers and football and basketball All-Americans.

Among Rickey's bonus babies were Heisman trophy winner Vic Janowicz out of Ohio State, who could make a fair catch but had trouble catching a pop fly, and basketball's twin All-Americans Johnny and Eddie O'Brien out of Seattle University, who found hitting a curveball much harder than dribbling a basketball. By 1957, when baseball finally ended its bonus rule, the Pirates system was littered with bonus babies who had mostly sat and rusted on the bench in their first two years in baseball.

• • •

In 1957, Bob Zuk, who'd been the director of baseball for the Oakland park district and had responsibility for ballpark scheduling and maintenance, signed on as a bird dog (they sniffed out players for scouts) for the Chicago White Sox. The following year he became a full-time scout for the Pittsburgh Pirates. Zuk claimed that he landed his first scouting jobs through the recommendation of George Powles, a legendary coach at McClymonds High School in Oakland. He also credited Powles, who was aggressive in finding and recommending black high school athletes to scouts in the Oakland area, for developing his own interest in signing minority players.

Willie Stargell always gave credit to his high school coach, George Reed, for convincing Zuk to take a look at his underdeveloped and unpolished first baseman, while other scouts were watching the more physically mature Tommy Harper and Curt Motton; but Zuk said it was George Powles who told him about Stargell's raw power and potential. It took three tryouts, but Zuk, who would later sign George Foster and Reggie Jackson to professional contracts, saw enough in Stargell to take a gamble and offered him a contract with the Pittsburgh Pirates.

While the bonus-baby rule, which had expired a year earlier, was no longer an obstacle for scouts interested in signing a high school star like Tommy Harper to a big contract, it wouldn't have been a problem for Zuk in the signing of Willie Stargell, who got a bonus of only $1,500. It was far less than the bonuses the Pirates had been doling out for the past few years, including the $25,000 paid out to Vic Janowicz, who hit two home runs and drove in 10 runs in his two years with the Pirates.

When Zuk signed Stargell in the summer of 1958, he was so worried about Stargell's thin physique and awkward play that he recommended to the Pirates that they not assign him to a minor league team until the following season. So Stargell, who had planned to attend Santa Rosa with Tommy Harper and play baseball there, ended up playing American Legion ball that summer until he cracked his hip while practicing his sliding, and doctors had to insert a pin.

Stargell loved socializing and dancing when he was in high school, but, by the time he graduated, he'd developed a steady relationship with Lois Beard, a girl two years younger, whom he described in his autobiography as "petite with a shapely figure and a radiant smile." Stargell spent time with Lois, who would become his first wife, while recuperating from his hip surgery and waiting for the start of spring training.

• • •

Willie Stargell was 19 years old when he arrived at the Pirates minor league spring training camp in Jacksonville, Florida, in 1959. The camp preceded the Pirates' regular spring training camp at Fort Myers and gave Pirate managers and coaches an opportunity to evaluate players and decide where to assign them in their minor league system for the coming season. That could mean an assignment to Class D for new players like Stargell or AAA for more seasoned players close to breaking through to the major leagues.

The Pirates were impressed by Stargell's quick bat and potential as a power hitter, but they were so concerned about his lack of defensive skill that they assigned Tony Bartirome, one of their most experienced first baseman, to teach him the proper footwork in handling bunts and throws. Bartirome was a Pittsburgh native who had been signed by the Pirates in 1951 right after his graduation from Connelley Vocational High School. After a year with the Class C Hutchinson (Kansas) Elks, he so impressed GM Branch Rickey at the Pirates' minor league camp that he was invited to the Pirates' major league camp in San Bernardino. He made the team out of spring training and became the Pirates starting first baseman in 1952, even though he was only 19 years old on Opening Day, the same age that Stargell was when he arrived in Jacksonville in '59.

Bartirome quickly developed a reputation as a flashy first baseman, finishing fifth in the National League in fielding average, but he batted only .220 in 1952, with no home runs. After serving two years in the military, Bartirome was assigned by the Pirates to Class B Burlington. By the time he met Stargell in 1959, he'd played at every level in the Pirates minor system and had finished the 1958 season at AAA Columbus. He would never, however, play in another major league game with the Pirates.

Years later, Bartirome remembered the 19-year-old Stargell as "a tall skinny kid" with "great bat speed" and a "Clemente arm." By the end of the minor league camp at Jacksonville, Stargell was assigned to play first base with San Angelo, Texas, in the Class D Sophomore League, while Bartirome ended up in the minors again, this time with both the AAA Columbus Jets and Denver Bears. Stargell and Bartirome wouldn't be together again until Bartirome became the Pirates trainer in 1967. At that point the player who had helped Stargell with his fielding in his first professional season took on the responsibility of helping Stargell get ready to play on bad knees that were "bone on bone." He'd packed them in ice so that Stargell could reduce the pain and play the next day, even though he sometimes had trouble just walking.

Stargell and Bartirome also became close friends over the years. Bartirome admired the way Stargell befriended and worked with younger players and remembered those who worked behind the scenes. He recalled that Stargell wouldn't accept a gift unless everyone in the clubhouse received one.

When Chuck Tanner was fired by the Pirates at the end of the 1985 season and was hired by the Atlanta Braves, Bartirome left the Pirates and joined Tanner and Stargell in Atlanta, where, missing his hometown, he spent "the worst three years of [my] life" before returning to Pittsburgh.

. . .

When Stargell reported to the Jacksonville minor league spring training camp in 1959, the Pirates were coming off their first winning season in nine years. From 1950 to 1957, the Pirates had finished either in last place or next-to-last place in the National League, including four straight years in the cellar from 1952 to 1955. But, with a sensational year from Pittsburgh native Frank Thomas, the improved pitching of Vernon Law, Roy Face, and Bob Friend (who won 22 games in 1958), and the strong hitting of Bob Skinner, Dick Groat, Roberto Clemente, and Bill Mazeroski (who hit a career high of 19 home runs), the Pirates finished with a record of 84–70, good for second place behind the repeat National League–champion Milwaukee Braves.

There seemed little room with the Pirates in the foreseeable future for a first baseman. Even though the Pirates had acquired veteran Ted Kluszewski in late July of 1958, the team called up first baseman Dick Stuart, a home run sensation in the minor leagues. Stuart hit 16 home runs in little more than half a season and sparked the Pirates to a 48–29 finish in 1958. Also that season, rookie first baseman R.C. Stevens—one of five black players on the roster—had a solid campaign, hitting .267 with seven home runs in a part-time role. The outfield was also young and solid with Bob Skinner, Bill Virdon, and Roberto Clemente as starters and Roman Mejias in a backup role.

. . .

The Pirates didn't do Stargell any favors when they assigned him to their Class D San Angelo farm club for the 1959 season. At the age of 19, he'd be facing a sweltering summer of long bus rides and bad food on his way to segregated towns and cities in a southwest area of the country as hostile to black players as the Deep South. He'd also end up playing for three different managers, including legendary minor leaguer Joe Bauman, who famously hit 72 home runs and drove in 224 runs in 1954 while playing for Roswell,

New Mexico. Roswell, incidentally, was where the San Angelo team moved in the middle of the 1959 season, before finishing in last place with a record of 48–77.

At Roswell, Stargell stayed in the home of a black Air Force sergeant stationed at nearby Andrews AFB, but on the road he often faced deplorable conditions. On a trip to Artesia, New Mexico, he and three of his black teammates had to stay in the home of a fish bait dealer who kept her house dark and boarded up to protect her bait. The air inside was so "stale and muggy" that Stargell and his teammates sat outside "before finally surrendering to fatigue and entering the smelly bait house to sleep." His meals on the road were so irregular and unpredictable that he bought food at a local market, packed some sandwiches, and took the responsibility for feeding himself: "I consumed many a Spam and salami sandwich in the Sophomore League."

But despite the harsh climate, the segregated living conditions, the bad food, and the racial taunts and threats, Stargell, while still struggling at first base and striking out 100 times in 118 games, managed to have a respectable year. In his first season of professional baseball, he hit .274 with seven home runs and an impressive 87 RBIs. While he didn't hit many home runs and had little command of the strike zone, his clutch hitting and raw power earned him a promotion to the Class C Grand Forks (North Dakota) Chiefs in the Northern League for the 1960 season.

♦ ♦ ♦

When Stargell arrived at the minor league spring training camp in 1960, the Pirates, unhappy with his lack of development as a first baseman and wanting to take advantage of his strong throwing arm and improving speed, decided to convert him into an outfielder. While the Pirates, after a disappointing drop to fourth place in 1959, headed to Pittsburgh for what turned out to be a championship season, Willie Stargell headed to the upper Midwest, where he encountered a cooler and wetter climate and far less racism in an eight-team league that spread from Wisconsin and Minnesota to the Dakotas and Canada. At Grand Forks, Stargell lived with several white teammates at the YMCA and often ate meals at the integrated counter at Don's Cafe.

In 1960, Stargell was playing in a competitive league that had several future major leaguers on its teams, including Joe Torre, who'd end up hitting .344 with Eau Claire, Wisconsin. In 1971, Torre, now playing with the St. Louis Cardinals, would win the National League MVP Award, even though Stargell was heavily favored for the honor after leading the Pirates to the World Series. Another future major leaguer was Stargell's teammate Gene Alley, who remembered their "days together in Grand Forks…living in the YMCA, the long bus rides into Canada and other cities. Eating at Don's Cafe in Grand Forks." Alley and Stargell would advance together through the Pirates minor league system and become teammates on the 1963 Pirates team. They'd remain teammates for the next 11 years.

Without the advantage of the thinner air of Roswell and facing tougher competition, Stargell's batting average dropped to .260 and his RBIs fell to 61, but he hit 11 home runs and struck out only 66 times in 107 games. While playing on a mediocre team that struggled under .500 for most of the season, he closely followed the Pirates' miracle run to the World Series in 1960 and dreamed of playing in the major leagues and becoming a World Series hero. At the end of the season, he was promoted from Class C to the Class A Asheville (North Carolina) Tourists in the South Atlantic League, and moved a little closer to fulfilling his dream.

• • •

The 1960 World Series champion Pittsburgh Pirates opened the 1961 season in San Francisco by beating the Giants 8–7 on a three-run homer by Bill Virdon in the top of the ninth. After a season of come-from-behind victories that ended with Bill Mazeroski's dramatic home run in the seventh game of the 1960 World Series, the thrilling Opening Day victory seemed like a harbinger of things to come in 1961. The Opening Day lineup was exactly the same as it was against the Yankees in Game 7 of the World Series, with the exception of the starting pitcher. Instead of Cy Young Award–winner Vernon Law on the mound, the Pirates opened the season with 18-game-winner Bob Friend.

Unfortunately for the Pirates, the Opening Day starting pitcher assignment was an indication that things weren't right with the 1961 Pirates. Law had injured his shoulder late in the 1960 season and would be ineffective in 1961, winning only three games and losing four. The Pirates pitching staff appeared strengthened by the addition of Bobby Shantz, who'd pitched so effectively against them in the World Series, but Bob Friend, Vinegar Bend Mizell, and Roy Face had losing seasons, and rookie-hopeful Earl Francis ended up with a 2–8 record. While Roberto Clemente had a sensational season and won his first batting title with a .351 average and Dick Stuart established himself as a legitimate power threat with 35 home runs, most of the Pirate hitters had subpar seasons. The Pirates struggled all season and ended up with a disappointing 75–79 record and a sixth-place finish.

One bright spot and hopeful sign for the Pirates in 1961 was the performance of its new Class A Asheville club in the South Atlantic League. In the first year of its affiliation with the Pirates, Asheville fielded the best team in its baseball history, finishing its championship season with a 87–50 record. The Asheville roster was loaded with young and talented players, including history-making Rex Johnston, who had been drafted and played briefly with the Pittsburgh Steelers after signing with the Pirates in 1959. Johnston, who'd played college football and baseball at Southern California, hit 18 home runs, stole 13 bases, and batted .283 at Asheville in 1961.

Rex Johnston, however, was hardly the brightest Pirates talent at Asheville. The player named the best prospect in the South Atlantic League in 1961 was catcher Orlando McFarlane, who hit 21 home runs and stole 27 bases, a remarkable total for a catcher. On a visit to Asheville, Pirates manager Danny Murtaugh called McFarlane the best catcher "from the neck down" he'd ever seen, probably a reaction to McFarlane's 20 errors behind the plate. He'd make his debut with the Pirates near the end of the 1962 season, but he never achieved the success predicted for him at Asheville.

At mid-season, Asheville had an even more ballyhooed prospect when 18-year-old shortstop Bob Bailey signed a $175,000 bonus contract, the largest in Pirates history, and was immediately assigned to the team's

Class A affiliate. Bailey became the starting shortstop for Asheville, but he struggled and committed 27 errors in just 75 games. He showed some power by hitting nine home runs, but batted only .220.

Naming Bob Bailey the starting shortstop had no impact on Gene Alley, who was playing second base for Asheville at the time and was having an outstanding season. With the All-Star Mazeroski a fixture at second base with the Pirates, Alley would soon be converted to a shortstop and eventually become a part of the greatest double-play combination in Pirates history. Bob Bailey, who soon showed he lacked the skills to play shortstop, would eventually be converted into a third baseman by the Pirates.

When the 21-year-old Willie Stargell took the field for the home opener at Asheville, he was playing in a city far different from the towns and cities he'd encountered in the Sophomore and Northern leagues. Asheville was a southern city with a segregated population, but it was also a culturally diverse city with a thriving tourist business. While Stargell found himself in a better social and cultural environment, he was also in a better frame of mind. During the off-season, his father, who was living in Los Angeles, called Stargell's mother and asked if he could see his son. Stargell could have refused to see his father, but he met him, forgave him, and developed a close relationship that lasted until his father's death in 1982, just months after Stargell's retirement as a player.

While Stargell's acceptance of his father showed a developing emotional maturity, he also was becoming physically stronger, though he still looked like that tall skinny kid who first arrived in Jacksonville in 1959. No player on Asheville's team was more aware of Stargell's development than Bob Priddy, a Pittsburgh native who grew up in McKees Rocks. Priddy was Stargell's teammate at San Angelo/Roswell and, after spending 1960 pitching with Class B Burlington, had advanced with Stargell to Class A Asheville. Priddy would pitch for AAA Columbus in 1962, where he'd be a September call-up, with Stargell and Bob Veale, and win his first major league game that season.

Stargell found the social atmosphere in Asheville interesting, but the most inviting part of his season was a short right-field fence at his home ballpark that stood at only 301 feet from home plate. Stargell hit so many home runs on the hill behind the fence that fans began calling him "On the

Hill Will." He ended up with 22 home runs, double his total at Grand Forks. He also drove in 89 runs and had a .289 batting average, both his personal bests in the minor leagues.

By the end of the season, the Pirates' front office, aware of Stargell's physical development and his improved batting statistics, especially his power numbers, no longer regarded him as a marginal prospect. He was invited to play with Chandler in the Arizona Instructional League and to report directly to the 1962 major league spring training camp at Fort Myers. For Stargell, the invitation looked like an opportunity to make the Pirates team and open the 1962 season in Pittsburgh.

• • •

The 22-year-old Stargell who arrived at Fort Myers in 1962 now stood nearly 6'3" and weighed close to 200 pounds. When Dick Groat first watched Stargell, the rookie was in the batting cage hitting against a pitching machine: "He was so impressive that I went to Joe L. Brown and asked him where he got that kid. Willie had the best looking swing of any young player I'd ever seen in our organization." Bill Mazeroski remembered that you could tell when Stargell was in the batting cage because of "the different sound of his bat" when he hit the ball.

When Bob Skinner, the Pirates starting left fielder, took a good look at Stargell he realized that his days in a Pirates uniform were numbered because Stargell was bound to become his eventual replacement in left field. Skinner remained with the Pirates in 1962 and, hitting a career-high 20 home runs, had one of his best years, but he'd end up traded early in the 1963 season to the Cincinnati Reds for bench player and clutch pinch-hitter Jerry Lynch.

Bill Virdon, the Pirates starting center fielder, recognized that Stargell still hadn't matured enough to play major league baseball, but, like Groat and Skinner, he thought the young rookie was "something special." After watching Stargell hit and throw, Virdon, who had played alongside Roberto Clemente since 1956, believed that Stargell had as much talent and potential as Clemente when he first arrived as a rookie at the Pirates' spring training camp in 1955.

• • •

By 1962, the Pirates had one of the most integrated spring training camps in baseball—on the field. But off the field, black players were subjected to the same segregated facilities and living conditions at Fort Myers that were still common in the early 1960s to all spring training sites in the South. Steve Blass remembered that in Fort Myers the white players would board a bus at their hotel and would then head to "colored town" to pick up the black players for practice or meals. In his book *October 1964*, David Halberstam wrote that, in the 1950s and 1960s, "Nothing highlighted the differences between the white and black experiences in the major leagues as much as spring training. Almost all veteran white players loved spring training—it was a chance to be in the sunshine with their families, to go fishing, and to recover from a long difficult winter. They thought of it as a kind of paid vacation. The black players, by contrast, hated it."

Having grown up in the projects and endured racial taunts and threats in his first season in the minor leagues, Stargell was all too familiar with the segregated conditions surrounding the Pirates' spring training camp at Fort Myers. He remembered waiting on the bus, while the white players, like Blass, got off and entered "the Bradford Hotel, known as the finest hotel in Fort Myers. From there our bus would proceed to our separate living quarters." He also remembered eating in the "kitchens of restaurants," using "the Negro bathrooms," and drinking "water from the filthy Negro fountains."

Stargell's focus, however, was on making the team and traveling north to Pittsburgh for Opening Day: "I sat at the back of the bus. I played the role." He had a solid spring, but, unfortunately for Stargell, the Pirates were still a year away from rebuilding with young talent from their farm system. They kept first baseman Donn Clendenon as a replacement for Rocky Nelson and added Bob Veale to their pitching staff after he'd struck out 208 batters in 201 innings with Columbus in 1961; but, by mid-season, Clendenon and Veale were sent back to Columbus, where they joined a disappointed Willie Stargell.

• • •

The Pirates AAA affiliate in Columbus played in the geographically challenging and highly competitive eight-team International League. The league fielded teams in major cities ranging from Toronto, Buffalo, and Syracuse in the north to Richmond, Atlanta, and Jacksonville in the South. They also had rosters filled with talented prospects and former major leaguers. The 1962 Columbus Jets, managed by Larry Shepard, barely finished over .500, but the team had one of the most powerful hitting lineups in the International League. Led by Bob Bailey, who bounced back from his poor showing in Asheville to win the International League Player of the Year Award, the Jets finished second in the league in runs scored and home runs.

Stargell's Columbus teammates included Ron Brand and Bob Priddy, who were with him at San Angelo/Roswell in 1959. Gene Alley and Rex Johnston, with him at Asheville in 1961, were also on the team, as was Orlando McFarlane, who'd had such an outstanding season in 1961 at Asheville. But his teammates also included player-coach and 1960 World Series veteran Gene Baker, who, with Ernie Banks, had crossed the color line with the Chicago Cubs in late 1953.

In 1961, after playing briefly with the Pirates, Baker had become the first African American in baseball history to manage an affiliated minor league team, when he took over the Batavia Pirates in the Class D New York-Penn League. One of the players on that team, in just his second year of professional baseball, was Steve Blass. In 1963, when Baker became the first-base coach for the Pirates, he became only the second African American, after Buck O'Neil with the Cubs in 1962 , to join a major league coaching staff.

It was a great advantage for Stargell to have Gene Baker on the coaching staff to prepare him for the challenges he'd faced as a black player once he moved up to the major leagues; but the player who probably had the most influence on Stargell and became one of his closest friends was not even on the Columbus roster at the beginning on the 1962 season. After his dominating season at Columbus, Bob Veale had fully expected to be on the Pirates' roster for 1962. He made the team out of spring training but, after a few brief appearances in relief, was sent back to Columbus to work on his control.

Believing that the demotion was "a slap in the face" and that Joe L. Brown had told him "one thing and done something else," Veale could have pouted on his return to Columbus, but instead he became even more aggressive and dominant on the mound, striking out 179 batters in 105 innings. When he returned to the Pirates for a September call-up, he struck out nine batters in the first five innings of his debut as a starter and, in his second start, pitched a no-hitter for 6⅔ innings and ended up with a complete-game three-hitter.

If Gene Baker was a father figure for Stargell on the Columbus team, someone who could share his early experiences in the big leagues with racism, Veale, nearly five years older than Stargell, was like an older and, at 6'6" and 212, bigger brother. Veale believed that discrimination was still a barrier for black players, and while Baker preached calm and patience to Stargell, Veale showed him, by example, how to turn adversity into motivation. Ron Brand, Stargell's teammate since their days together in Class D ball, remembered, "We played together at Columbus in 1962 and Willie showed the greatest class I've ever seen. He was in the most horrible slump, but he never quit hustling…. He never hung his head and never quit or complained. When he finally broke out of it, the entire club was as happy as he was."

Even with his prolonged slump, Stargell had the best year of his minor league career. He hit 27 home runs, drove in 82 runs, and batted .276. He did strike out 111 times, but he also hit eight triples, stole six bases, and had 10 outfield assists. His strikeout total was a concern, but he had the speed and the throwing arm to play the outfield in spacious Forbes Field, as well as the bat speed and power to become a legitimate long-ball threat.

• • •

The Pirates, even after their losing record in 1961, had kept the core of their 1960 World Series champion team together for one more year. They bounced back in 1962 with a 93–68 record and a fourth-place finish in what was now a 10-team league, with the addition of the New York Mets and the Houston Colts, but, after the season, the team was ready to rebuild. The Pirates organization was particularly concerned with the team's lack of power. Bob Skinner's team-leading 20 home runs was the lowest total since the pre-Kiner year of 1945.

The Pirates called up several young power hitters in September, including Willie Stargell. On September 13, a UPI photograph was taken at Forbes Field with Danny Murtaugh at the batting cage with three of the club's most promising home run hitters. The caption read, "Pittsburgh Pirates in dire need of offensive strength for next yr. have brought up to the parent club from minor league farm three home run hitters, L to R Wilver Stargell 27 HRs, Bob Bailey 28 HRs, and Elmo Plaskett 29 HRs, and Danny Murtaugh, the Pgh. manager." In the photograph, Murtaugh, with a wad of tobacco firmly in place, looks ready to initiate the spikes of the newcomers with a stream of tobacco juice, but his quizzical and concerned gaze in the photo appears directed at Stargell.

A few days earlier, after Columbus manager Larry Shepard told Stargell that the Pirates were calling him up to Pittsburgh, Stargell had packed his bags and crammed himself into the passenger seat of Bob Veale's beat-up Studebaker for the 200-mile drive to Pittsburgh. When Ralph Kiner was a rookie with the Pirates in 1946, he remembered arriving in Pittsburgh by train at noon, after opening the season in St. Louis: "It was so smoky from all the coal-burning factories, it looked like the middle of the night." For Stargell, who arrived by car in the middle of the night, the first sight of Pittsburgh was far more dazzling.

Once Stargell and Veale made the passage by car down from the mountainous terrain of West Virginia and southwestern Pennsylvania, entered the greater Pittsburgh area, and drove through the Fort Pitt Tunnel, they emerged on a brilliantly lighted scene that, in his autobiography, Stargell described as "reaching out to greet us." For Stargell, that drive through the Fort Pitt Tunnel must have seemed like a trip down the rabbit hole and into a baseball Wonderland. Emerging out of the tunnel, Stargell saw, in the "glimmering" Pittsburgh skyline, an invitation to a world of fabulous encounters and amazing adventures. For Bob Veale, who had made this journey before, it was more like a trip through a baseball Looking Glass, where lurking behind the invitation were sinister characters who had already made up their mind about you no matter what your talent or character.

Now Batting for Pittsburgh

Willie Stargell made his major league debut on September 16, 1962, when Danny Murtaugh summoned the rookie from the bench to pinch hit against the San Francisco Giants. Stargell's first at-bat was a baseball matchup of biblical proportions between a towering, powerful Goliath and a crafty, undersized David—and the result turned out exactly the same.

Stu Miller, the Giants pitcher facing the nearly 6'3" and 190-pound Stargell, stood at under six feet and weighed only 165 pounds. He was so lacking in athletic strength and skill that his first manager, Eddie Stanky, called him "the stenographer." Miller was known as a "junk pitcher" whose repertoire of breaking balls was once described as "slow, slower, and slowest." His junk pitches, however, were good enough for 105 wins and 154 saves in a career spanning 16 years.

Miller's most memorable moment on the pitching mound had come a little more than a year before he faced Stargell. In the 1961 All-Star Game at Candlestick Park, a gust of wind pushed his shoulder forward and caused him to balk just as he was about to deliver a pitch to Detroit's Rocky Colavito. While he finished the year with 14 wins and 17 saves and won *The Sporting News* Fireman of the Year award, he'll always be remembered in baseball's fabled history as the undersized pitcher who was blown off the mound by a gust of wind, even though he protested, over the years, that, while the wind caused him to balk, he "didn't get blown off the mound as the story goes."

In his autobiography, Stargell claimed that, as he was walking to the batter's box, he passed Dick Stuart, who told him, "When you KO, rookie, don't feel bad." It was an easy prediction for Stuart and good advice for the rookie. Like Stargell, Stuart was a power hitter who feasted on fastballs. He'd hit 66 home runs in one of his minor league seasons and once launched a ball so far over the center-field wall at Forbes Field that he made the mammoth ballpark look like a Little League field. But, with his big swing, he also led the Pirates in strikeouts for four seasons in a row, including a National League high of 121 in 1961.

Stargell's first at-bat in the big leagues, as Stuart predicted, was no contest. Miller, who would go on to save 19 games that season for a Giants team that was on its way to the World Series, threw a variety of slow curveballs, and Stargell, like the Mighty Casey, struck out. Twenty years later, when he stepped into the batter's box for the last time, only Reggie Jackson prevented Stargell from holding the major league record for career strikeouts. He'd also, however, have 475 homers, including some of the most prodigious home runs in baseball history.

Stargell must have taken Stuart's advice to heart because he recovered well enough to record his first major league hit four days later: a triple at Forbes Field, against the Cincinnati Reds. Though he didn't hit a home run in the 10 games in which he appeared at the end of the 1962 season, he had nine hits, including three doubles and a triple, for a batting average of .290. He also struck out 10 times in his 30 at-bats.

While Bob Veale had warned his young friend not to take anything for granted, Stargell felt he'd proven to Pirates management that he was ready for the big leagues and would be with the team when it headed north for the 1963 season. He was confident in his own ability, but the Pirates off-season activity also gave him reason to be optimistic. The Pirates' fourth-place finish in 1962 had convinced Joe L. Brown that it was time to dismantle the 1960 world champion team and make room for some of the young talent in their minor league system.

• • •

Just before the November baseball meetings, Brown began making major changes when he traded Dick Groat to the Cardinals and Dick Stuart to the Red Sox in a matter of two days. The trade of the popular Groat was a shock for Pirate fans, but Brown believed that the 1960 National League MVP no longer had the range to play shortstop. He also wanted to create an opportunity for Groat's backup, Dick Schofield, to play regularly.

The Stuart trade was less of a shock and, for many Pirate fans, something of a relief after watching "Dr. Strangeglove" routinely lead the league's first basemen in errors and, if positioned in the outfield, play fly balls on the bounce. After Stuart's numbers dropped from 35 home runs and 117 RBIs in 1961 to 16 home runs and 64 RBIs in 1962, Brown decided that the flamboyant Stuart was no longer worth the trouble and traded him to make room for Donn Clendenon at first base. Clendenon was an all-around talent who could hit for average and power and steal bases.

Brown made one more major trade, and this one seemed to have a potentially negative impact on Stargell's chances of making the Pirates squad in 1963. A week after he traded Groat and Stuart, Brown sent 35-year-old third baseman Don Hoak to the Philadelphia Phillies for 25-year-old outfielder Ted Savage. The move made room for Bob Bailey to play third base, but, with outfield regulars Bob Skinner, Bill Virdon, and Roberto Clemente still on the team, Stargell's goal of winning a spot on the Pirates roster now seemed more challenging. When Brown acquired outfielder Manny Mota from Houston at the beginning of the 1963 season, the outfield became even more overcrowded.

One of Brown's reasons for acquiring Savage may have been the lingering doubts about Stargell's ability to hit major league pitching, especially left-handers, on a consistent basis. The trade for Mota, however, probably had more to do with Brown's unhappiness with Stargell's expanded waistline when he arrived at Fort Myers. After spending the fall playing ball for Chandler in the Arizona Instructional League, Stargell returned to the Bay Area, but this time as a husband and a father. On May 14, 1962, while he was playing for Columbus, he'd married Lois Evelyn Beard, his high school girlfriend and mother of his daughter, Wendy. When Stargell arrived for spring training, it was obvious that he'd spent the winter enjoying his new domestic life.

With the help of medicine balls, outfield sprints, rubberized sweat shirts, as well as the nagging of Danny Murtaugh and Joe L. Brown, Stargell managed to get into playing shape, though his weight would become a chronic spring training problem. After coming to camp overweight, he worked hard enough and hit well enough in spring training games to convince Murtaugh and Brown to keep him with the team, but more as a platoon player in the outfield and at first base than as a regular. When the Pirates opened the season on April 8 in Cincinnati, Stargell watched from the bench as Skinner, Virdon, and Clemente trotted out in the bottom of the first to their starting outfield positions, while rookies Bob Bailey and Donn Clendenon took the field at third and first base.

• • •

Joe L. Brown's player trades going into the 1963 season produced a major change in fortune for the Pirates, but it was a change for the worse. The Pirates ended the season with a 78–88 record and finished in eighth place, ahead of only the expansion Houston Colts and New York Mets. It was the team's worst record since Danny Murtaugh took over the Pirates in mid-season from Bobby Bragan in 1957. The ballclub also experienced a dramatic drop in attendance from 1,090,648 in 1962 to 783,648 in 1963, the Pirates' lowest home attendance since the 1955 season.

With the acquisitions of Don Schwall and Don Cardwell in the Stuart and Groat trades, the Pirates starting pitching seemed to be the team's strength going into the season, but, with the exception of Bob Friend, the Pirate starters, plagued by the team's lack of offense, struggled to win games. Schwall and Cardwell ended up with losing records, as did lefty Joe Gibbon and Opening Day starter Earl Francis. Vernon Law continued to be hampered by injuries, and veterans Roy Face and Harvey Haddix were inconsistent in the bullpen. Danny Murtaugh had assigned Bob Veale to the bullpen at the beginning of the season, but, by August, he finally moved Veale into a starting role where he became the Pirates' best pitcher.

Roberto Clemente had a solid year, but other veterans, like Bill Mazeroski and Smoky Burgess, were hampered by injuries. Rookie Bob Bailey hit a home run in the Pirates home opener against the Milwaukee Braves, but he struggled during the season and finished with a .228 average. Ted Savage came off the bench to win the home opener with a pinch hit, but he batted only .195. Desperate for offensive help, Brown traded Bob Skinner, who had failed to hit a home run in the first month of the season, to the Cincinnati Reds for one of baseball's premier pinch-hitters, Jerry Lynch.

Willie Stargell also struggled at the plate and, like Bob Bailey and Donn Clendenon, was striking out at an alarming pace. He had trouble hitting the sweeping curveballs of left-handers, but right-handers were also striking him out by going "up the ladder" with fastballs. Stargell was a low-ball hitter, but he couldn't resist a high fastball. So pitchers would start him off with a fastball around the letters, then move each pitch a little higher until Stargell struck out on a pitch around the shoulders and out of the strike zone.

Stargell got his chance to play more when Brown traded Bob Skinner for Jerry Lynch. While Lynch was a clutch pinch hitter, he was a mediocre outfielder with a poor throwing arm. With Skinner gone, Savage struggling, and Lynch proving that as an outfielder he'd be great coming off the bench as a pinch hitter, Stargell received more and more playing time in left field as the season moved along.

Appearing in 108 games, he finished the season with a disappointing .243 average, but he hit 6 triples, 11 home runs, and drove in 47 runs. Going into the 1964 season, Stargell with his power hitting, and his close friend Bob Veale with his power pitching, looked like the most promising young talents to come out of the 1963 campaign.

◆ ◆ ◆

The 1971 and 1979 World Series years are so monumental in Stargell's career that it's easy to overlook the importance of the 1964 season. Once Murtaugh decided to give Stargell an opportunity to play every day and inserted him into the clean-up spot, he gave the Pirates their first consistent power threat in the lineup since the days of Ralph Kiner. He'd go on to lead the Pirates in home runs in 1964; he lead the team in homers for 10 of the next 11 years. He'd also established himself, in only his second full major league season, as one of the best players in the National League. In July, he was selected for the 1964 All-Star Game, his first of seven appearances during his career.

The Willie Stargell who came to the 1964 Pirates spring training camp at Fort Myers was not the same ballplayer who arrived out of shape in 1963. Instead of spending the winter months with his family, he signed a contract to play winter ball in the Dominican Republic, where he competed against a number of major leaguers. By the time he arrived in Fort Myers, he was more experienced and ready—physically and mentally—to assert himself as a team leader.

Stargell made it easy for Murtaugh to select him as the new Pirates clean-up hitter by homering in each of the Pirates first two exhibition games and banging out six hits in 14–7 and 15–7 victories against the Kansas City Athletics. He went on to have an outstanding spring with six home runs and 24 RBIs. One of his old minor league teammates also played against the Athletics and actually out-homered Stargell. Gene Alley hit four home runs, three in the second game, and was on his way to making the Pirates team as a backup to Dick Schofield and Bill Mazeroski.

• • •

In 1963, the Pirates had trouble scoring runs, but their pitching staff had one of the best earned-run averages in the major leagues. At the beginning of 1964, their pitchers, hampered by injuries and inconsistency, struggled to win games, but their hitters were hot throughout the first month of the season. While Clemente, Clendenon, and Bailey hit over .300, Stargell led the way with five home runs and a .373 batting average.

No one was more surprised than Stargell at his early hot streak. Following an early-season game, after his towering home run helped the Pirates defeat the Reds, he told a reporter, "This is a new experience for me. I've never been a spring hitter. Even the year I hit 22 home runs in Asheville, and the next season when I hit 27 at Columbus, I hit most of them after the season was well underway." His home run against the Reds, described by Stargell as "the best ball I ever hit" came within a foot of clearing the right-field roof at Forbes Field.

Stargell continued his hot hitting into May and, by the end of the month, after driving in four runs against the Dodgers, trailed only Willie Mays for the National League lead in RBIs. By Memorial Day, he had 28 RBIs and a batting average of .358, second on the Pirates to Clemente's .375. There was an ominous moment, however, in a game against the Dodgers. He dove head-first into third base in an attempted steal and badly bruised his left knee. After taking a cortisone shot, he had to sit out the next three games against Houston.

His injury forced Murtaugh to use Stargell at first base occasionally, but Murtaugh also worried about Stargell's inconsistency against left-handers. Going into the All-Star break, he was batting only .208 against left-handers, though two of his eight hits were home runs off Mets lefty Al Jackson. In an interview with Pittsburgh sportswriter Les Biederman, Stargell admitted, "I'm the first to know left-handers bother me," but he added, "If I see enough of them I'm going to hit them."

After Stargell finished second in the National League All-Star balloting for left field behind the Cubs' Billy Williams, he was selected by Dodgers manager Walter Alston as an All-Star reserve. His appearance in the game, won by the National League in the bottom of the ninth on a dramatic home run by the Phillies' Johnny Callison, came early and was hardly the stuff of drama. In the bottom of the third, he pinch hit for the Dodgers' Don Drysdale and bounced weakly back to Angels pitcher Dean Chance, who threw him out at first base.

A few weeks after the All-Star break, Stargell had his greatest game in the 1964 season when he hit for the cycle against the St. Louis Cardinals. Stargell joined 13 other Pirates in hitting for the cycle, the most by one team in baseball history. The Pirates list included Hall of Famers Fred Clarke, Honus Wagner, Arky Vaughan, and Ralph Kiner.

After contending through the first half of the 1964 season, the Pirates, with veteran pitchers Friend, Law, and Face struggling to win games and Cardwell and Schwall on the disabled list, slumped badly over the last two months of the season. They finished in sixth place with a disappointing

80–82 record, despite Bob Veale's 18 wins as a starting pitcher, Al McBean's 22 saves, and an impressive debut by rookie Steve Blass, who, in his first start, out-pitched the Dodgers' Don Drysdale.

Though he finished the 1964 season with a team-leading 21 home runs, 78 RBIs, and a .273 batting average, Stargell, battling knee and elbow injuries, also slumped in the last two months of the season. In three games on September 24 and 25 (there was a doubleheader on the 24th), after aggravating his left knee in a collision at first base, he tied a National League record by striking out seven consecutive times. Stargell already had surgery scheduled for the off-season to remove the steel pin that had been inserted in his hip after a high school football injury, but, with one week left in the season, the Pirates decided to move up Stargell's surgery to have additional work done on his knee and his elbow. On September 29, he had bone chips removed from his left elbow and a torn cartilage repaired in his left knee

• • •

Besides recuperating from major surgery in the off-season, Stargell faced a considerable separation in his personal life and in his professional career. By the time he returned to Oakland after his surgery, his wife Lois had filed for divorce. In his autobiography, Stargell claimed that "Lois wanted a normal husband and father for our children, someone who would always be around.... I had been married to Lois and married to my career." Facing a choice, Stargell accepted the divorce, thereby ending a marriage that had lasted a little more than two years.

The second major loss in Stargell's life came in his marriage to baseball. During the 1964 season, Pirates manager Danny Murtaugh had undergone several tests during the season for what had been publicly described as stomach problems, but really had to do with a heart condition. Near the completion of a season-ending road trip, the 47-year-old Murtaugh shocked his players by announcing his retirement. Writing in the *Post-Gazette*, Al Abrams claimed that "only his family and friends knew that the Buc manager has been bothered by a heart condition for a little more than two years. While the doctors do not consider it serious, Murtaugh wisely made the decision that health and family came first."

The Pirates' new manager for the 1965 season was just the opposite of Murtaugh in personality and approach to the game. After Eddie Stanky declined an invitation to interview for the Pirates job, general manager Joe L. Brown hired the talkative, energetic Harry "the Hat" Walker to replace Murtaugh. Walker, who was nicknamed "the Hat" because of his habit, when he was a player, of nervously fiddling with his cap in the batter's box between pitches, had first become a manager in the St. Louis Cardinals minor league system in 1951. He'd replaced Eddie Stanky as Cardinals manager during the 1955 season but, after losing the job to Fred Hutchinson at the end of the year, went back to managing in the minors, where he led AAA Jacksonville to the International League pennant in 1964.

Harry Walker believed he could talk any player or team into becoming a success, but he faced a daunting challenge going into the 1965 season. Stargell wasn't the only key Pirate recovering from surgery when the Pirates arrived in Fort Myers for spring training. Clemente, after having an operation in Puerto Rico to relieve a blood clot in his thigh, had come down with a malaria-like ailment and wouldn't be able to play in an exhibition game until late March. Bill Mazeroski was healthy when he came into camp, but he broke his foot rounding third base in an exhibition game and wouldn't play again until early May. Stargell, the team's leader in home runs in 1964, was still recuperating from knee surgery and wouldn't hit a home run until the beginning of May.

With their team leaders struggling or out with injuries, the Pirates, who were picked to finish in the second division, proved their critics were optimists by getting off to a horrendous start under Walker. At one point they were 9–24 and dead last behind the New York Mets. Once Clemente and Stargell rounded into shape and Mazeroski returned to the lineup, however, the Pirates went on a 12-game winning streak and won 23 of their next 27 games. They also had a new shortstop during their streak. Gene Alley had played so well at second base during Mazeroski's absence that when Mazeroski returned to the lineup the Pirates decided to make Alley the regular shortstop, replacing Dick Schofield, who was then traded to the Giants for utility infielder Jose Pagan.

After his early home run drought, complicated by Harry Walker's decision to bench him against lefties, Stargell snapped out of his slump in May and went on a spectacular home run streak in June. On June 8, he became only the third left-handed hitter to clear the left-field scoreboard at Forbes Field, when he homered off Houston's Dick Farrell. On June 24, he had one of the most spectacular nights of his career when he became the first player to hit three home runs in one game at Dodger Stadium. In his last at-bat he narrowly missed hitting a fourth, a feat accomplished in baseball history by only a handful of players, including Lou Gehrig and Willie Mays.

In the Dodger game, won by the Pirates 13–3, Stargell hit his first two home runs off starter Don Drysdale. He struck out against left-hand relief pitcher Nick Willhite, but hit his third home run off right-hander John Purdin. In his last at-bat in the top of the eighth inning against left-hander Mike Kekich, he swung late on a 3–2 pitch and drove the ball deep down the left-field line, where it hit off the wall just a few inches from the stands. Stargell had to settle for a double to go with his three home runs and his six RBIs.

After the game, Stargell told Les Biederman, "Those three home runs were the thrill of my life." They also gave Stargell a total of 20 for the season, second only to Willie Mays, who was leading the National League with 22 home runs. He was also second in the National League in RBIs with 54. His 10 home runs and 35 RBIs in June earned him the National League's Player of the Month Award, an honor he shared with his teammate Vernon Law, who was making a remarkable comeback in 1965 after four injury-plagued seasons. Law won six games in June and had an ERA of 0.87.

The recognition was gratifying for Law, who'd struggled with arm trouble since 1960, but it was also a pleasure for him to share the honor with Stargell. He'd watched Stargell quietly "learning the game" and "feeling his way" through his first years with the Pirates. From the very beginning Law thought Stargell was a "likable person" with a world of potential, but it took a few seasons for him to become a team leader. In 1965, Law saw a

Stargell that the team could now rely on, and someone who also showed that, like Law, he could "play through injuries."

On July 13, Stargell appeared in his second All-Star Game, but this time he was voted in as the starting left fielder in an outfield with Hank Aaron and Willie Mays. He singled in his first at-bat, then homered off the Twins" Mudcat Grant, his only home run in All-Star competition. After striking out in his third at-bat, he was replaced in left field by Roberto Clemente.

Years later, when asked about his favorite home runs, Stargell smiled and mentioned the one he hit at Metropolitan Stadium in Minnesota in the 1965 All-Star Game, but not because it was one of the most dramatic or longest in his career. Stargell claimed that it was the most unusual because the ball sailed over the fence and into the bullpen, where it scattered members of a band before landing in a tuba.

After the All-Star break, the Pirates, with key players completely recovered from injuries and an improved pitching staff, led by strong repeat seasons from Bob Veale and Al McBean and bounce-back performances by Don Cardwell and Don Schwall, worked their way into contention before finishing in third place with a 90–72 record, seven games behind the pennant-winning Los Angeles Dodgers.

The only major disappointment for the Pirates in the second half of the season was the decline in home run production by Willie Stargell after his hot streak in June and early July. On July 3, just before the All-Star Game, Stargell hit his 21st home run, equaling his career personal best in 1964, but in only his 77th game of the season. In his final 67 games in 1965, he hit only six more home runs and finished with just 27 on the year.

The 27 home runs tied Stargell with Dale Long for the most in a single season by a Pirates left-handed batter. His 27 home runs, 107 RBIs, and .272 batting average were close to the 30 home runs, 100 RBIs, and .300 average he wrote into the lining of his batting cap in spring training as his goals for 1965, a practice he'd continue for the next few years until it became a distraction. His falloff in home runs in the second half of the season, however, was disappointing and unexpected.

Stargell had developed an early reputation for hitting home runs in streaks, but his extended power outage in the second half of the season puzzled him. He thought that his home run surge in June probably had something to do with it. "The only thing I can figure out is that I tried too hard after I got the first 21 and kept pressing. I kept trying to hit homers and, no matter how often you're told it can't be done, you have to learn the hard way."

• • •

Following a visit with Stargell in the hospital after he'd just had more off-season surgery, this time to remove scar tissue from his right knee, Les Biederman wrote a mock-letter to Harry Walker that appeared in the November 13, 1965, *Post-Gazette*. Biederman told Walker not to worry about the physical condition of his star slugger. He claimed that Stargell would be as "good as new" in a few weeks and shouldn't have any trouble being "a 30-homer and 100-RBI man for some years to come." He also had a suggestion for Walker: "Harry, I have a hunch you're going to be using Stargell as an every-day player next year. He stands right up there against left-handers and the more he sees of them the better he's going to hit 'em."

The irony of Biederman giving hitting advice to the Pirates manager was that Walker built his reputation in baseball on his knowledge of hitting and his ability to help batters improve their swing. After the 1965 season, he was given major credit for the Pirates' offensive improvement and the team's strong finish. In 1966, Walker would look even more like a hitting genius when the Pirates scored more than 100 runs than they had in 1965, improved their home run total from 111 to 158, and raised their team batting average from .265 to .279.

While several Pirate hitters had outstanding years in 1966, Walker's major success story was the hitting of Matty Alou and Manny Mota. When Bill Virdon retired at the end of the 1965 season, Joe L. Brown traded left-hand pitcher Joe Gibbon to the San Francisco Giants for Alou, who was a good center fielder, but, at best, a mediocre hitter. After Walker convinced Alou to use a heavier bat and hit to all fields instead of pulling the ball, Alou went on to win the NL batting title in 1966 with a .342 average. Walker used the same approach with Manny Mota who improved his average from

.279 to .332 and became one of the best bench players and pinch-hitters in baseball.

Walker worked his magic with several other players in 1966, including Donn Clendenon, who doubled his home run total from 14 to 28, and Gene Alley, whose average jumped from .252 to .299. He wasn't, however, all that confident of Biederman's forecast because he still had his doubts about Stargell's ability to hit left-hand pitching consistently. After his struggles in the second half of the 1965 season, Stargell admitted that, after hitting three home runs in Los Angeles and narrowly missing a fourth, he made the mistake of trying to pull the ball too much. "He [Walker] keeps me concentrating on the fact that I can hit the ball out of left field as easily as right."

Stargell felt that, despite Walker's lingering doubts, he was a much improved hitter going into 1966 and wrote 35 home runs, 120 RBIs, and a .320 batting average into the lining of his batting helmet as his goals for the season. He also made an effort during the off-season to keep his weight down after Joe L. Brown warned him that he'd be fined for every pound over 210 that he weighed coming into spring training. With his knees feeling better after his second off-season surgery, Stargell believed he was ready to have the best season of his career.

Going into his fourth full season in the majors, Stargell had also developed a healthier mental approach to the game. He once told Mike Easler that you didn't become a complete player until you failed and learned to live with your failure. His Pirate teammates, including veteran players like Vernon Law and Bill Mazeroski, noticed that Stargell never offered an excuse when he had a bad game or fell into a slump and that, no matter how he was playing, he was a positive force in the clubhouse. The positive attitude paid major dividends in 1966, beginning with a June 4 game at Forbes Field against right-hander Robin Roberts and the Houston Astros.

After flying out to center field in his first time at bat, he singled to left field off Roberts. In his following three at-bats, against Astros relievers, Stargell singled to center field, singled again to left field, and then topped off his day with a three-run homer into the right-field stands to give the Pirates a close 9–6 victory after trailing 0–6. The next day Stargell homered into the right-field stands off Dick Farrell, another right-hander, in his first at-bat, then singled to right field, doubled down the right-field line, and then hit a towering home run over the 406 mark in left-center field, before finishing his day with a line-drive single to right field. By the time the Pirates jogged off the field with an easy win against Houston, Stargell, in two games, had banged out nine consecutive hits, one short of the National League record, held by several players, and three shy of the major league record of 12, achieved in 1952 by Detroit Tiger first baseman Walt Dropo.

Stargell's streak began against a future Hall of Fame pitcher, and it came to an end against another future Hall of Famer when he faced Bob Gibson of the St. Louis Cardinals. In his first time at bat, he grounded the ball to shortstop Jerry Buchek, who threw out Gene Alley trying to score from third base. Stargell said he swung at "a hard moving fastball that really hopped at the end." All he could add was, "And that was that." Later, he expressed amazement at what he had done: "This can't be happening to me. I can understand Roberto Clemente getting nine hits in a row, but not Willie Stargell."

Stargell's hitting streak and his impressive numbers in the first half of the season earned him a spot on the National League All-Star team for the third straight year. He was selected as a reserve after losing out in the balloting for a starting outfield positions to Hank Aaron, Willie Mays, and his teammate Roberto Clemente. Bob Veale, who was leading the Pirates in victories and was second only to Sandy Koufax in strikeouts, was selected to the All-Star Game for the second consecutive year, but, as was the case in 1965, he did not appear in the game. After starting the 1965 All-Star Game and hitting his memorable "tuba" home run, Stargell didn't appear in the 1966 game until the eighth inning when he pinch hit for Reds shortstop Leo Cardenas and fouled out to third base.

The Pirates entered the All-Star break as one of the hottest teams in baseball with a record of 52–33 and were only a game out of first place behind the Giants. At one point in the season, they had four of the top seven hitters in the league, with Mota at .352, Alou at .338, Stargell at .337, and Clemente at .328. Stargell, Clemente, and Clendenon were also having career years in home runs and RBIs. The hot hitting continued after the All-Star break, and by the end of July, the Pirates were in first place.

They managed to stay in first place through most of August and into mid-September, until back-to-back losses to the Cardinals dropped them into second place. They never regained first place and finished in third behind the Giants and the pennant-winning Dodgers, but only three games behind the Dodgers. After a 90–72 record under Harry Walker in 1965, the Pirates, with their 92–70 record in 1966, seemed poised, going into the 1967 season, to capture their first pennant since 1960.

◆ ◆ ◆

Willie Stargell had set the lofty goals of 35 home runs, 120 RBIs, and a .320 batting average for 1966 and came very close to reaching those figures. He homered 33 times, his career high, and broke Dale Long's Pirates single-season record of 27 home runs for a left-handed hitter. He drove in 102 runs and hit .315. It was the first time in his professional career that he'd batted over .300 in a season. For all his success, however, his season was overshadowed by the performance of Roberto Clemente.

Responding to Walker's challenge to hit with more power, Clemente, while his average dropped to .317, his lowest in four years, had a career-high 29 home runs and drove in a team-leading 119 runs. It was the first time he'd driven in over 100 runs in a single season. In a close race for the National League MVP Award, he edged out the Dodgers' Sandy Koufax and finally won the honor he felt he deserved in 1960. Stargell finished 15th in the balloting, just behind his teammate, Gene Alley, who won his first Gold Glove in 1966 for his stellar play at shortstop.

The Pittsburgh Pirates and their fans had every reason to be optimistic going into the 1967 season. Led by MVP Roberto Clemente and the explosive Willie Stargell, the Pirates had the best hitting team in the league and one of baseball's most powerful lineups. With the Gold Glove combination of Gene Alley and Bill Mazeroski anchoring the infield and the rifle-like arms of Clemente and Stargell in the outfield, they also had a solid defense to back up their pitching staff.

While critics worried about Walker's lack of interest in his pitchers, the Pirates staff, while not as strong as those with the Dodgers and the Giants, had a healthy Vern Law, a dominating Bob Veale, a promising rookie in Woodie Fryman, and an improving Steve Blass, who won 11 games in 1966. The Pirates also had a strong bullpen led by Roy Face, who bounced back after two disappointing seasons to lead the Pirates with 18 saves, and Pete Mikkelsen, who, after being acquired from the Yankees for the popular Bob Friend, pitched in 71 games, and nearly matched Roy Face in saves.

All the Pirates needed for 1967 was the right trade or two by general manager Joe L. Brown, whose 1959 deal sending Frank Thomas to the Cincinnati Reds for Harvey Haddix, Don Hoak, and Smoky Burgess, as well as his mid-season acquisition of Vinegar Bend Mizell, were the keys to the Pirates winning the National League pennant in 1960. Barely two months after the 1966 season ended, an eager Brown made the first and most dramatic of several moves that would turn the Pirates from contenders to odds-on favorites with bookies and sportswriters to win the National League pennant.

You Have to Fail

On December 1, 1966, Joe L. Brown announced he'd traded Bob Bailey and Gene Michael to the Los Angeles Dodgers for Maury Wills, the major league single-season record holder for stolen bases. It was a bold but risky move by Brown. In acquiring Wills, who, in the early 1960s, had single-handily revived the stolen base as an offensive weapon, Brown added speed to a powerful lineup. Wills would open the season batting second behind Matty Alou, the National League's top hitter in 1966, and in front of Roberto Clemente, the reigning National League MVP. A Gold Glove winner at shortstop in 1961 and 1962, Wills would also improve an already solid Pirates defense. The Pirates had a Gold Glove shortstop in Gene Alley, so Wills would move to third base and give the Pirates a fourth Gold Glove performer in their starting lineup, along with Alley, Mazeroski, and Clemente.

The biggest risk for Brown in the trade was Maury Wills' age and his declining numbers since his record-breaking 104 stolen bases in 1962. Now 34 years old, Wills had stolen only 38 bases in 1966, his lowest total since 1961, and been thrown out 24 times, the second highest number in his career. There was a further risk for Brown in trading away Bob Bailey to acquire Wills. In 1961, at the age of 18, Bailey had received the highest signing bonus in Pirates history. While Bailey had yet to live up to the lofty expectations that the Pirates had for him, he'd been a steady performer since he struggled in his 1963 rookie season.

The Maury Wills trade thrilled Pirate fans, but Brown wasn't finished strengthening the Pirates for their pennant run in 1967. He acquired Juan Pizarro from the Chicago White Sox to give manager Harry Walker an experienced left-hand pitcher to complement Roy Face and Pete Mikklesen in the bullpen. He then traded starting pitcher Don Cardwell, a disappointment since he came to the Pirates in the Dick Groat trade, to the New York Mets for 25-year-old right-hander Dennis Ribant, who could start or pitch in long relief.

• • •

While Brown was busy strengthening the Pirates during the winter for a pennant run in 1967, Wille Stargell had an off-season that, in the words of baseball's master of the malapropism, Yogi Berra, was "déjà vu, all over again." He married Dolores Parker, a Pittsburgh native he met a few years earlier at an *Ebony* fashion show. Stargell's second marriage had the same physical effect on him as his first marriage. When he arrived at Fort Myers for spring training, Stargell's weight had ballooned from 210 to 225 pounds.

Stargell tried to explain to the Pirates brass that his new wife was an excellent cook and, now that he was in camp, he'd have no problem getting back into playing shape. Brown and Walker, however, weren't buying it. An infuriated Brown fined Stargell $1,500, or $100 for each pound over his projected playing weight, and ordered Stargell to go on a crash diet prepared by Pirates team physician Joseph Finegold. He also put Stargell on an exercise program, in addition to his baseball workouts, to sweat off the extra pounds.

Despite his extra weight, Stargell, coming off the best season of his career, was optimistic about the 1967 season and wrote 40 home runs, 120 RBIs, and a .320 batting average into the lining of his batting helmet. Once the season started, however, it was clear that Stargell wasn't ready physically to play baseball. While the Pirates got off to an expected good start in April, Stargell slumped badly and was hitting only .156 by the end of the month. By the middle of June, his average had climbed to only .235. He was also having trouble hitting home runs and driving in runs. During a stretch from June 15 to July 15, he hit only two home runs, while driving in eight.

When Stargell did connect, however, he hit balls that were electrifying. During the 1967 season, he victimized pitchers Jack Fisher and Jim Maloney with the first two of his seven home runs over the 86-foot right-field roof at Forbes Field. He was the ninth player to accomplish the feat since Babe Ruth cleared the roof back in 1935 and the first to hit two balls over the roof in one season. He also had Pittsburgh sportswriters wondering if the ball that he hit that season over the 436 mark near the Barney Dreyfuss monument had gone farther than Dick Stuart's towering home run that cleared the Schenley Park trees bordering Forbes Field's brick outfield wall.

• • •

While Stargell struggled and failed to make the National League All-Star team for the first time in four years, his teammates, with the exception of Donn Clendenon, were having solid offensive seasons. Clemente, who'd win his fourth batting title in 1967, was voted to start in the All-Star Game, as were Bill Mazeroski and Gene Alley. With four regular position players hitting over .300 for the season, including Maury Wills, who hit .302 and stole 29 bases, the Pirates would finish with a league-high .277 batting average, though their home run total, largely because of Stargell's and Clendenon's off-years, had fallen off from 158 to 91.

• • •

The 1967 Pirates were hitting well, but scoring less, so they needed help from what looked like an improved pitching staff. Juan Pizarro and Dennis Ribant didn't have great seasons, but, used as starters and relievers, they managed to win 17 games and save another nine between them. Bob Veale led the Pirates again with 16 wins and Roy Face had another solid season out of the bullpen. Veteran Vern Law, however, struggled with injuries again, and the promising Steve Blass and Woodie Fryman could manage only 11 wins between them, after winning 35 games in 1966.

After the Pirates performed erratically through the first half of the season, Brown decided he needed to make a dramatic move. Though he'd blamed the players for the club's failure to live up to expectations and had recently given Harry Walker a vote of confidence, he fired Walker on July 18 and announced that Danny Murtaugh had "reluctantly" agreed to give up his position as scout and advisor to manage the Pirates for the remainder of the season.

Chet Smith, the sports editor of the *Pittsburgh Press* since 1931, wrote in his "Village Smithy" column that Brown had finally decided to replace Walker because he'd lost the confidence of his players. The team had been bothered by "one irritation after another," but most frustrating was Walker's frequent clubhouse meetings before and after losses. Walker, who prided himself on his gift of gab, had apparently talked himself out of a job.

When Murtaugh took over the team, it had a 42–42 won-lost record and was mired in sixth place. If Brown thought that Murtaugh's calming effect in the clubhouse would translate into victories on the field, he overestimated his 1967 Pirates. Under Murtaugh, the Pirates had a 39–39 mark and finished the season in sixth place, 20½ games behind the pennant-winning Cardinals. At the end of the season, Murtaugh, who admitted he wasn't ready to manage again, stepped down to take a front-office position in player development, and Joe L. Brown began the search for a new Pirates manager.

• • •

Stargell wasn't the only Pirate happy to see Walker fired, but he was certainly among the happiest. Stargell felt that Walker had no confidence in his ability to hit left-hand pitching and, by frequently benching him against left-handers, had never given him a chance to prove himself. When Murtaugh took over from Walker, he told Charley Feeney of the *Post-Gazette* that he planned to play Stargell every day: "I'll bat him sixth or seventh against lefthanders."

When Murtaugh announced that Stargell would now start against right-handed and left-handed pitching, Stargell was thrilled, but perhaps he was too excited and eager to prove himself to Murtaugh. On July 18, during Murtaugh's first game back as Pirates manager, Stargell crashed into

Manager Danny Murtaugh (right) eyes rookie prospects (from left)Willie Stargell, Bob Bailey, and Elmo Plaskett at the Pirates' 1963 spring training camp.

General manager Joe L. Brown put Willie Stargell on several crash diets and exercise programs in spring training. Here, he playfully tugs at Stargell's sweat jacket at the Pirates' 1966 camp.

Vernon Law helps Willie Stargell celebrate his 27th birthday on March 6, 1968. Stargell, born in 1940, was actually 28 years old at the time.

Often batting behind Roberto Clemente, Willie Stargell had many opportunities to congratulate "the Great One" at the end of his home run trot.

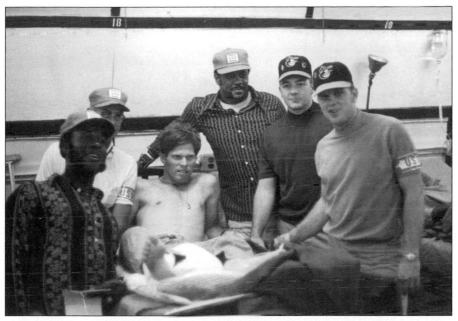

Willie Stargell visits a wounded soldier in a military hospital at Chu Lai, Vietnam, in December 1970. With him are (from left) teammate Mudcat Grant, Pirates broadcaster Bob Prince, and Orioles Eddie Watt and Merv Rottenmund.

The Pirates had their own Murderers Row in the 1971 championship season. Left to right: Manny Sanguillen, Willie Stargell, Al Oliver, Dave Cash, Roberto Clemente, Richie Hebner, and Bob Robertson.

Willie Stargell and the Orioles' Jim Palmer look on as Steelers quarterback Terry Bradshaw handles a bat at a workout before the 1971 World Series.

Willie Stargell and Bill Mazeroski in a moment of celebration in 1971.

Danny Murtaugh with Willie Stargell and Roberto Clemente. They were co-winners of the 1971 Dapper Dan Sportsman of the Year honor at the annual banquet.

The Pirates wore No. 21 on their uniform sleeves in 1972 to honor their teammate Roberto Clemente, who died on New Year's Eve in a plane crash while delivering aid to earthquake victims in Nicaragua.

Playing on damaged knees, Willie Stargell won baseball's Comeback Player of the Year Award in 1978. Here he is, scoring from first base on a triple by Phil Garner.

the right-field wall as he was chasing a fly ball and injured his left thigh. Two days later, he crashed into the left-field wall and aggravated the injury.

Stargell was already dealing with tendinitis in his right shoulder, so the injury to his thigh made it even more of a challenge to bounce back from his poor start in the first half of the season. He struggled for the next few weeks, but on August 13 banged out two hits against Mets left-hander Bob Henley (and a third after Henley was pulled). The next day, he had the game-winning hit against Reds left-hander Billy McCool. Over the last several weeks of the season, he batted over .300 and finished the season with a respectable .271 batting average, but still significantly lower than his .315 average in 1966. He'd improved his home run production over the last month or so, but his season-ending 20 home runs and 73 RBIs were his lowest totals since his 1963 rookie season.

• • •

Brown's first task and his biggest challenge in the off-season was hiring a new Pirates manager. Two years before, he looked outside the Pirates organization and found a manager with a reputation as a hitting coach. This time he stayed within the organization and found a manager who built his reputation helping young pitchers. Larry Shepard had spent the 1967 season as the pitching coach for the Phillies, but before that he'd spent several years managing in the Pirates' minor league system and had tutored most the pitchers on the current major league staff, including Bob Veale and Steve Blass.

In hiring Shepard, Brown clearly acknowledged that the Pirates couldn't hit their way to a pennant and needed a manager who would concentrate his energy on improving their pitching. Brown was also reaching out to a far less talkative but far more organized and disciplined personality in Shepard, someone that Steve Blass described as "tough and blustery." To emphasize the need for a tougher approach, the Pirates added ex-Marine Bill Virdon as their hitting coach and the disciplined Vern Law, who announced his retirement when the season ended, as their pitching coach. Both Virdon and Law were highly respected in the organization for their work ethic.

After hiring Shepard, Brown made a blockbuster trade similar to the one that had brought Maury Wills to the Pirates a year ago, but this time, instead of adding to his offense, he went after an All-Star pitcher with Hall of Fame credentials. The Phillies' Jim Bunning had been one of the National League's most consistent and successful pitchers for over a decade and in 1967 had finished second in the Cy Young Award balloting. To get Bunning, Brown had to give up Woodie Fryman, one of the Pirates' most talented young pitchers, and Don Money, a highly regarded shortstop whom Brown had recently declared an untouchable prospect. Despite the loss of Fryman and Money, Pirate fans were thrilled with the trade, and the new Pirates manager, who'd coached Bunning in 1967, predicted the Pirates would win the pennant in 1968.

• • •

While Brown was busy hiring a manager whom he hoped would bring a more disciplined approach to running the Pirates, he hadn't forgotten the Pirate he regarded as one of his most undisciplined players. Near the end of the 1967 season, the *Post-Gazette*'s Charley Feeney wrote in his "Roamin' Around" column that Willie Stargell "was thinking ahead to next spring and he's wondering if he'll be allowed to play himself into shape. Willie hated those non-baseball exercises that were forced on him last March…. They put him in a bad frame of mind. It took him more than half a season to be happy Willie again."

Stargell wouldn't have to wait until next March to find out what Brown had in mind, and the news wasn't going to make him happy. Just before Brown headed to the December winter meetings where he made the trade for Bunning, *The Sporting News* ran a story by Les Biederman with the headline, "Buccos' Stargell Enjoys a Joke But His Extra Suet Isn't Funny." The story ran with a photograph of Stargell exercising with a medicine ball and a caption reading, "Taking no chances on being out of condition by the 1968 season, Willie Stargell works out with the help of Alex Martella of the Pittsburgh Athletic Association."

Stargell planned to spend the off-season relaxing in his new home in the Point Breeze suburb in Pittsburgh's East End with his wife and his son,

Willie Jr., but Brown was not going to allow Stargell to arrive at spring training out of shape again. He ordered him to spend the winter in a strict conditioning program with strength coach Alex Martella of the Pittsburgh Athletic Association. The idea was not only to keep Stargell's weight at 225, but to turn flab into muscle. When Stargell arrived at Fort Myers, Brown wanted to see a firm and muscular slugger ready to have a great year after his disappointing 1967 season.

Stargell's conditioning program worked exactly as planned, but that was the problem. When Stargell arrived for spring training, he was in the best shape of his career, but his new firm and muscular torso was better fit for a body-building contest than hitting a baseball. Since his earliest days as a ballplayer, Stargell's strength as a hitter was in his long arms and quick wrists, but now he was so muscle-bound that he'd lost some of the bat speed in his swing. An alarmed Brown and Shepard quickly ordered Stargell to drop the medicine ball and start on a new exercise program to improve his flexibility.

. . .

If ever there was a season when a hitter needed flexibility at the plate, it was 1968, which became known as the Year of the Pitcher. It was an extraordinary season for pitchers, but a dismal one for batters. Both the American and National leagues saw their pitchers' ERAs drop below 3.00 for the first time since the end of the dead-ball era in 1920. The St. Louis Cardinals' Bob Gibson finished the season with an extraordinary 1.12 ERA, while pitching 13 shutouts and 28 complete games. The Detroit Tigers' Denny McLain struck out 280 batters and won 31 games, becoming baseball's first 30-game winner since Dizzy Dean in 1934.

Pitchers so dominated the 1968 season that only one American League batter, the Red Sox's Carl Yastrzemski, hit over .300; and he barely made it with a .301 average. Ken Harrelson and Frank Howard were the only American League batters to drive in 100 runs, and in the National League only the San Francisco Giants' Willie McCovey, who led the league with 36 home runs, reached 100 RBIs. The Pirates' Matty Alou managed to hit .332 and finish second to Pete Rose at .336 in the batting race, but Roberto

Clemente hit only .291. A muscle-bound Willie Stargell batted only .237, the lowest average of his major league career.

• • •

Despite his struggles in spring training with his flexibility and bat speed, Stargell began the 1968 season with high hopes. He was so thrilled by new manager Shepard's announcement that he'd be playing against right-handed and left-handed pitching and batting fourth behind Roberto Clemente, that Stargell predicted he'd hit .330 with 50 home runs and 140 RBIs. It was the worst prediction of the 1968 season besides Shepard's optimistic view that the Pirates were going to win the National League pennant.

After major league baseball delayed the 1968 season for Martin Luther King's funeral, the Pirates opened at Houston with their new ace, Jim Bunning, on the mound. The Pirates lost to Houston, but, four days later, Bunning made Brown look like he'd made the right trade when he shut out the Dodgers in Los Angeles. Unfortunately, in the Year of the Pitcher, Bunning would struggle with injuries, win only three more games for the Pirates, and finish the season with a dismal 4–14 record.

Bunning wasn't the only Pirate hampered by injuries in 1968. The Pirates' three All-Stars and Gold Glove winners from 1967 all missed significant playing time. Clemente came to spring training with an injured shoulder he'd suffered in a fall at home and never completely recovered during the season. Mazeroski was hampered by pulled leg muscles, and Alley developed a sore arm that forced him to throw sidearm. Even Alley's backup at shortstop, Freddie Patek, missed playing time when Don Drysdale hit him in the arm with a pitch.

Stargell had twice injured himself in 1967 by running into outfield walls, and, in 1968, the Don Quixote of left fielders was at it again. In a June 23 loss to the San Francisco Giants at Forbes Field, Stargell made a spectacular catch, but crashed into the left-field scoreboard and knocked himself out. He ended up with a severely lacerated face, a stiff and sore neck, and recurring headaches. He wore a neck brace for a time and tried wearing the glasses he used off the field, but he gave up when the glasses became too much of a distraction. His face healed and his neck improved, but the headaches persisted for the rest of the season.

The major headache for Larry Shepard during the season, beside his injury-plagued and underperforming offense, was the team's erratic pitching. What was supposed to be a strength turned into a nightmare when veteran pitchers like Bob Veale and Al McBean failed to overcome the loss of Jim Bunning and had losing seasons. Steve Blass, benefitting from the tutelage of Shepard and Law, had a breakthrough season with an 18–6 record and seven shutouts, but Law felt that some of his veteran pitchers had developed bad habits and weren't working hard enough to prepare themselves for a game.

• • •

The Pirates started the season well enough with an 8–8 record, but they had a five-game losing streak in May and finished the month at 18–23. The one bright spot for Stargell came on May 22 in a 13–6 victory at Wrigley Field against the Chicago Cubs. With the wind blowing out to left field, he just missed hitting four home runs for the second time in his career.

In his first two times at bat against Joe Niekro, he went to the opposite field and homered deep into the left-field bleachers. In his third at-bat against Niekro, he singled in a run, and in his next at-bat against Bill Stoneman, he doubled high off the left-field wall, barely missing a home run. In his last at-bat in the eighth inning, he homered to left-center field off Chuck Hartenstein. As he circled the bases, Cub fans rose and gave him a standing ovation.

Stargell felt that he "never had a better day" in baseball and claimed he was feeling "good physically" and was "eager to get going." The Pirates and Stargell continued, however, to play erratically for the rest of the season. After a five-game losing streak at the beginning of June dropped the team to nine games under .500, the Pirates went on a nine-game winning streak and finished the month with a 36–36 record. After winning their first three games in July, however, they turned around and lost 10 games in a row and fell out of contention. They spent most of the second half under .500 and, after losing their last four games, ended the season at 80–82, good for sixth place, 17 games behind the pennant-winning Cardinals.

After Stargell's home run binge against the Cubs, he went on a hot streak and was near the league leaders in home runs and RBIs until he ran into the wall at Forbes Field in that game against the Giants in late June. After that, he struggled at the bat. When the Pirates went into their July swoon, Shepard lost confidence in Stargell and started benching him against left-hand pitching. Thanks to his mid-season heroics, Stargell still managed to lead the Pirates with 24 home runs, but he drove in only 67 runs. After three All-Star seasons, Stargell, at the age of 28, had his second subpar season on a team loaded with underachievers. With the Pirates' attendance dropping off to 693,485, the lowest total since 1955, Brown knew the time had come to remake the Pirates for the 1969 season, just as he had done in the early 1960s.

• • •

After the Year of the Pitcher, baseball tried to help hitters by lowering the pitching mound from 15 inches to 10, as well as shrinking the strike zone from between the shoulders and the knees to between the armpits and the knees. That, however, wasn't the only dramatic change going into the 1969 season. After adding new franchises in Montreal, San Diego, Kansas City, and Seattle, baseball divided each league into two divisions and introduced divisional playoffs. The Pirates were placed in the East Division with the Cardinals, Cubs, Mets, Phillies, and the expansion Expos.

The immediate impact of expansion on the Pirates was the loss in the National League expansion draft of four veteran players, though each had been a disappointment in 1968. The Expos selected Manny Mota, Maury Wills, and Donn Clendenon from the Pirates' unprotected list, while the Padres picked up Al McBean. Leaving Mota, Wills, Clendenon, and McBean unprotected was a clear signal from general manager Brown that the Pirates would be different in 1969, and much younger.

After the 1962 season, Brown broke up his 1960 world championship team by trading veterans Dick Groat, Don Hoak, and Dick Stuart to make room for some of the young talent in his farm system, including

Willie Stargell. After his 1967 and 1968 Pirate teams failed to live up to expectations and produce a championship, he decided it was time for another dramatic infusion of youth.

There would be no blockbuster trade for a Maury Wills or a Jim Bunning going into the 1969 season. Instead a rookie, Richie Hebner, would replace Maury Wills at third base, and either of two rookies, Al Oliver or Bob Robertson, would step in for Donn Clendenon at first base. Al McBean, Juan Pizarro, and Dennis Ribant were gone, but the Pirates had several young, talented pitchers, including Bob Moose, Dock Ellis, and Luke Walker ready to join Steve Blass, Bob Veale, and, hopefully, a recovered Jim Bunning.

The 1969 season was also critical for Willie Stargell. After three All-Star years from 1964 to 1966, he'd failed to live up to the Pirates' and his own expectations in 1967 and 1968. Struggling with injuries and his weight, he was coming off two disappointing seasons and, after six full seasons in the major leagues, still hadn't convinced the Pirates that he could hit left-hand pitching consistently. At a time when he should have been reaching the peak of his career, Stargell, approaching the age of 29, gave the appearance that his best years were already behind him.

• • •

The Pirates certainly needed Stargell to bounce back on the playing field in 1969, but they also needed him to assume a leadership role with its young players. The team still had the veterans Roberto Clemente and Bill Mazeroski to set the tone in the clubhouse, but Clemente would turn 35 in the 1969 season, and Mazeroski, slowed down with recurring leg injuries, would be 33. The Pirates needed Stargell, with his physical presence and outgoing personality, to become the emotional leader in the clubhouse, draw the team's younger players together, and instill a sense of confidence in them.

That Stargell was finally beginning to mature was evident during the off-season when he told Les Biederman in an interview for *The Sporting News* that he intended to spend time during the off-season working with teenagers in Pittsburgh's black districts: "I believe I can help some young fellows who need guidance." Recalling his own experiences in Alameda and his good fortune in playing his way out of the projects, he added that he liked to show kids "how to get more out of life. I feel I owe it to them.... So many kids want to be something, to make something out of themselves, but they have nothing to start with, nothing to look forward to."

The Pirates hoped that the Willie Stargell who spoke to Les Biederman would show up for spring training not only with a renewed sense of dedication to his own career, but a new sense of responsibility for the success of his younger teammates. The Pirates also hoped their new spring training site would help team cohesion. After several years at Fort Myers with its limited training facilities and segregated housing, the Pirates were moving to Bradenton, Florida, and their newly constructed Pirate City, where they had housing for all of their players, a cafeteria for their meals, and four playing fields, easily accessible from the clubhouse.

Arriving at Bradenton were several young players who'd go on to develop a close relationship with Stargell for the rest of their lives and form the core of the Pirates family a decade before Willie Stargell became the legendary "Pops." What an older Bob Veale had been emotionally to an inexperienced Stargell in the early 1960s, Willie Stargell now became for young players with personalities as different as an intense Al Oliver, an excitable Manny Sanguillen, and a rebellious Dock Ellis.

While Clemente still dominated the Pirates clubhouse and infused a sense of pride and a will to win in his younger teammates, Stargell was there to listen to their doubts and concerns and loosen things up with a practical joke, usually at his own expense. When necessary he was also willing to offer some calming advice or even a stern word or two, but always in confidence. The quality that Al Oliver most admired in Stargell, besides his ability to keep himself under control under even the worst of circumstances, was the trust that he instilled in his teammates: "He never went public with private conversations."

Al Oliver had actually first met Willie Stargell back in 1964. A week after signing his contract with the Pirates right out of high school, Oliver had knee surgery, and while he was recuperating in a Pittsburgh hospital, Stargell, only in his second full season with the Pirates, paid Oliver a visit.

In late 1968, when Oliver was called up from Columbus by the Pirates, he first had to attend to his father's funeral before joining the team. Stargell, who was nearly 20 years old before he met and reconciled with his own father, was there to comfort a grieving Oliver. They became such close friends that, when the still-single Oliver confided to Stargell that he was yearning to start a family, Stargell introduced Oliver to the woman he would later marry and was the best man at Oliver's wedding.

• • •

One of the things that Oliver noticed when he joined the Pirates was the presence of so many African American and Hispanic players in the Pirates clubhouse and the way that Stargell seemed to thrive on the diversity. With Clemente setting the example on the field and Stargell drawing the team together in the clubhouse, the 1969 season brought a new unity and purpose to the Pirates.

Clemente, coming off a subpar season, had been criticized in the press for not being a team player. Stung by the criticism, he bounced back in 1969 and led the team in batting with a .345 batting average, second only to Pete Rose for the league lead. Stargell, criticized for his lack of commitment in 1968, had a spectacular first half of the season and led the National League in hitting after 81 games with a .349 average. Early in the season, when Shepard benched the hot-hitting Stargell against Mets left-hander Jerry Koosman, he was criticized for the move by the same press that claimed for years that Stargell would never develop the consistency to be an everyday player.

Stargell batted only .264 in the second half of the season, but he finished with a .307 average, good for eighth among National League hitters, and fifth in extra-base hits, behind Hank Aaron, Willie McCovey, Lee May, and Tony Perez. He was disappointed with his 29 home runs, but, when he began experimenting with a heavier bat, he hit 17 home runs in the second half of the season. He also reasserted himself as one of the game's most powerful and dangerous hitters. After becoming the only player to hit two home runs over the right-field roof at Forbes in a single season in 1967,

Stargell launched three more home runs over the right-field roof in 1969, including a towering shot against the Mets' Tom Seaver.

Stargell also hit what observers claim was the longest ball ever hit out of Jarry Park in Montreal, but the home run that stunned the baseball world and attracted the attention of the national press came on the night of August 5 at Dodger Stadium. The commonly held view was that it was physically impossible to hit a ball out of the Dodger ballpark, but Stargell, playing with a sore thumb, hit a pitch from the Dodgers' Alan Foster in the top half of the seventh inning that sailed an estimated 525 feet and easily cleared the right-field stands.

. . .

With Clemente and Stargell leading the way, several of the younger Pirates had solid years in 1969. Richie Hebner and Manny Sanguillen hit over .300 in their rookie seasons, and Al Oliver hit 17 home runs, good for third on the team behind Clemente and Stargell. Another promising rookie, Dave Cash, came up from Columbus in September to fill in for Bill Mazeroski, who was still struggling with leg injuries. The biggest surprise among the Pirates' young players, however, was the hitting of an unheralded Carl Taylor, who'd batted a weak .211 in 1968. In a backup role to Stargell, Alou, and Clemente in the outfield, Taylor hit .348 in just 104 games. His performance caught the eye of the St. Louis Cardinals and set the stage in the off-season for one of the most lopsided trades in Pirates history.

If the Pirates' pitching in 1969 had matched an offense that led the National League in hitting and finished second in runs scored, the Pirates might well have run away with the East Division instead of finishing third behind Leo Durocher's Cubs and the Miracle Mets. Steve Blass led the Pirate starters with 16 wins, and Bob Moose, pitching brilliantly as a starter and reliever, had a 14–3 record that included a no-hitter against the Mets. The rest of the pitching staff, however, struggled to win games. Bunning's pitching improved, but he was so inconsistent that the Pirates traded him in August to the Los Angeles Dodgers. Veale led the staff in strikeouts again, but he also pitched erratically and finished with more losses than wins. A disappointing Dock Ellis led the staff in losses with 17. The bullpen, without Roy Face, who was sold to the Detroit Tigers near the end of last season, and Al McBean, lost in the expansion draft, had no one with more than 10 saves.

• • •

The Pirates had started well in 1969 with a 13–8 record, but the team played under .500 in May and June and were a game below .500 at the All-Star break. They'd played better in August and September, but it was too late to save Larry Shepard's job. He'd been under so much strain during the season that he lost weight and, at one point, was hospitalized a few days for nervous exhaustion. He was increasingly criticized in the press for making poor decisions during games and ridiculed for going from a four-man to a five-man rotation to keep his starters from wearing down.

With only two weeks left in the season, Shepard had dinner with Joe L. Brown in New York and asked him about the Pirates' plans for next season. When Brown said he wouldn't make a decision on the Pirates' manager until the season was over, Shepard asked that Brown let him know as soon as possible if he wasn't bringing him back. On September 26, Brown told Shepard that he decided the Pirates needed a change in leadership. Though he thought he was prepared for the decision, Shepard later told the press he was devastated by his firing. With five games left in the season, Brown named coach Alex Grammas as acting manager. Under Grammas, the Pirates won four of their last five games and finished the season with an 88–74 record and a third-place finish.

Since the retirement of Danny Murtaugh, Joe L. Brown had hired two managers with strong minor league records, but with little experience at the major league level. Brown felt that neither manager had proven a strong leader and, as a result, Pirate teams over the past four years had not played up to the level of their talent. Determined not to make the same mistake, Brown turned to Danny Murtaugh, his closest friend in the Pirates organization, and asked for his advice in hiring the next manager.

Pittsburgh sportswriters speculated that Brown was ready to hire Don Hoak, the fiery leader of the 1960 Pirate world champions, to lead the underachieving Pirates after Hoak's successful year as manager at AAA

Columbus. A few days after the end of the season, while at the Pirate City training facility in Florida, Brown discussed the three leading candidates for the manager's job, including Hoak, with Danny Murtaugh. He recalled that "about seven o'clock the next morning there was a rat-a-tat-tat at my door. It was Danny. He came in and said, 'What's the matter with me?' He said, 'You talked about those three guys last night, what about me?'" Brown told Murtaugh he could have the job any time he wanted it, but he'd need medical clearance and the blessing of his wife. When Murtaugh assured Brown that he had both, Brown said, "Okay, you're the manager."

• • •

Brown and Murtaugh weren't the only ones conducting business at Bradenton in the early days after the 1969 season. In the last month of the season, Willie Stargell, at the recommendation of Manny Sanguillen, had switched from a 33-inch, 35-ounce bat to a heavier 36-inch, 38-ounce bat and saw an increase in power. He batted only .212 for the month, but 12 of his 22 hits were for extra bases. Instead of staying in Pittsburgh, he spent the first month of the off-season at Bradenton adjusting to the heavier bat.

Stargell also knew that he wouldn't have to worry about pulling the ball so much to hit home runs because, by mid-season, the Pirates were scheduled to move from mammoth Forbes Field to the friendlier confines of Three Rivers Stadium. He told Pittsburgh sportswriter Bill Christine, "I hope to wait longer on a lot of pitches and hit 'em to the opposite field more." Stargell's former manager Larry Shepard was a poor prophet at picking the Pirates to win championships, but Stargell hoped Shepard had it right when he told reporters, "Next year, when Willie gets into the new ballpark with its normal dimensions, he will challenge Ruth, Maris, and all home run records."

Stargell had also decided to do something about the weight problem that had plagued him for the past several seasons. Instead of waiting for Joe L. Brown to fine him and put him on a crash conditioning program, Stargell decided to head back to Bradenton in late January, a month before the start of spring training, to work himself into playing shape. In the past few seasons, he'd never been able to keep his weight below 225 pounds, and, at times, his weight ballooned to 240 pounds. He was determined to drop 10 pounds in Florida by trying "to run it off."

Stargell had more than a heavier bat, a friendlier ballpark, and the return of the confidence-building Murtaugh for incentives going into the 1970 season. He would become 30 years old before the beginning of spring training and had yet to establish himself among baseball's top echelon of players. He wanted to put himself in position to demand the salary paid out to an Aaron, Mays, or Clemente, whose contract in 1971 was for $125,000. For his rookie season in 1963, Stargell had signed a contract for $6,000. Just before heading to Bradenton in late January, he signed a contract for $35,000. After seven years in the major leagues, his salary had increased by a little less than $30,000 dollars or, on average, about $4,000 a season.

Adding to Stargell's financial concerns were the growing demands of his personal life. With the birth of his daughter Kelli in the off-season, Stargell was now the father of five children. He had the responsibility of providing for his second wife, Dolores, and their two children, Willie Jr. and Kelli, but he had alimony payments and child support checks to write as well. Stargell had also decided to branch out into some business ventures, including an All-Pro Chicken franchise in Pittsburgh's black Hill District.

With all his growing responsibilities and investments, Stargell knew that his financial future was dependent upon his achievements on the ballfield and the success of the Pirates. After writing his season goals inside his batting helmet for several spring trainings before finally concealing them in an envelope in 1969, he openly declared his goals for the coming season: "For 1970, I'd like to see the Pirates win all the marbles and for myself to be named MVP."

CHAPTER 6

Going for
All the Marbles

On March 1, the Pirates played the first intrasquad game of their 1970 spring training camp. It had little practical purpose beyond giving the players a chance to work out under game conditions, but the mood during the game indicated a more relaxed and confident atmosphere than in previous years.

Danny Murtaugh selected Willie Stargell and Bill Mazeroski to manage the two teams, choices that reflected the team's diversity, but also recognized two veterans who had worked hard during the off-season. Like Stargell, Mazeroski had come to Bradenton in January to get into shape before the beginning of spring training. Frustrated by a muscle tear in his thigh that restricted him to 67 games in 1969, Mazeroski ran four miles a day and swam with a kickboard in the Gulf of Mexico to strengthen his legs for the coming season.

During the game, Stargell and Mazeroski spent more time poking fun at Murtaugh and his predecessors than managing their teams. Picking up on Murtaugh's "dumb as a fox" routine with the press, Mazeroski told reporters that he wasn't going to try to outsmart Stargell: "I can't outsmart anyone. I'm the quiet type, remember. I've been around Murtaugh too long. We can't outsmart anybody."

Mimicking Walker's system of fines and Shepard's demand for discipline, Stargell told his players they had a curfew and "must be in their rooms before breakfast." He threatened to fine and trade Richie Hebner when he caught him eating sunflower seeds, but Mazeroski refused Stargell's offer of Hebner and $200,000 for a rookie infielder who'd played in the lower minor leagues last season. When a reporter asked Stargell to explain his bizarre behavior, he said, "I have big pressure on me. I'm the first black man to manage in the South."

Murtaugh, who'd offered a box of cigars to the winners, rooted for a tie so he could keep the cigars, but the Stargells won the game 2–1 on an infield dribbler off the bat of Al Oliver. A jubilant Stargell took credit for the victory and, according to a tongue-in-cheek summary of the game by the *Post-Gazette*'s Charley Feeney, "Stargell headed to the clubhouse where he awaited a phone call from the president. Willie was still waiting for the call at midnight. Somehow Mr. Nixon didn't think this game between all Pirates was important enough."

• • •

Joe L. Brown believed that the 1970 Pirates, under the calm and experienced leadership of Murtaugh, had the talent for a championship season, but sportswriters, remembering the disappointment of recent years, picked the team to finish no better than third behind the World Series–champion Mets and the Cubs. Brown made no blockbuster deals during the off-season, but he did trade outfielder Carl Taylor, who hit .348 in his first full season with the Pirates, to the St. Louis Cardinals for pitcher Dave Giusti and catcher Dave Ricketts, a member (with his older brother, Dick) of the 1955 NIT champion Duquesne Dukes.

Trading a young talented hitter for an inconsistent pitcher and a backup catcher was puzzling for Pirate fans and Pittsburgh sportswriters. Brown, however, knew that with first baseman Bob Robertson, who'd hit 34 home runs at Columbus in 1969, added to the roster, the Pirates had a surplus of young, talented hitters. Robertson could platoon at first base with Oliver, while Oliver spelled Stargell, Alou, and a still-ailing Clemente in the outfield. Trading a .348 hitter for a pitcher with a 50–60 career record (including a 3–7 mark with the Cardinals the previous year) and a catcher who played in only 30 games in 1969, however, seemed a one-sided deal; especially after Giusti struggled in spring training, giving up 21 hits in 15 innings and finishing with a 6.60 ERA.

Brown's critics were right about the trade being lopsided, but it was the Pirates who were the big winners. Carl Taylor never lived up to expectations in St. Louis, but Dave Giusti, who'd actually been recommended to Brown by Roberto Clemente, became one of the premier relief pitchers in baseball once Murtaugh decided to move him to the bullpen. In a season plagued by injuries to Steve Blass, Bob Moose, and Dock Ellis, and a subpar performance by Bob Veale, Giusti became the Pirates' most consistent and clutch performer, winning nine games and saving 26. As for Dave Ricketts, when Tim McCarver, who had played with Ricketts on the Cardinals, heard that his former backup had been traded to Pittsburgh, he told his friends on the Pirates, "You just won the pennant. You got Dave Ricketts. He's going to make a change in your ballclub just by being in the clubhouse."

• • •

After a solid spring training camp, the Pirates started the season with a 10–5 record in April. They didn't, however, get much help from Willie Stargell, who predicted he'd have an MVP year in 1970, but went hitless in his first 22 at-bats. Unlike his two predecessors, Murtaugh didn't panic and kept Stargell in the lineup.

Murtaugh's patience paid off when Stargell gave the Pirates two dramatic wins in late April with towering home runs over the right-field roof at Forbes Field. On April 20, he had only one hit in 29 at-bats when he faced Jim Bouton in the bottom of the sixth inning; but he launched a two-run homer, his first of the season, that easily cleared the right-field roof and gave the Pirates a 3–1 victory over the Houston Astros. On April 25, a still-struggling Stargell came into the Pirates' game against the Atlanta Braves with only three hits in 43 at-bats. His .070 batting average was the lowest in the National League. In the bottom of the seventh inning, with Clemente on first base and the Pirates trailing the Braves by a run, Stargell lofted his second home run in a week over the right-field roof, this time off

Hoyt Wilhelm, to give the Pirates an 8–7 victory and Dave Giusti his first win as a Pirate.

The two home runs, Stargell's first in the 1970 season, were the 17th and 18th to clear the right-field roof in the history of Forbes Field and the sixth and seventh of Stargell's career. Only Bob Skinner and Eddie Mathews, each with two home runs, had hit balls over the roof more than once. The home runs were also parting shots for Stargell at a ballpark that, with its daunting outfield dimensions in the power alleys, had kept him from becoming one of the National League leaders in home runs. As the season entered May, the Pirates were less than two months away from moving into Three Rivers Stadium, with its friendlier dimensions for home run hitters.

• • •

The Pirates played their final games at Forbes Field on June 28 in a doubleheader against the Chicago Cubs. The Cubs were a fitting opponent because they were the visiting team when the Pirates played their first game at Forbes Field on June 30, 1909. The 1909 Cubs, managed by Frank Chance, defeated the Pirates 3–2, but Leo Durocher's 1970 Cubs were much more accommodating. After the Pirates swept the Cubs 3–2 and 4–1, they were in a virtual tie with the New York Mets for the division lead. By the time the Pirates returned to Pittsburgh to open Three Rivers Stadium on July 16, they had climbed into sole possession of first place.

Three Rivers Stadium was lavishly praised in the Pirates' souvenir book for its multi-level seating, all-weather Tartan Turf, computer-operated scoreboard, and glass-enclosed Allegheny Club. It was also lauded as fan friendly, with its wider aisles and seats and its unobstructed view of the playing field.

For Pirate fans, however, it was a wonder that the stadium was finally finished after years of fruitless planning, false starts, cost overruns, and labor problems. They'd also soon discover, that for all its space-age look, Three Rivers, wedged in a corner of land located between the Allegheny and the Ohio rivers, was an old-fashion traffic nightmare for those heading to the stadium. Once inside, instead of finding a friendly atmosphere waiting for them, fans encountered six levels of color-coded, elevated seating that made the new Pirates home feel distant and sterile.

Many baseball fans hated the move from Forbes Field, with its pastoral setting, to Three Rivers, surrounded by empty lots and dilapidated and abandoned buildings. They mockingly described the new stadium as a steel donut, better suited for football than the national pastime. For Willie Stargell, however, Three Rivers Stadium, with its symmetrical, "cookie-cutter" shape, looked like a power hitter's dream. After several seasons of watching the vast dimensions of Forbes Field's power alleys limit his long drives to doubles and triples, Stargell finally had a park perfectly constructed for his straightaway power.

Down the foul lines, Three Rivers measured 340 feet, shorter than Forbes Field's left field by 25 feet, but longer in right field by 40 feet. There were, however, no towering obstacles like Forbes Field's scoreboard in left field and its high fence in right field that pull hitters had to clear for home runs. For Stargell, who was not a natural pull hitter, the most exciting dimensions at Three Rivers, however, were in center field and the power alleys. Forbes Field's center-field dimensions ranged from 420 to 440 feet in its power alleys, out to 457 feet in its deepest recess in left-center field. Three Rivers ran only 385 feet to the fences in its power alleys and 410 feet to center field. Stargell would have no trouble following Harry Walker's advice of a few years before to go with the pitch and drive the ball to all fields.

As the Pirates prepared to move out of Forbes Field, there were a number of estimates of how many home runs Stargell would have hit had he played his early career at Three Rivers Stadium. Most Pittsburgh writers estimated he'd have averaged between 20 and 25 more home runs per year for an additional 150 in his career. His wife Dolores, who charted his long drives in 1969, claimed that her husband would have hit 22 more home runs that season, for a total of 51, the same number that Ralph Kiner hit in 1947, with the help of Greenberg Gardens.

When Three Rivers opened on July 16, Stargell had his own response to those who were estimating how much of a difference the Pirates' new stadium would make in his home run numbers. The 48,846 fans attending the first game at Three Rivers watched Hall of Famer Pie Traynor, one of the heroes of the 1925 World Series champions, throw out the first ball, and listened to Pittsburgh-native Billy Eckstine sing the national anthem, as he had at the 1960 World Series. They then looked on as the Cincinnati Reds, with Tony Perez hitting the first home run at Three Rivers, defeated the Pirates 3–2.

The loss was disappointing, but Stargell managed to thrill the crowd by homering deep into right field in the bottom of the sixth to tie the score at 2–2. It was the first home run by a Pirate at Three Rivers and earned Stargell a $1,000 check from Babcock Lumber Company for accomplishing the feat. It was the first of a record 147 home runs Stargell would hit at Three Rivers Stadium and the beginning of Stargell's emergence as one of baseball's premier power hitters. Playing his home games at Three Rivers for the rest of the decade, he would hit more home runs in the 1970s than any other player in the major leagues.

• • •

Buoyed by their new home, the Pirates played well enough in July to stay at the top of their division, but near the end of the month they lost five out of six games and fell into second place. At the beginning of August, with a win against the Braves, they moved back into first place, where they stayed for the rest of the month. Helping the Pirates keep afloat in August was the hot hitting of a rejuvenated Willie Stargell. Besides becoming the first player to hit a home run that reached the facade of the sixth deck at Three Rivers, he went on a hitting spree, topped by his two homers and three doubles in a 20–10 win over the Atlanta Braves on August 1. His five extra-base hits tied a major league record for the most in one game, and his two home runs gave him 20 for the season after his horrendous start.

After a three-game losing streak in early September dropped the Pirates into a tie for first place, they won 12 of the next 17 games and finished with a 17–10 record for the month. On September 27, the Pirates clinched their first East Division title with a 2–1 win over the now-dethroned New York Mets. Stargell was the team leader on offense for the season with 31 home runs and 85 RBIs, but he had plenty of help from Pittsburgh's core of young players, including Bob Robertson, who nearly matched Stargell by hitting

27 home runs and driving in 82 runs. Manny Sanguillen and Dave Cash hit over .300, and Al Oliver and Richie Hebner also had solid years.

Struggling with injuries, Steve Blass and Bob Moose failed to match their success in 1969, but Luke Walker had his best season and led the Pirates with 15 wins. Dock Ellis, who'd pitched a no-hitter in June, bounced back from a sore elbow, and finished as the Pirates' best pitcher down the stretch drive. Rookies John Lamb, Steve Blass' brother-in-law, and Jim Nelson also contributed, but it was a veteran, Dave Giusti, who was the dominant presence on the Pirates pitching staff. His 26 saves were the second best in the National League and his nine wins were tops for NL relief pitchers. After the season was over, he finished fourth in the balloting for the Cy Young Award and sixth for the National League MVP Award.

The Pirates, after winning 19 of their last 29 games, finished with a record of 89–73, five games better than the second-place Chicago Cubs. Their opponents in the 1970 National League Championship best-of-five playoffs would be a powerful Cincinnati Reds team that had run away with the NL West Division and finished with a 102–60 record. Pittsburgh had its young offensive guns, but the Reds had 22-year-old Johnny Bench, who led the National League with 45 home runs and 148 RBIs. The Pirates had Dave Giusti ready in the bullpen, but the Reds had Clay Carroll with 16 saves and Wayne Granger, who led the National League with 35 saves. It was a clash between a team on the rise after its early season struggles and a team that had dominated its opponents for most of the season, then coasted the rest of the way. The Reds were the heavy favorites to win the playoffs, but the Pirates appeared to have momentum.

· · ·

For the first game of the playoffs, Danny Murtaugh, aware of the Reds' right-handed power, passed over left-handers Luke Walker and Bob Veale and named right-hander Dock Ellis as his starting pitcher. Much to Stargell's relief, the Reds' manager, Sparky Anderson, passed over left-hander Jim Merritt, who'd won 20 games in the 1970 season, and named 22-year-old right-hander Gary Nolan as his starting pitcher. The matchup between

103

Dock Ellis and Gary Nolan was a repeat of the inaugural game at Three Rivers Stadium.

The battle between the two best offensive teams in the National League and the teams with the best bullpens should have been the lead story going into the playoffs, but, instead of writing about Roberto Clemente, Willie Stargell, Pete Rose, and Johnny Bench, the national press was covering an umpires strike that forced the National League to use replacements from the AAA International League for the first game in Pittsburgh. There were no incidents or disruptions in the first game, but, when union workers at Three Rivers threatened a walkout in support of the strike, baseball's management agreed to go back to the bargaining table, and the umpires returned for the second game in Pittsburgh.

The umpire controversy, however, was in sharp contrast to Willie Stargell's high hopes going into the playoffs. Ever since his teenage ball-playing days on Alameda's project fields, he'd dreamt not only of becoming a big-league ballplayer, but of playing some day in a World Series. When the Pirates won the 1960 World Series on Bill Mazeroski's dramatic home run, a 20-year-old Stargell, in only his second year in the minor leagues, saw himself duplicating Mazeroski's feat some day. When he finally made it to the major leagues, he spent season after season in the 1960s on teams that seemed to have the talent to play in a World Series, but always fell short. Now he was about to take the field at Three Rivers only three wins away from fulfilling his boyhood dream.

The general assumption of sportswriters and fans was that the playoffs between the Pirates and the Reds would turn into a slugfest, with the outcome, as Stargell had dreamt it, decided by a dramatic home run. The games, however, turned into pitching duels with neither team generating much offense. In the first game, Dock Ellis became only the third pitcher in 1970 to shut out the Reds in nine innings, but Nolan matched Ellis with nine shutout innings of his own. In the 10th inning, after Pete Rose drove in the lead run and Lee May drove in two more with a double, Clay Carroll retired the Pirates in the bottom of the tenth for a 3–0 Reds victory.

In the second game, Murtaugh went with left-hander Luke Walker, his top winning pitcher for the season, but Anderson countered with his own top winner, left-hander Jim Merritt. The Pirates had struggled to hit Merritt's assortment of breaking pitches all season and would not fare better in the playoffs. They failed to score on Merritt through the first five innings and trailed the Reds 2–0 going into the bottom of the sixth. When Merritt gave up a one-out double to Dave Cash, Anderson, who was called "Captain Hook" because he yanked his starting pitchers at the first sign of trouble, brought in Clay Carroll, who retired two batters but gave up singles to Clemente and Sanguillen.

With the Reds leading only 2–1 and the tying and lead runs on base for the Pirates, Anderson went to his bullpen once again and brought in 19-year-old left-hander Don Gullett to face Willie Stargell. This was the moment Stargell had been waiting for throughout his entire career. While Gullett was a left-hander, his strength was his fastball, and Stargell was a fastball hitter. With one swing of the bat, Stargell could give the Pirates the lead and turn the playoff series around. Stargell pinwheeled his bat, looked for a fastball, and, when he got it, drove the ball deep into right field—but not deep enough. Rose drifted back, caught the fly ball near the wall, and ended the inning. The Reds added a run in the eighth and won the game, 3–1.

With the Pirates down two games, the playoffs shifted to Cincinnati, but with the same result. After the Pirates scored a run in the first inning off Tony Cloninger, Bob Moose gave up back-to-back home runs by Tony Perez and Johnny Bench in the bottom of the first. The Pirates tied the game in the fifth inning on a hit by Stargell, but the Reds scored a run in the bottom of the eighth and went on to a 3–2 victory and a three-game sweep in the playoffs.

In the three games with the Reds in the National League Championship Series, the powerful Pirates offense scored only three runs and hit no home runs. They had the lead for only one inning in the entire series, and Dave Giusti, who appeared in two games, never had a save opportunity. Stargell fell short in his one dramatic moment in the playoffs, but he led the Pirates in hits with six and batted .500. He'd finally had a chance to play in a major league baseball postseason and did well, but he ended up tasting failure and defeat. Next season, he'd be playing his first full season in Three Rivers

Stadium. He would have the chance to prove that he was capable of leading the National League in home runs, while also leading his team beyond the playoffs and into the World Series.

• • •

After the 1970 season, Joe L. Brown was eager to improve the Pirates for 1971, but it was a deal he'd made late in 1970 to help the team win the division that would have a direct bearing on Willie Stargell during the off-season. Looking to improve his bullpen, Brown acquired Mudcat Grant from the Oakland A's in September for a player to be named later. Grant, who gave up Stargell's "tuba" home run in the 1965 All-Star Game, won two critical games for the Pirates in the last few weeks of the 1970 season and was re-signed by the Pirates for 1971. In early December, Bob Prince invited Grant and and his teammate Stargell to join him on a tour, sponsored by the USO, to visit military hospitals in Vietnam. Baltimore Orioles pitcher Eddie Watt and outfielder Merv Rettenmund, who would make the last out in the 1971 World Series, were also a part of the tour.

Grant's stay with the Pirates lasted less than a year. On August 10, 1971, after appearing in 42 games, while winning five and saving seven, Grant was sold back to the A's on the same day they acquired relief pitcher Bob Miller from the San Diego Padres. During his trip to Vietnam, however, Grant became close friends with Stargell. He'd later help him with the sickle cell anemia initiative Stargell established after learning that his daughter Wendy had the sickle cell trait.

When the tour ended, Grant told the press that Stargell, after visiting so many badly wounded soldiers in the hospitals, would be different when he returned home: "It was as if he realized we had it pretty good, and he was going to take full advantage of it." Even Bob Prince noticed the change in Stargell: "Willie's attitude was always good, but now it's even better. I think what he saw over there built up his resolution."

Stargell had worked hard to get in shape for the 1970 season, but, during his tour of Vietnam, he lost a significant amount of weight in the jungle heat, while moving from base camp to base camp. By the time he returned to Pittsburgh, he felt he'd lost several pounds, but Prince believed

Stargell had shed "about 20 or 25 pounds sweating over there." Stargell didn't know how much weight he'd lost, but he did notice he was able to wear clothes he usually couldn't wear "until July."

Once he was home, he went on a "strict diet of broiled meat and boiled vegetables" to keep his weight down and avoided his favorites, "sweet potato pie and fruit cobblers." To stay in shape, he also took long walks "in a graveyard near his house. I'd walk about three times a week, about four miles every day. Some of those cold days, I was tempted to go back in the house, but I managed to keep going."

The long walks strengthened Stargell's ailing knees and the right heel he'd freakishly injured in a game in Houston the previous May. He said that after he swung and missed a pitch "the bat came round and hit my heel. I figured it was a just a bad bruise. It wasn't until August that I knew it was a tendon tear." By the time he arrived at Bradenton, he felt he was in the best physical shape and the best frame of mind of his career. His weight was down, his legs and heel felt sound, and, at the age of 31, he believed he had finally gained the emotional maturity to match his physical talent.

When Murtaugh saw Stargell for the first time at the 1971 spring training camp, he was so impressed that he told reporters the time Stargell "used to spend running off fat" he could now spend "at batting practice." That extra time he'd spend in the batting cage would pay off when the 1971 season opened with an offensive explosion that even Stargell, with his perennial optimism at the beginning of each season, could never have predicted for himself.

• • •

Stargell wasn't the only one feeling healthier when he arrived at Bradenton. After the 1970 season, Joe L. Brown met with Danny Murtaugh to check on the health of his manager, whose heart problems had forced him to retire after the 1964 season. Brown was prepared to offer the manager's position to Bill Virdon, who'd been a coach with the Pirates for the past few years and had the respect of players and management.

He hoped, however, that Murtaugh, who'd won *The Sporting News* Manager of the Year Award, would feel well enough to return for the

1971 season. After a few weeks of rest and talking matters over with his family, Murtaugh, surrounded by Brown and a group of happy players, including Stargell, announced at a November 12 news conference that he felt "healthier and wiser" and had agreed to a one-year contract to manage the Pirates in 1971.

After re-signing Murtaugh, Brown made two trades to improve the Pirates for 1971. Even though the Pirate offense had faltered in the playoffs against the Reds, Brown knew that the team's talented balance of young and veteran hitters was its strength. With Giusti anchoring a solid bullpen, Brown decided that the Pirates' most important need was starting pitching. The Pirates had an impressive nucleus of young pitchers, including Ellis, Blass, Moose, and Walker, but, because of injuries and inconsistency, none had put together consecutive solid seasons. With veteran Bob Veale fading, Brown felt that Murtaugh needed more options on his pitching staff for the coming season.

In each of the two trades, Brown acquired a pitcher who would play a pivotal role in 1971. His main target was the Kansas City Royals' 27 year-old right-hander Bob Johnson. In 1970, while finishing with a losing record on a poor Royals team, Johnson led all right-handers in the American League with 206 strikeouts and finished second for *The Sporting News* Rookie of the Year Award to the Twins' Bert Byleven, a future hero for the Pirates in the 1979 World Series.

To get Johnson, Brown had to give up shortstop Freddie Patek, pitcher Bruce Dal Canton, and catcher Jerry May, but in Johnson, Brown believed he had found a dominating fastball pitcher to replace Bob Veale in the starting rotation. His only concern was that in giving up Patek, he'd left the team vulnerable at shortstop if the injury-prone Gene Alley couldn't play everyday. To protect himself, he had the Royals throw in their good-field, no-hit shortstop Jackie Hernanadez. It would turn out to be one of the smartest moves that he made during the off-season.

After acquiring Bob Johnson from the Royals, Brown turned to the St. Louis Cardinals, his key trading partner from last year. He offered former batting champion Matty Alou to the Cardinals for versatile pitcher Nelson Briles and veteran outfielder Vic Davalillo. Briles had proven himself a clutch pitcher in 1967 when he won 14 games and helped lead the Cardinals to the World Series, but he'd became expendable after the 1970 season because of a crowded Cardinal starting pitching staff. The Cardinals, looking for center-field help after the loss of Curt Flood, jumped at the chance to get Alou and threw in Davalillo, who had reached an age where he no longer could play regularly.

The trade not only gave Brown another starting pitcher, it created room for the Pirates to keep Al Oliver and Bob Robertson in the starting lineup by moving Oliver into center field to replace Alou. In 1970, Oliver had rotated between first base and the corner outfield positions, but he told the *Post-Gazette*'s Charley Feeney that he thought he could play center field: "One thing I'd like for next year. I'd like to have one regular position."

When Bill Virdon, one of baseball's best center fielders in his playing career with the Pirates, told Brown he thought Oliver could make the adjustment, Brown sent Oliver to play center field for the San Juan winter league team managed by Roberto Clemente. When Clemente, after watching Oliver play his new position, gave his endorsement to the move, Oliver became the Pirates' regular center fielder on a team that had future Hall of Famers in left and right field.

• • •

When the Pirates arrived at Bradenton for spring training, they were a talented, diverse, and confident ballclub. Brown had improved the pitching staff through trades, and the shift of Oliver to center field had solidified the starting lineup. Brown went so far as to declare that "this Pirate team is the best rounded, most talented team since I've been in Pittsburgh."

The Pirates had so much talent that there was no room on the roster for outstanding prospects like Bruce Kison, Rennie Stennett, and Richie Zisk, though Kison and Stennett would be brought up from the minors during the season and contribute to the Pirates' drive to the division title. The team was so balanced on the field and so diverse and relaxed in the clubhouse that even the aloof Clemente joined in the racial banter and the practical jokes.

The Pirates suffered a few injuries during spring training, but Gene Alley, with a broken hand, was the only regular out of the lineup on Opening Day. The Pirates played well during the exhibition season, and seemed poised to improve on their success in 1970. Willie Stargell, in particular, seemed on the brink of his greatest season since joining the Pirates late in 1962. After nearly a decade in the major leagues, he was finally going to play an entire season in a home run–friendly ballpark.

At the age of 31, Stargell felt in good health and in great shape for the coming season. During the off-season, especially after visiting the military hospitals in Vietnam, he believed that he had learned "a lot" about himself and "matured like a fine wine." The only question now, as the Pirates headed to Pittsburgh in April, was whether or not Stargell and his teammates would be drinking champagne in October.

CHAPTER 7

If He's Going to Be a Man

It didn't take long for Willie Stargell to face his first challenge in the 1971 season. The Pirates opened at Three Rivers on April 6 against the Philadelphia Phillies and veteran left-hand pitcher Chris Short. After a day off, they'd face another veteran left hander, their former teammate Woodie Fryman. When Murtaugh made out his lineup card, he adjusted the batting order by moving Manny Sanguillen into Stargell's clean-up spot in the order and dropping Stargell down to sixth. It was a clear indication that Murtaugh, while keeping Stargell in the lineup against left-handers, still believed Stargell had trouble hitting left-handed pitching.

The major story in the Pirates' 4–2 and 2–0 wins against the Phillies in the first two games of the season was the complete-game performances of Dock Ellis and Luke Walker. It was Stargell, however, who sparked a sluggish offense in the second game by hitting a two-run double off Fryman in the bottom of the sixth to give the Pirates their margin of victory. When the Pirates played their next game on the road in Atlanta, Stargell, back in the clean-up spot in the order against right-hander Pat Jarvis, led the Pirates to an 8–2 victory with three hits, including his first home run of the season, off Ron Herbel.

The next night the Pirates lost their first game of the season in extra innings to the Braves in Atlanta, but Stargell exploded for three more

111

homers on the way to a record-breaking home run spree in April. He hit two home runs off Phil Niekro knuckleballs, then homered against left-hander George Stone. It was the third time in his career that Stargell had hit three home runs in one game, but not the last. When the Braves came to Pittsburgh 11 days later, Pirate fans finally had their own chance to see Stargell hit three home runs in one game. On April 21, in his first two times at bat, he homered against right-hander Jim Nash, and in the sixth inning he homered again, this time against relief pitcher Tom Kelley. It was the fourth time in Stargell's career he'd hit three home runs in one game. Only Johnny Mize, Lou Gehrig, Ernie Banks, and Ralph Kiner had accomplished the feat before Stargell.

When Stargell homered the next night in the third inning against Braves right-hander Ron Reed, it was his 10th for the season and tied the major league record for most home runs hit in April, held by Frank Robinson with the Orioles and Tony Perez with the Reds. On April 27, in a night game against the Los Angeles Dodgers, Pirate fans had a chance to see Stargell set the record, but only if they stayed around to watch the end of the game. In the bottom of the ninth, with the Pirates trailing 7–4 and no one on base, Stargell hit his record-breaking 11th home run of the season off former teammate Pete Mikkelsen.

Stargell accepted the congratulations of his teammates, but he was in no mood to celebrate after the Pirates lost the game 7–5. He told Phil Musick of the *Pittsburgh Press*, "If I could trade it for a win, I'd give it up." When a fan offered Stargell the historic baseball, he responded, "Let him keep it." Stargell asked Musick, "What's it mean, really?" But before Musick could answer, Stargell responded to his own question, "Next time someone will hit 20 in a month."

Stargell had good reason to be frustrated by the Pirates loss. On the night Stargell hit his record-breaking 11th home run, Richie Hebner, coming out of an 0-for-24 slump, also homered, but it was only the eighth of the season for the rest of the Pirates lineup. While fans and sportswriters buzzed about the prospects of Stargell breaking the single-season home run records of Babe Ruth and Roger Maris, the Pirates had generated little buzz about their own prospects for the season because of their anemic hitting. With Hebner slumping and Clemente hitting well below his .316 lifetime average and struggling to drive in runs, the Pirates, even with Stargell's home run barrage, were barely playing above .500. At the end of the month, Stargell was hitting .347 to go along with his 11 home runs, but the Pirates, with a win over the San Diego Padres on the last day in April, finished the month with a modest 12–10 record.

• • •

It didn't take long for Stargell to hit his 12th home run of the season. After increasing their record to 14–10 with two more wins in a sweep of the Padres, the Pirates headed to the West Coast for series with the Giants, Dodgers, and Padres. In the first of two games with the Giants, Stargell homered in the eighth inning to cap a lopsided 10–2 victory. The 10-run scoring spree, led by Manny Sanguillen's four hits, ignited the Pirates offense and sent the Pirates on their way to a 17–9 record in May and a 29–19 record for the first two months of the season. They had a scare in early May when Dock Ellis developed a sore elbow, but Ellis quickly recovered and became the ace of the Pirates pitching staff. Luke Walker was struggling after his impressive shutout of the Phillies, and an inconsistent Bob Veale was sent to the bullpen; but Steve Blass, Nelson Briles, and Bob Moose were off to solid starts, as was the team's closer, Dave Giusti.

Ellis' sore elbow was a concern at the beginning of May, but the biggest scare for the Pirates came late in the month. On May 20, before the start of a game against the Cincinnati Reds, Pirates manager Danny Murtaugh experienced chest pains. With his history of heart trouble, he was rushed to a Cincinnati hospital. While a cardiologist found no signs of a heart attack, Murtaugh remained in the hospital for four days before he was transferred to Presbyterian University Hospital in Pittsburgh for more tests. During his two-week stay in hospitals, Murtaugh made no public comment, but he privately admitted to friends that he felt weak and tired: "These games are tough on my boiler."

After resting at home for a week, Murtaugh returned to the Pirates on June 6 for a game at Three Rivers against Houston. During Murtaugh's absence the team had gone 9–7 and were in second place behind the

Cardinals under interim manager Bill Virdon. With Murtaugh back in the dugout, the Pirates defeated Houston with the help of Stargell's 18th home run. Stargell also homered the next day in an 11–6 romp over the Cubs. A few days later, after defeating the Cardinals, the Pirates moved into first place. They finished June with a 49–29 record and would never fall out of first place for the rest of the season.

• • •

No one was happier to see Murtaugh back than Willie Stargell. When asked by reporters in the past if he had an interest in managing, he always said no, but also told them that if he ever did become interested, he'd model himself after Danny Murtaugh. Two months after Murtaugh's health scare, with the Pirates well on their way to the playoffs, Stargell told a reporter, Murtaugh "doesn't demand respect, he commands it. He knows how to handle players, to get the most out of them. He doesn't say much, but when he does you listen because you know it means something."

With Murtaugh back in the dugout, Stargell went on another home run binge that had reporters predicting, once again, that he would easily break Hack Wilson's National League single-season home run record of 56 and probably challenge Ruth at 60 and Maris at 61 for the all-time record. By the end of June, Stargell had set a new major league record for the most home runs at that juncture in a season with 28. By the All-Star break, Stargell had 30 home runs and 87 RBIs, and the Pirates were sitting comfortably in first place with a 10-game lead.

In the first half of the 1971 season, Stargell was not only hitting home runs at a record pace, he was launching shots into the upper deck at Three Rivers and hitting balls so far out of ballparks around the league that they were becoming the stuff of legends. His home run on June 25 at the Phillies' newly opened Veterans Stadium against his former teammate Jim Bunning was hit so hard and so far that it seemed to defy the physics of baseball. Those who witnessed the home run turned to the language of another sport when they tried to describe what they had just seen. Phillies shortstop Larry Bowa said, "It sounded like a golf ball coming off a metal driver." Picking up on Bowa's comment, *Philadelphia Inquirer* columnist

Frank Dolson described Stargell's blast as "a Jack Nicklaus tee shot." Even Stargell seemed amazed: "I knew it had distance and height, but I had no idea it would carry that far."

◆ ◆ ◆

At the beginning of July, Stargell was selected as the starting National League left fielder for the All-Star Game, but it was Oakland Athletics—slugger Reggie Jackson who stole the spotlight on July 13 with a home run blast at Tiger Stadium off Pirates pitcher Dock Ellis that hit a light tower. There were six home runs in the game, an All-Star Game record, but the only Pirate to homer in the National League's 6–4 loss was Roberto Clemente. Stargell went hitless in the game, while striking out twice.

The Pirates were in the middle of an 11-game winning streak at the All-Star break, and, when play resumed, they defeated the San Diego Padres in 17 innings for their seventh win in a row. The extra-inning win against the Padres was one of the most dramatic games of 1971. Trailing 1–0 in the bottom of the ninth, they tied the score on Gene Alley's sacrifice fly. After the Padres went ahead 2–1 in the top of the 13th, Willie Stargell tied the score in the bottom of the inning with his 31st home run. When the Padres scored a run in the top of the 16th, Richie Hebner hit a home run to tie the game again. In the bottom of the 17th, Roberto Clemente, who was hitless on the night, hammered his ninth home run of the season to give the Pirates an exhausting, but thrilling, 4–3 victory.

With the help of their 11-game winning streak, the Pirates ended July in first place with an 8½-game lead over the St. Louis Cardinals. Stargell finished the month with 36 home runs, tying the major league record for most home runs through July, and had already reached 100 RBIs for the season. There was, however, a potential jinx lurking when Stargell appeared on the cover of a sports magazine that arrived on August 2 at newsstands and bookstores around the country.

◆ ◆ ◆

Over the years a number of sports figures went into mysterious slumps when they appeared on the cover of *Sports Illustrated*. It had happened so often that it became known as the *Sports Illustrated* jinx. Anyone picking up a copy of the weekly *SI* magazine dated August 2 saw a striking color photograph of Willie Stargell about to release his bat after hitting—what the intense gaze in his eyes suggests—was a home run. The title on the cover read, "Pittsburgh Overpowers the East: Slugger Willie Stargell."

The featured article on the Pirates, titled "On the Lam With the Three Rivers Gang," was by Roy Blount Jr., who went on to write *About Three Bricks Shy of a Load* on the 1973 Steelers season. In the article, Blount, for the most part, had fun with the irreverent humor of the Pirates clubhouse, where not even Roberto Clemente escaped the clowning and the ribbing. Blount wrote that when Dock Ellis found out that Clemente was the one who turned down the volume on his "funky" music tape, he broke "into his Clemente imitation. Hobbling, twitching his neck and saying in a Latin accent, 'Oh, I not like I used to be. I a little bit of an old man now.'"

The article also took note of the relaxed atmosphere of the clubhouse, where even the team's rich diversity was part of the clowning: "Altogether, with seven American blacks, six Latins, and a white minority which included one Polish American, one Texas American and two redheads, the Pirates had perhaps the richest assortment of ethnic strains ever to heap threats, obloquy and even full nelsons on each other." Years later, however, Blass, the "clown prince" in the clubhouse in 1971, had to admit "it was great fun because we were good. None of that shit would be fun if we weren't, because when you're not good, nothing's funny."

For all the humor in the article, its focus was the Pirates' offensive depth, led by Willie Stargell, its "batting bulwark." Blount's colorful portrait of Stargell ranged from his imposing physical presence ("He has an enormous trunk that seems to swell visibly in the batter's box") to a touching scene where he asks his four-year-old son, Wilver Jr., called "Son-Son," if he's ready for an upcoming father-son game ("Kin you pole it?"). There was also a brief history of Stargell's struggles to hit home runs at Forbes Field and his power surge at Three Rivers ("Stargell is heading toward fifty plus homers"). The most telling detail of Blount's portrait, however, was his description of the condition of Stargell's knees: "His knees are puffy, pitted, and dumpy looking, and the ravaged cartilages in them apparently make it an ordeal for him to play."

Three Rivers' home run–friendly dimensions may have been a blessing for Stargell, but its Tartan Turf was turning into a curse. The constant pounding and cutting on the artificial outfield surface was taking such a toll on Stargell's surgically repaired knees that he contemplated an operation on at least one of them in the off-season. With Bob Robertson playing well at first base and hitting with power, Murtaugh had no option other than playing Stargell in left field, but, during the last two months of the season, Stargell's knees worsened to the point that Joe L. Brown thought Stargell should go ahead and have the surgery before doing even more damage to himself.

With the Pirates driving toward the playoffs and a possible trip to the World Series, Stargell decided to play out the season, though he wasn't the same hitter who broke home run records in the first half of the season. He had a decent second half and set personal highs with a league-leading 48 home runs (his previous best was 33 in 1966) and 125 RBIs, second best in the National League. The numbers, however, fell short of the lofty expectations and predictions that had surrounded Stargell as late as the All-Star Game and that still lingered in Blount's *Sports Illustrated* article when it appeared in early August.

• • •

With Stargell hobbled by bad knees, the Pirates had their worst month of the season in August. At one point, they lost 15 out of 22 games and ended with a record for the month of 14–17. It was their first and only losing month of the 1971 season. Stargell wasn't the only Pirate struggling with physical woes in August. In the first week of the month, Jose Pagan was hit by a pitch that fractured his arm and put him on the disabled list until late September. Later in the month, Richie Hebner came down with a viral infection that briefly hospitalized him, and Gene Alley had to sit out games when he severely twisted the same knee he had injured back in 1968. At one point the Pirates were so depleted of players, especially infielders, because of injuries that Murtaugh had to use Bill Mazeroski at third base.

In mid-August, the Cardinals swept the Pirates in four games at Three Rivers (in a series that featured a no-hitter by Bob Gibson) and moved to within four games of the first-place Pirates. Now at their lowest point in the season, Bob Robertson issued a challenge to his teammates: "Stargell's been carrying us all year and now that his shoulders have gotten tired, it's up to somebody to take over." The Pirates responded to the challenge with the help of strong performances by pitcher Bruce Kison and infielder Rennie Stennett, who were called up from the minors to fill in for injured players. They won seven of their last nine games in August and held a 4½-game lead on the Cardinals going into September.

While Kison and Stennett were becoming valuable additions to the team, two other player moves by Brown actually caused some discontent in the clubhouse, a rarity in the 1971 season. On August 10, Brown sold Mudcat Grant back to the Oakland Athletics, even though Grant, after playing a key role in the Pirates East Division title run in 1970, had won five games and saved seven in a backup role to Dave Giusti. On the same day that he sold Grant, Brown traded two minor leaguers for San Diego Padres relief pitcher Bob Miller, whose record was similar to Grant. Miller was then assigned to take Grant's spot in the Pirates bullpen. Grant was one of the most popular players in the Pirates clubhouse, and his departure puzzled and angered his teammates, especially Willie Stargell. Stargell's response to the trade: "What the hell is going on?"

For Stargell, it was a reminder that players had little control over their careers, something Bob Veale had warned him about back in 1962, when they were driving to Pittsburgh after being called up from AAA Columbus. Stargell believed this was especially true for black players because in 1971, over 20 years after Jackie Robinson crossed baseball's color line, there were still no black managers in the major leagues, very few coaches, and no one in a position of authority in a major league front office. In an interview published just a month before Grant was sold, Stargell told a reporter that he wondered "if baseball would ever have a black manager.... Maybe someday the people will come around and realize that we're all one, that we are all equal in ability. When the people are ready to accept it, then it will happen."

• • •

On September 1, the Pirates started off the last month of the season at Three Rivers with a 10–7 victory over the Philadelphia Phillies. The win was an encouraging display of the Pirates' offensive power, but it also solidified the 1971 Pirates' reputation as the most integrated ballclub in baseball. With a left-handed Woodie Fryman pitching for the Phillies, Murtaugh decided to sit out Richie Hebner and play Dave Cash at third base. He also decided to start Al Oliver at first base for Bob Robertson, who had slumped in the last few games. With Willie Stargell, Gene Clines, and Roberto Clemente in the outfield and Jackie Hernandez and Rennie Stennett replacing the ailing Gene Alley and Bill Mazeroski at shortstop and second base, all that Murtaugh had to do was write in the names of Manny Sanguillen and Dock Ellis as his starting catcher and pitcher for the Pirates to take the field with the first all-black lineup in baseball history.

The victory against the Phillies ignited the Pirates. After a three-game sweep of the Cubs, helped along by Stargell's grand slam, his 44th home run of the season, they swept two games from the Cardinals. By mid September, the Pirates had increased their division lead to 8½ games. On Wednesday, September 22, at Busch Stadium, after losing to the Cardinals the night before, the Pirates defeated their nemesis Bob Gibson 5–1, behind the pitching of Luke Walker and Dave Giusti, and clinched the division title.

In the clubhouse, as players doused themselves with champagne, Murtaugh told reporters, "It's poetic justice that Giusti should wrap it up. He has closed the door so often." Giusti, who had appeared in 58 games and had 30 saves and five wins, had only one complaint about his physical condition going into the playoffs. His locker was next to Stargell's, and every time he wasn't looking, Stargell would pull out some of his chest hairs. Years later, he'd claim, "To this day, I have less hair on the 'Willie side' of my chest." During the season, he did get even with Stargell, who was developing a taste for big cars and fine wines. After he lost a bet with Stargell in which the winner was to receive "a nice bottle of wine," Giusti gave his tormentor "a non-vintage bottle of watermelon wine."

• • •

The Pirates opened the best-of-five playoffs for the National League pennant at wind-swept Candlestick Park against the San Francisco Giants. After dominating the West Division in the first half of the season, the Giants had struggled in the second half and nearly collapsed in the stretch drive. It took a strong pitching performance by Juan Marichal in the final game of the season for the Giants to beat the Padres and finish one game ahead of the Dodgers. But, even with their late-season struggles, the Giants were a dangerous hitting team with future Hall of Famers Willie Mays and Willie McCovey in a lineup led by rising star, Bobby Bonds, who'd hit 33 home runs and had 102 RBIs, while batting leadoff. They also had two veteran (future Hall of Fame) starters in Marichal and Gaylord Perry.

What made matters worse for the Pirates was their poor performance against the Giants during the 1971 season, and their inability over the past few seasons to win at Candlestick Park. They'd lost nine of their 12 regular season games against the Giants in 1971, and, dating back to 1969, had lost 11 of their last 13 games at Candlestick. Adding to the challenge were the nagging knee injuries to Gene Alley and Willie Stargell. Alley's left knee was so bad that Murtaugh, realizing that his All-Star shortstop would be limited to coming off the bench, decided to replace hot-hitting rookie second baseman Rennie Stennett for the playoffs with the veteran Jose Pagan, who could fill in at shortstop.

Stargell was clearly excited by the opportunity to return to the playoffs after last season's sweep by the Cincinnati Reds; but the wear and tear of a full season on the hard artificial turf at Three Rivers had further damaged his knees and affected his ability to drive the ball. He'd managed to hit four more home runs after his clutch grand slam against the Cubs in early September for a league-leading 48 for the season, but his batting average had dropped below .300 by the end of September. He was in the starting lineup and batting clean-up for the first game at Candlestick, but it would be up to a resurgent Roberto Clemente, who hit .341 for the season, and younger hitters, like Bob Robertson, Al Oliver, and Richie Hebner to provide the power needed to outscore the San Francisco Giants and carry the team into the World Series.

• • •

For the opening game of the NLCS, Murtaugh passed over an ailing Dock Ellis, who'd won 19 games but struggled with a sore elbow during the season, and started 15-game winner Steve Blass against the Giants' Gaylord Perry. Blass was excited, but, by his own admission, "too pumped up" for the game: "I remember thinking, 'Okay, postseason is more important than regular season, so maybe I've got to be better than I was in the regular season.'" He tried to be perfect with his pitches, and, with the Pirates leading 2–1 in the bottom of the fifth, he threw pitches that were too perfect to Tito Fuentes and Willie McCovey, who hammered them into the right-field stands. Each home run was hit with a man on base, and, by the end of the fifth inning, the Giants had a 5–2 lead. Al Oliver's two-run single in the top of the seventh, after Willie Stargell popped out with the bases loaded, closed the gap, but Gaylord Perry shut down the Pirates in the last two innings to give the Giants a 5–4 victory.

Murtaugh, who had yet to win a game in the postseason since the seventh game of the 1960 World Series, gave the starting assignment to Dock Ellis for the second game. With Ellis struggling early in the game, the Pirates trailed the Giants 2–1 after two innings. Bob Robertson, the young Pirate slugger who'd challenged his teammates to pick up the burden that Stargell had carried most of the season, then responded by hitting three home runs, a NLCS record, to lead the Pirates to a 9–4 victory. Robertson's record-breaking performance was badly needed because Stargell, who went hitless in four at-bats in the first game, failed to get a hit in five at-bats in the Pirates' win and was now 0-for-9 in the series.

• • •

Stargell was sure he'd snap out of his slump once the playoffs shifted to Pittsburgh, but, once again, it was Robertson who provided the spark. The Pirates had to face the Giants' ace, Juan Marichal, in the third game, and their task was made even more daunting when Pirates starter Nelson Briles injured his groin while warming up. Murtaugh turned to Bob Johnson, a disappointment for the Pirates during the season after coming to the team in a trade from Kansas City, but Johnson pitched the game of his life. In the bottom of the second inning, Bob Robertson homered for the fourth time in the series and gave the Pirates a 1–0 lead. Johnson held the lead until the Giants tied it in the sixth. In the bottom of the eighth, another young Pirate hitter, Richie Hebner, homered to give the Pirates a 2–1 lead. Murtaugh brought in Dave Giusti, who retired the Giants in the ninth to preserve the victory and move the Pirates to within one game of clinching the National League pennant.

Stargell went hitless again and had yet to score or drive in a run in the three games against the Giants. Later, when a reporter asked him if the slump had him down, Stargell replied, "When I was going good I didn't get excited, so when I'm going bad I'm not going to hit the bottom of the barrel." He still had confidence he'd come out of it, and when asked why he was struggling, he offered no excuses: "I have an idea what I'm doing wrong. I'm not hitting the ball."

◆ ◆ ◆

One game away from clinching the pennant, Murtaugh went back to Steve Blass to start the fourth game, but Blass struggled again. The Pirates took a 2–1 lead in the bottom of the first on a two-run single by Clemente, but McCovey victimized Blass once again, this time with a three-run homer, and put the Giants ahead 5–2. In the bottom of the second, with a man on base, Bill Mazeroski came off the bench and singled to set up more Richie Hebner heroics. Hebner, who'd won the third game with a home run, launched a three-run homer to tie the score at 5–5 heading into the third inning.

In the top of the third, Murtaugh brought in Bruce Kison, who'd pitched well since being called up by the Pirates at mid-season. The 21-year-old Kison had such a baby face that when Murtaugh saw the tall, lanky right-hander for the first time, he said he looked older than Kison on the day he was born. Kison, however, with his long arms and sweeping motion, had a reputation for pitching inside and intimidating batters. He shut down the Giants for the next four innings and set the stage for the Pirates' pennant-winning victory.

In the bottom of the sixth, Clemente drove in Dave Cash with a single to give the Pirates a 6–5 lead. After Clemente advanced to second base, the Giants chose to walk Stargell intentionally, even though he was hitless on the day and for the series. With two men on base, Al Oliver, who was upset with Murtaugh for platooning him in center field with Gene Clines, lined the ball into the right-field stands for a 9–5 Pirates lead. When Kison struggled in the top of the seventh, Murtaugh summoned Dave Giusti out of the bullpen. Giusti closed out the Giants without giving up a run and pitched two more shutout innings to give the Pirates their first National League pennant since 1960 and their eighth in the team's history.

There were plenty of heroes to douse with champagne in the Pirates clubhouse. Bob Robertson had set a NLCS record with his four home runs, and Al Oliver and Richie Hebner had also homered in clutch situations. Dave Cash led the Pirates with eight hits and had a .421 average, and Clemente had six hits and drove in key runs in the series. Starter Bob Johnson pitched the best game in the series, and Dave Giusti, Bruce Kison, and Bob Miller were outstanding in relief.

There were a few disappointments for the Pirates, including the pitching struggles of Steve Blass and Dock Ellis, but the most glaring problem during the series was the performance of Willie Stargell, who went 0–14 and failed to drive in a run. Dock Ellis remembered that during the season, when the Pirates fell into a slump, Stargell, with a wry smile, would chide them, "You're losin' it boys. You're losin' it." He'd need that same attitude and perspective going into the World Series. He could have very easily lost it and been down on himself, but he was so thrilled at going to his first World Series that he "felt like a kid again." He remembered that Ernie Banks once told him that "he'd go 0-for-50 just to get into a World Series." Banks would never get that chance to play in a World Series, but Stargell was just days away from fulfilling his childhood dream.

• • •

Willie Stargell would need all the optimism and confidence he could muster because the Pirates were facing a powerful and heavily favored Baltimore Orioles team that had won three straight American League pennants and were the defending World Series champions. They'd finished the 1971 season with 11 straight wins and swept the Oakland Athletics in the ALCS. They had a powerful offense, led by Frank Robinson and Boog Powell, and an outstanding defense, featuring perennial Gold Glove–winner Brooks Robinson. But the Orioles' strength was its starting pitching with its four 20-game winners: Jim Palmer, Dave McNally, Mike Cuellar, and Pat Dobson.

If the Pirates needed an incentive going into the first World Series game in Baltimore, all they had to do was read the papers. A chorus of baseball writers believed that the Pirates had little chance to beat Baltimore, and Orioles manager Earl Weaver chimed in, by adding, "A team cannot win a World Series with Jackie Hernandez at short stop." An article in the *New York Times* declared that the Pirates had already "lost the series on paper," but Stargell, speaking for his teammates, decided they'd show up anyway: "From what I'm reading in the papers, we shouldn't even have bothered coming here. We've lost it already. But we're not going out there with the idea that they have a superior team. They have to prove it." Danny Murtaugh added that the Pirates "fear no one. If they have any sense, they'll respect us."

• • •

The first ominous sign for Willie Stargell that he would continue his postseason batting woes in the World Series was Earl Weaver's announcement that he was passing over right-handed Jim Palmer, the ace of his staff, and pitching his left-hander Dave McNally in the first game of the World Series to counteract the bats of Oliver, Hebner, and Stargell. Murtaugh responded to Weaver's move by starting Clines and Pagan in place of Oliver and Hebner, a decision that infuriated Oliver. Murtaugh also decided to start his ace Dock Ellis, even though Ellis was still suffering with a sore elbow. He kept Stargell in the lineup and in the key clean-up position in the batting order, even though Stargell would be facing one of the best left-handers in baseball.

Playing under threatening weather conditions and on a playing surface so chopped up by a Colts football game that the field crew sprayed parts of the outfield to make it look green, the Pirates jumped off to a 3–0 lead in the second inning on some aggressive base running and unexpected Oriole fielding misplays. Ellis, however, struggled in the early going and in the bottom of the third served up a three-run homer to outfielder Merv Rettenmund to give the Orioles a 4–3 lead. McNally went on to keep the Pirates hitless in the last six innings to give the Orioles a 5–3 victory and a 1–0 lead in the World Series.

Stargell had another miserable game, going 0–3 with two strikeouts and a walk, and extended his hitless streak to 0–17 in the 1971 postseason. He had plenty of company, including Clines and Pagan, who were a combined 0–8, and Bob Robertson, the hero of the NLCS, who also went hitless. Only Clemente provided an offensive spark with two hits, including a double. As bad as the offense was in the first game, the worst news came from Dock Ellis. After the game, Dock Ellis admitted that his "arm was gone."

When the second game of the World Series was delayed a day by a rainout, Murtaugh had the option of pitching a rested Steve Blass, but, remembering Blass' shaky performance in the NLCS, he decided to go with Bob Johnson, who'd pitched so well in the pivotal third game against the Giants. Any hope that Bob Johnson would pitch as well against Jim Palmer as he had against Juan Marichal was quickly dashed when he lasted fewer than four innings and gave up four runs. Kison, Moose, Miller, and Veale fared no better as the Orioles hammered out 14 hits and scored 11 runs.

The Pirate offense continued to sputter against Jim Palmer and failed to score until Richie Hebner, now back in the lineup with Al Oliver, hit a face-saving three-run homer in the top of the eighth in a lopsided 11–3 loss. Willie Stargell managed to get his first hit of the World Series to go along with two walks, but the only Pirate who seemed to be playing with any passion was Roberto Clemente, who had two hits, including a double, and made a electrifying throw from right field that many regarded as one of the greatest throws in World Series history.

• • •

Trailing 2–0 in the Series, the Pirates headed back to Pittsburgh, while sportswriters proclaimed that the World Series was all but over. Nationally syndicated columnist Jim Murray wrote that if the Pirates showed up they should at least be offered blindfolds before the execution. A headline in a Baltimore paper echoed Murray's sarcasm by declaring, "May Be Baltimore in Three." When Murtaugh saw the headline, he cut in out and posted in the clubhouse. He told a doubting press, "The world has yet to see the real Pirates." Murtaugh's blunt and confident statement would be engraved on the Pirates' 1971 World Series rings.

While Murtaugh was providing motivation for the Pirates, they also had three leaders in the clubhouse to help them deal with adversity. In his autobiography, Stargell remembered Bill Mazeroski calmly talking about the Pirates' lopsided defeats in the 1960 World Series and telling the press, "It was much easier to rebound from losing by a lot of runs rather than just one." As for Stargell, who would be booed the first time he came to bat at Three Rivers in Game 3, he remained relaxed and confident and seemed no different from the Stargell who had carried the team through the first half of the season. For all the calm and confidence of Mazeroski and Stargell, however, it was Roberto Clemente, after playing so well in defeat, who, with his fierce pride, would will the Pirates to victory with one of the most spectacular performances in World Series history.

• • •

In 1925, the Pirates became the first team to come back from a 3–1 deficit and win a World Series, but no team in World Series history had ever come back from a 3–0 deficit. Down 2–0 to the Orioles, the Pirates had to win Game 3 to have a realistic chance of turning the series around against the streaking Orioles. Facing left-handed Mike Cuellar, Murtaugh decided to play Al Oliver, but he angered Richie Hebner, the only Pirate with a home run, by benching him again for Jose Pagan. Murtaugh dismissed Hebner's complaint, but he couldn't shake his concern about his starting pitcher Steve Blass, who seemed to be struggling with his nerves in the postseason.

Blass showed no sign of nerves when he retired the Orioles in order in the top of the first inning. In the bottom of the first, Dave Cash led off with a double and scored on a force-out by Clemente. Staked to a 1–0 lead, Blass was nearly flawless against the Orioles and didn't allow a hit until the fifth inning. The Pirates nearly scored again in the bottom of the fifth when, with one out, Clemente singled Oliver to third base and took second on an error by Brooks Robinson. But Stargell, who'd walked in his first two times at bat, struck out, as did Robertson, who was hitless so far in the World Series. In the bottom of the sixth, Pagan made Murtaugh look good, when he singled in Sanguillen for a 2–0 lead after Sanguillen had led off the inning with a double.

In the top of the seventh, the Orioles finally broke through when Frank Robinson hit a Steve Blass slider deep over the left-field fence. Robinson's home run cut the Pirates' lead to 2–1 and set the stage for the pivotal moment in the 1971 World Series. When Clemente led off the bottom of the seventh, he tapped the ball weakly back to Cuellar for what looked like a routine out. When Cuellar fielded the ball and went to make a lob throw to first base, he noticed that Clemente was sprinting down the line. Cuellar hurried his throw and pulled Powell off first base. Cuellar was so unnerved by his error that he walked Stargell, sending Clemente to second base, and bringing up Bob Robertson.

With Bob Robertson hitless in the series, Murtaugh decided to have his slugger bunt the runners along, but the move appeared to backfire when Robertson missed the sign. With Clemente frantically waving for a time out, Robertson swung at the next pitch and lined it deep into the right-field stands for a three-run homer. When Stargell greeted Robertson at home plate, he leaned over and whispered, "That's the way to bunt the ball." With the Pirates ahead 5–1, Blass had little trouble retiring the Orioles in the eighth and ninth innings to preserve the victory. After the game, Stargell told a sportswriter, "It was a helluva bunt. A perfect bunt. A beautiful bunt. You can be in this game all your life and never get a chance to bunt three runs in."

• • •

The Pirates had already made history in 1971 with baseball's first all-black lineup, and were about to make history again by hosting the first night game in the history of the World Series. While the pregame atmosphere at Three Rivers for the occasion was festive, Murtaugh and Weaver had a tough decision to make on their starting pitchers. With Ellis nursing a sore arm, Murtaugh decided to go with Luke Walker, who'd bounced back in the second half of the season, but hadn't pitched for three weeks because of the breaks in the playoff schedule. Weaver had the option of bringing McNally back, but decided to go with 20-game winner Pat Dobson, who, like Walker, hadn't pitched for weeks.

When the game started, both pitchers, after weeks of inactivity, struggled in the first inning. After Walker surrendered three runs, Murtaugh went to his bullpen and brought in Bruce Kison to finish the top of the first. In the bottom of the inning, Dobson walked leadoff hitter Dave Cash. After Dobson retired Hebner and Clemente, Stargell, who'd been booed the day before in his first at-bat, responded to the sell-out crowd's cheers and lined the ball into right-center field for a run-scoring double. When Al Oliver followed with a bloop double, Stargell scored and cut the lead to 3–2 going into the second inning.

With the baby-faced Kison pitching inside and intimidating Oriole batters (he hit three, including Frank Robinson in the stomach) over the next six innings, the Pirates tied the game in the bottom of the third inning on a single by Oliver after Stargell flied out to center field. They loaded the bases with one out in the bottom of the fifth on singles by Clemente and Stargell and an intentional walk to Oliver, but Robertson and Sanguillen failed to bring home the lead run. They loaded the bases again in the bottom of the sixth, this time with two outs, but Stargell, who had two hits on the night, grounded out to second base.

Finally, in the bottom of the seventh, with Robertson in scoring position, the Pirates took the lead when Murtaugh called on 21-year-old rookie backup catcher Milt May to pinch-hit for his roommate, Bruce Kison. The nervous and excited May, using Willie Stargell's heavier bat because his bat felt too light, singled home Robertson to put the Pirates ahead 4–3. Dave Giusti came out of the bullpen to retire the Orioles in the eighth and the ninth, and the Pirates, who just two days ago had been buried by the national press, had tied the World Series at two games a piece.

• • •

The good news for the Pirates in the first two games at Three Rivers, along with the excellent pitching performances of Steve Blass and Bruce Kison, was the revived offense. Robertson had snapped out of his slump and hit a key home run; Clemente, who'd vowed not to lose the World Series, was batting .471; and even Willie Stargell, though he was only hitting .115 for the postseason, had his first multi-hit game and drove in his first run.

For the critical fifth game, Murtaugh turned to Nelson Briles, who had to be scratched, because of injury, from his start against the Giants in the NLCS. Briles pitched in two World Series when he was with the Cardinals, so he was not intimidated by the assignment or by the prospect of facing Dave McNally, who had dominated the Pirates in Baltimore. In Game 5, Briles was the dominant pitcher. After Brooks Robinson singled in the second inning, the Orioles had only one more hit the rest of the game and never had a runner in scoring position. Briles faced only 29 batters, just two more than Yankee Don Larsen faced in his perfect game against the Dodgers in the 1956 World Series. When he came to bat in the bottom of the eighth inning, he broke into tears when Pirate fans gave him a standing ovation.

The Pirates scored the only run they needed when Bob Robertson, after his "bunt" home run in Game 3, homered in the bottom of the second inning. The Pirates scratched out three more runs on RBI singles from Briles and Clemente and a wild pitch, and won the game 4–0. Stargell, once again, was not a factor in the Pirates offense. He tried to take McNally (and then righty-reliever Dave Leonhard) to the opposite field, but went 0–3 with a ground out, pop out, and fly out. He did single off right-hander Tom Dukes in the bottom of the seventh for his fourth hit in the last three games, but he was hitting a modest .250 with only one RBI for the World Series and an anemic .133 for the postseason as the Pirates headed back to Baltimore with a 3–2 lead and one win from a World Series championship.

• • •

Murtaugh's choice to pitch a healthy and experienced Briles in the pivotal fifth game surprised no one, but his decision to start Bob Moose in Game 6 seemed an odd choice. Moose's only appearance in the World Series came in the embarrassing second game loss when he relieved a shaky

Bruce Kison and gave up five runs in one official inning of work. Murtaugh, however, told sportswriters, that Moose was his choice, win or lose, in the sixth game: "I told him that before the fifth game. It's a sign of how much confidence I have in Moose."

Murtaugh's confidence in Bob Moose seemed to be paying off when he shut out the Orioles on two hits over the first five innings. The Pirates wasted an opportunity to break on top against Jim Palmer in the top of the first inning after a Clemente triple, but a still struggling Stargell struck out on his way to another hitless game. They did take a 1–0 lead in the second inning on Robertson's RBI single after an Oliver double, and extended their lead to 2–0 on an opposite-field home run from Roberto Clemente in the top of the third. It was fitting that Frank Robinson had to watch Clemente's home run sail over the right-field fence because Robinson had taunted Clemente after hearing him complain about the poor outfield conditions at Baltimore's Memorial Stadium: "Maybe we should give him a ticket, and have him get a seat in the stands." To Robinson's credit, he tipped his cap in Clemente's direction as he rounded the bases.

The Pirates were 12 outs away from their first World Series championship since 1960, but the 2–0 lead didn't hold up. In the bottom of the sixth, Moose gave up a solo home run to left-fielder Don Buford to cut the lead in half, and, in the bottom of the eighth, Dave Giusti, in relief of Bob Johnson, gave up a game-tying single to second baseman, Dave Johnson. The Orioles had a chance to score in the bottom of the ninth, but another electrifying throw from Clemente kept the winning run at third base. The Pirates loaded the bases in the top of the 10th on a Cash base hit and walks to Clemente and Stargell, but Dave McNally, pitching in relief, got Oliver on a fly-out to end the inning. In the bottom of the 10th, the Orioles sent the World Series to a seventh and deciding game when Frank Robinson tagged up on a short fly ball to Vic Davalillo and narrowly beat the throw to home plate for a 3–2 Orioles win.

• • •

Willie Stargell had dreamt of playing in the seventh game of a World Series ever since he was a child living in the Alameda projects. When Mazeroski hit his dramatic home run in the 1960 World Series, Stargell fantasized about matching Mazeroski's heroics. He was now about to play in the deciding game of a World Series. In the previous six World Series games, he had only four hits in 20 at-bats, and no home runs, but with one swing of the bat he could transfer his poor showing into a moment of triumph.

Murtaugh told Steve Blass back in Pittsburgh that if the Pirates lost Game 6 he'd be pitching the seventh game. He also decided that, with the left-handed Cuellar scheduled to start for the Orioles, he'd start right-hand-hitting Gene Clines and Jose Pagan in place of Al Oliver and Richie Hebner. Murtaugh kept Stargell in the lineup, but dropped his slumping slugger to sixth in the order. He batted Robertson in Stargell's customary clean-up position behind Clemente and moved Sanguillen into the fifth spot in the batting order.

Blass was so nervous he had trouble sleeping the night before the game, and his attack of the nerves carried over into his first inning on the mound. Mike Cuellar opened the game by easily retiring the Pirates in order, but a shaky Blass walked the Orioles' first batter. Earl Weaver, sensing an opportunity to rattle Blass, ran out of the dugout and yelled at the home plate umpire, "Rule 8.01, Rule 8.01." He argued that Blass was violating a rule that stated a pitcher had to have his foot on the pitching rubber when he delivered the ball. Weaver's tactic disrupted the game, but if he hoped to completely unnerve Blass he'd made the same mistake that Frank Robinson had made when he insulted Clemente. An angry Blass pitched out of the inning and went on to dominate Oriole hitters over the next several innings.

After a frustrated Stargell struck out on three straight pitches to lead off the second inning, Cuellar retired the Pirates in order again. When Clemente came up in the top of the fourth with two outs, Cuellar had retired 11 batters in a row. Cuellar, however, made his first mistake of the game when he hung a high breaking pitch, and Clemente hammered the ball into the left-center-field bleachers to give the Pirates a 1–0 lead. While Clemente rounded the bases, Stargell joined his teammates in celebrating in the dugout. Any hope he had of joining Clemente in World Series heroics, however, seemed to slip farther away when he struck out in the top of the fifth.

In the top of the eighth inning, with the Pirates hanging on to a 1–0 lead, Stargell led off the inning with what looked like his last at-bat in the 1971 World Series. Reaching out for a Cuellar breaking ball, he hit a routine grounder to the left side of the infield, but Oriole shortstop Mark Belanger, expecting Stargell to pull the ball, had shifted near second base and couldn't reach the grounder with his back-handed stab. With Stargell on first base after only his fifth hit of the World Series, Jose Pagan came to home plate. Murtaugh had the option of bringing in a faster runner for Stargell and having Pagan sacrifice the runner into scoring position; but with the weak-hitting Hernandez and Blass following Pagan, he signaled for the hit-and-run.

As Stargell took off, Pagan lined the ball deep into the left-center-field gap. Stargell hesitated at second base, but when he saw the ball go through to the fence, he took off on his wobbly knees for third base. What followed was like a slow-motion repeat of the famous play in the seventh game of the 1946 World Series when the Cardinals' Country Slaughter took off from first base on a ball hit into the left-center-field gap by Harry Walker and scored the winning run when Red Sox shortstop Johnny Pesky hesitated on his relay throw to home plate.

Stargell was a much slower runner than Slaughter, so it took two blunders, one physical and one mental, to get him home. As center-fielder Rettenmund retrieved the ball and went to relay it to Oriole shortstop Belanger, he bobbled the ball before throwing it. Belanger, unlike Pesky, didn't hesitate with his throw to home plate, but Boog Powell cut off the ball and allowed a sliding Stargell to score what turned out to be the winning run. The video of Stargell's "mad dash" around the bases showed him lumbering around third base and stretching out his stride as if to compensate for his lack of speed as he headed home. He almost appeared to be running in slow motion in his last few strides, and his sprawling slide across home plate seemed more an act of relief than a moment of triumph.

After Blass gave up a run to the Orioles in the bottom of the eighth to cut the lead to 2–1, Stargell had one more chance at World Series glory when he batted with two outs and two runners on against Dave McNally, but he ended the inning by grounding out to second base. In the bottom of the ninth, Blass easily retired home run threats Boog Powell and Frank Robinson. With two outs, Rettenmund hit a sharp ground ball that appeared to be headed to center field until it took a high bounce off the pitching mound. Jackie Hernandez, who had been dismissed by Earl Weaver before the World Series, managed to reach the ball and, from the outfield grass, threw a strike to Bob Robertson to end the game and give the Pirates the World Series championship.

◆ ◆ ◆

In the clubhouse, while the Pirates popped champagne, Clemente, after his MVP performance, held court for reporters, while a giddy Steve Blass pranced around like a kid on Christmas morning. While soaking up the joy around him, Willie Stargell managed to hide his disappointment in his own performance in the World Series with the same wry humor that helped the team through its slumps during the season. When asked by Bill Christine of the *Pittsburgh Press* about scoring the Pirates' winning run, he replied, "I musta looked like a runaway beer truck going around the bases.... I don't know yet whether [Frank] Oceak [the Pirates' third-base coach] was holding or sending me. I had my head down as I was going to third." He smiled and added, "Course a guy with my wheels can afford to take chances. I stole 40 bases this year."

Stargell batted only .208 for the World Series and struck out nine times, but he also had seven walks to go with his five hits. As he spoke with reporters, he could have pointed out that his failure to hit home runs and drive in runs was at least partly the result of the Orioles decision to pitch around him. Instead, refusing to offer an alibi or excuse, he took responsibility for his poor performance. In a telling moment, he nodded in the direction of his four-year-old son, Willie Jr., and said, "There's a time in life when a man has to decide if he's going to be a man."

CHAPTER 8

Adios, Amigo Roberto

While Pirate fans savored the 1971 World Series championship during the off-season, Willie Stargell faced more disappointment.

After his spectacular year, he was a heavy favorite to win the National League MVP Award, but he finished a disappointing second in the voting to the Cardinals' Joe Torre, the National League batting champion and leader in RBIs. Stargell put a good face on his public reaction by saying that winning a World Series was far more important to him than any individual honor, but he was hurt by the decision and thought it was unfair. Though sportswriters were not supposed to take the postseason into consideration, Stargell believed they had in his case. Over a decade later, in his autobiography, he said, "I'm sure my poor showing in the playoffs and World Series cost me the award."

On November 23, Stargell had to deal with another disappointment when Danny Murtaugh, concerned about the pressure of managing on his fragile health, announced he was going back into retirement: "Although the doctors have assured me that my health was good, each succeeding season seems to take that much more out of me." Stargell had great respect for Bill Virdon, who was named by Joe L. Brown to succeed Murtaugh, but in Murtaugh, he'd found a father figure who gave him the confidence he needed to develop as a ballplayer and mature as a team leader.

In addition to his disappointment with the MVP voting and Murtaugh's decision not to come back next season, Stargell had to deal with the third knee surgery of his career. Dr. Joseph Finegold, who performed the surgery to remove cartilage from one of Stargell's knees, told the *Post-Gazette's* Al Abrams, "Few people know the pains and ache he went through the last half of the season. I had to drain the fluid out of his knee every week, or at least every 10 days, so he could play as much as he did." The good news for Stargell was Dr. Finegold's claim that "Willie's knee is perfect now."

• • •

There was an early bump in the road for the Pirates when a strike over the funding of the players pension fund delayed the start of the 1972 season and forced the cancelation of the first seven games. The Pirates, however, with their balance of veterans and youth in the starting lineup, depth on the bench, and an emerging strength in the pitching staff, felt confident that, once the season began, they would repeat as World Series champions.

During the brief strike, the *Post-Gazette's* Charley Feeney, covered a Pirates voluntary workout at Leech Farm, a baseball field located on the grounds of Pittsburgh's VA hospital. He reported on the happy, relaxed mood of the players as they waited for the players union and the owners to settle the strike. Willie Stargell was the first Pirate to step into the batting cage, though he was facing some daunting targets: "There was a fence in right field about 400 feet away and behind the fence in center field was a hill where a couple of youngsters were playing with their big, black dogs." When Stargell lined a ball just short of the center-field fence and in front of the hill, Dave Cash yelled out, "Chicken on the hill, Will" in mocking tribute to Stargell's pledge of free chicken to the customers at his Hill District restaurant every time he hit a home run.

Before the work stoppage, the Pirates, led by Bob Robertson's torrid home run hitting, had completed an excellent spring training and finished with a 15–10 record in the Grapefruit League. There were, however, a few concerns going into the season opener in New York against the Mets. Willie Stargell, while recovering from his knee surgery, was in the Opening Day lineup, but Gene Alley, still rehabilitating his knee, wasn't ready to play. An ailing Clemente was in the starting lineup, but an aging Bill Mazeroski was on the bench for Opening Day for only the second time since 1957. Dock

Ellis was still bothered by what Dr. Finegold had diagnosed as a "tennis elbow," but he was still Bill Virdon's choice for the Opening Day starting pitcher.

• • •

After being shut out in their season opener in a combined effort by Tom Seaver and Tug McGraw, the Pirates, behind Steve Blass, bounced back to shut out the Mets. They lost their home opener to the Cubs, however, then fell into an early season swoon. They finished April with a 5–8 record and dropped to 5–9 after losing their first game in May. The turning point in the 1972 season came a few weeks later, when Bill Virdon, concerned about Stargell's slow start and Robertson's failure to come out of a horrible early season slump, decided to bench Robertson and move Stargell to first base, a position easier on his knees.

It was as if Virdon had waved a magic wand. The Pirates went on an eight-game winning streak, while Stargell went on a hitting binge. The team finished May at 24–15 and, after improving its record to 40–25 by the end of June, was well on the way to winning its third consecutive East Division title. In his initial month at first base, Stargell hit .376 with eight home runs and 27 RBIs, an average of nearly one RBI a game since Virdon's decision, and was well on his way to being selected for the All-Star Game, ironically, as an outfielder. He'd finish the season with 33 home runs and 112 RBIs, down from his totals from 1971, but impressive for a ballplayer coming back from major surgery to remove cartilage from a knee.

It may have taken Stargell longer to recapture his batting stroke in 1972, but the effect of his surge on the Pirates was the same as it had been in 1971. After being ineffective in April and early May, Dave Giusti returned to form, and by the end of the season he was among the league leaders in saves. With Stargell playing first base and Clemente still ailing, outfielder Gene Clines had the opportunity to play more and raised his average from .138 to a team-leading .334 by the end of the season. Clines was one of five Pirates to hit over .300 for the season, and Manny Sanguillen just missed making it six with a .298 average. The only Pirate hitter not to bounce back during the season was Bob Robertson. After hitting 27 home runs in 1970 and 26 in 1971, Robertson dropped to 12 home runs with a .193 batting average in 1972.

The Pirates romped through July with a 20–10 record for the month, and, with a rejuvenated Stargell going on another home run tear in early August, highlighted by four home runs, including a grand slam, in a three-game sweep against division-rival Expos, they roared through August and ended the month with a record of 77–46. On September 6, they beat the second-place Chicago Cubs and increased their lead over the Cubs to 13½ games. On September 21, they clinched the division title against another division rival, the New York Mets. The only mystery left in the 1972 season was whether or not Clemente would reach 3,000 hits before the end of the season. On September 30, he doubled off Met Jon Matlack and became the third Pirate, after Honus Wagner and Paul Waner, to achieve that goal, though he was the first to get all 3,000 of his hits in a Pirate uniform.

· · ·

With so many hitters over .300, the strength of the Pirates going into the playoffs appeared to be their offense, but the team, though it led the league in batting average, actually finished with 110 home runs and 691 runs scored, significantly lower than the team totals of 154 home runs and 788 runs scored in 1971. The loss of seven games to the strike accounted for some of the decline, but the Pirate offense just wasn't as powerful in 1972 as it had been in the previous season.

The Pirates' season was characterized by clutch hitting in close, often low-scoring games, but the reason hitters had the opportunity to win those games was the outstanding performance of a pitching staff that finished with an ERA of 2.81, second only to the Dodgers. The best of the Pirates' starting pitchers was World Series–hero Steve Blass, who completed 11 games and led the Pirates with 19 wins. Joining Blass with double-figure wins were Dock Ellis with 15, Nellie Briles with 14, and Bob Moose with 13. Giusti, after his slow start, saved 22 games and won seven, but he had plenty of help in what may well have been the strongest bullpen in baseball. With a 5–0 record and 11 saves, lefty Ramon Hernandez was a great complement to the right-handed Giusti, and Bruce Kison, Luke Walker, and Bob Johnson, when they weren't starting, pitched well in long relief.

The 1972 Pirates may well have been the most talented, experienced, and balanced team that Stargell had played on since his rookie season in 1963, but their opponent in the NLCS was a formidable Cincinnati Reds team that was stronger than the team that swept the Pirates in 1970. The Reds had four future Hall of Fame–level stars in their batting order in Pete Rose, Joe Morgan, Johnny Bench, and Tony Perez. Rose was the National League leader in hits, and Morgan led the league in runs scored and was second in stolen bases. Johnny Bench, who would be named the National League MVP, was the league leader in home runs and RBIs. Like the Pirates, the Reds had a group of young talented starters, including 21-year-old Don Gullett, who was scheduled to open the NLCS against Steve Blass, and an outstanding bullpen led by Clay Carroll, Pedro Borbon, and Tom Hall.

• • •

In the first game of the NLCS, Steve Blass picked right up where he'd left off in the 1971 World Series. With the help of Ramon Hernandez, who relieved him in the ninth inning, Blass held the Reds to a Joe Morgan home run in a Pirates 5–1 victory at Three Rivers. Murtaugh decided not to platoon Al Oliver against the left-handed Gullett and it paid off when Oliver, batting second in the order, tripled and homered. After Oliver tripled in Rennie Stennett in the first inning, Clemente failed to bring him home; but Stargell, batting fourth against Gullett, doubled home Oliver and scored on a Richie Hebner single. After Stargell's disappointing postseason in 1971, the double in his first time at bat against the Reds and their star left-hander seemed an encouraging sign.

For the second game of the series, Virdon passed over Ellis and Briles and went with Bob Moose, but Moose didn't survive the first inning. The first five Reds batters reached base and, by the time Bob Johnson relieved Moose and ended the first inning, the Reds had a 4–0 lead. The Pirates crept back into the game, but, with the Reds leading only 4–2 in the bottom of the fifth, Stargell struck out with runners at the corners. The Pirates scored a run in the sixth, but, after Joe Morgan homered in the top of the eighth, the Reds went on to a 5–3 victory to even the series at 1–1.

As the Pirates headed to Cincinnati for the remaining games in the series, there were some worrisome signs for Virdon. After his spectacular play in the 1971 World Series, Clemente had gone hitless in the first two games of the NLCS and Stargell, after doubling in his first at-bat, had had also gone without a hit. With Nellie Briles on the mound in Game 3 against the Reds' Gary Nolan, the Pirates fell behind 2–0, but with the help of a Sanguillen home run, rallied to tie the score. In the top of the eighth, Stargell, still looking for his second hit in the series, managed to draw a walk off the Reds' top reliever Clay Carroll. Stargell never had a chance to reprise his mad dash around the bases in the seventh game of the 1971 World Series, but the walk did turn into the winning run when pinch-runner Gene Clines scored on a Manny Sanguillen force-out.

Up 2–1 in the series, Virdon finally turned to Dock Ellis, but he struggled against the Reds and left the game after five innings, trailing 3–0. The Reds scored four more runs against Johnson and Walker and went on to an easy 7–1 victory to tie the series. After getting his first hit in Game 3, Clemente had two hits, including a home run for the Pirates' only run. Stargell, however, facing left-hander Ross Grimsley, went hitless again and was now 1–12 with two walks in the four games against the Reds.

The deciding game of the 1972 NLCS was a rematch between Steve Blass and Don Gullett. The game started off well for the Pirates when they took an early 2–0 lead on consecutive hits by Sanguillen, Hebner, and Cash in the second inning. Pete Rose doubled home a run in the third to cut the Pirates' lead to 2–1, but consecutive hits again by Sanguillen, Hebner, and Cash pushed the Pirate lead to 3–1 at the end of four innings. Cesar Geronimo homered in the fifth inning to make it a one-run game again at 3–2, but Blass shut down the Reds for the next three innings.

In the top of the eighth, the Pirates had a chance to extend their lead when Rennie Stennett led off the inning with a single. After Oliver sacrificed Stennett to second base, the Reds, with left-handed Tom Hall on the mound, walked Clemente intentionally to pitch to Stargell. After popping up twice against Don Gullett, Stargell had struck against Hall in his last at-bat. With two men on and a chance to drive in insurance runs, Stargell looked at a called third strike. After doubling in his first at-bat in the series, Stargell had now gone 15 at-bats without a hit.

After Hall retired Sanguillen to end the Pirates' threat, Blass struggled in the bottom of the eighth, but Ramon Hernandez came in to get the last two outs of the inning and preserve the Pirates' 3–2 lead. After the Pirates failed to score in the top of the ninth, Dave Giusti came in to close down the Reds and send the Pirates back to the World Series. Johnny Bench, however, led off the bottom of the ninth with a towering home run to right field that stunned the Pirates and tied the score. After a shaken Giusti gave up back-to-back singles, Virdon summoned Bob Moose from the bullpen. Moose managed to get two Reds out, but with the winning run on third base, he threw a wild pitch that gave the Reds a 4–3 victory. It was the most devastating loss for the Pirates since the Cubs' Gabby Hartnett hit his famous "homer in the gloamin'" that knocked the Pirates out of a chance to go to the 1938 World Series

• • •

After the game, the Pirates clubhouse was like a tomb. While Stargell struggled to put a good face on a dismal 1-for-16 hitting performance, Moose and Giusti were devastated by their failure to stop the Reds. With a meaningless home run and a .235 average, Clemente had not been much of a factor in the series, but, facing his teammates, he had one of his finest moments as a Pirate. After telling them, "Get your heads up. We had a great year," he went around to each locker to congratulate his teammates on the success of their season. He then sat down beside a disconsolate Bob Moose and gently told him, "Don't worry about it anymore. It's gone. It's gone." When the Pirates flew back to Pittsburgh, there was no doubt in anyone's mind that Clemente would be returning next season to lead them back to the World Series.

• • •

Steve Blass and Dave Giusti lived only a few blocks from each other in Pittsburgh's Upper St. Clair suburb. On New Year's Eve, Blass and his wife, Karen, hosted a party for several close friends including the Giustis, who were staying over for the night. On New Year's Day, the two couples planned to go together to an annual gathering hosted by Bob Prince. About 3:00 AM, the phone rang. On the line was the Pirates' publicity director Bill Guilfoile with some horrifying news. He told Blass, "There was an unconfirmed report that there was a plane that went down in Puerto Rico and Clemente was on it."

Blass and Giusti dressed hurriedly and drove over to Joe L. Brown's house in nearby Mt. Lebanon, where they sat in disbelief and tried to get additional information. Finally the three of them drove across Pittsburgh to Willie Stargell's home in Point Breeze, where, as reports came in confirming the worst, they wept and told each other stories about Clemente's greatness as a ballplayer and his compassion as a human being. Eventually, they drove over to Bob Prince's house, where an annual party to celebrate the new year turned into a wake.

A few days later, a chartered flight with more than 60 members of the Pirates organization left for Puerto Rico to attend a memorial service for Clemente, whose body had not been found by divers. At the lobby of the San Juan International Airport, the Pirates held a news conference before boarding the two buses that would take them to the memorial service and mass. Brown was the first one to speak. He told reporters, "This plane from Pittsburgh contains many of Roberto's closest and dearest friends. There is one purpose in their visit: to show their love and respect for Vera and the Clemente family."

After Brown finished his remarks, Commissioner Bowie Kuhn and Pirates president John Galbreath expressed their regrets. Manager Bill Virdon, whose relationship with Clemente went back to 1956, when they first became teammates, was the first Pirate to speak; then Gene Clines, Al Oliver, and Steve Blass followed to talk about their sense of loss and grief. Finally, Willie Stargell stepped forward to speak about his love and respect for Clemente.

In his biography of Clemente, David Maraniss described, how "The room fell quiet as Stargell spoke. For nearly a decade, Stargell had been the other pillar on the Pittsburgh team. He towered over Clemente physically, but always looked up to him." Over the years, Stargell had inspired his teammates more by his physical presence than by what he had to say, but on this occasion, it was his words that moved them. He first spoke of Clemente the man: "He was proud, he was dedicated. He was in every sense you can determine, a man. And I think going the way he went really typifies how he lived. Helping others without seeking any publicity or fame." Stargell then spoke about the Clemente who was his friend: "I had the opportunity to play with him, to sit down and talk about the things that friends talk about. And I am losing a great friend. But he will always remain in my heart."

• • •

Three weeks after the memorial service for Roberto Clemente, Joe L. Brown addressed the dual issue of finding someone to replace Clemente in right field and finding someone to fill the leadership void in the clubhouse. In an Associated Press article, he admitted that the Pirates were "not going to put anybody in right field as good as Roberto." He did, however, point out that the Pirates had several options, including Gene Clines, rookie Richie Zisk, and even catcher Manny Sanguillen.

Filling the leadership void was another matter. Not only was Clemente gone, but Bill Mazeroski, while staying on as a third-base coach, had announced his retirement at the end of the season. Brown believed that there were players who "will take on an added dimension," but the only one he mentioned was "a fellow like Willie Stargell, who plays when he's hurt and gives everything he has."

Stargell seemed the obvious choice to become the team leader, but as the Pirates arrived at Bradenton for spring training, Bob Smizik, in his "Sports Beat" column in the *Pittsburgh Press*, claimed there were those "in some Pittsburgh circles" who felt that Stargell, in the postseason, had not performed "up to the standards of excellence that he had set, and for that he cannot be forgiven." Smizik went on to write that "Stargell is aware of the lack of esteem, but is a man of great inner peace and it bothers him little." As for the issue of leadership, Stargell told Smizik, "Some people say I should assume leadership. My opinion is if a person shines a little brighter that comes from the way he does things, not what he says.... I'm not going to tell anyone anything. If a guy asks me something, I'll be happy to tell him. That possibly is what they call leadership."

Shortly after Smizik's column appeared, Danny Murtaugh, who accepted the position of director of player acquisition and development after he stepped down as Pirates manager, asked Stargell to replace Bill Mazeroski as team captain. A reluctant Stargell told Murtaugh he was "honored" but would accept the position only if the Pirates didn't expect him to change. Murtaugh responded, "No, we won't ever ask you to change. We like you just as you are."

• • •

The big news at Bradenton during spring training was Virdon's decision to replace Roberto Clemente in right field with his closest friend, Manny Sanguillen. The Pirates kept the talented Richie Zisk on the roster as a backup and had a rising star in Dave Parker, who would start the season in the minors at AAA Charleston. Starting Sanguillen in right field, however, would give the talented Milt May a chance to become the team's regular catcher. As for the rest of the team's makeup, the Pirates felt that, even without Mazeroski, they still had enough depth and talent in the middle infield with Cash, Stennett, Alley, and Hernandez. Hebner was now a fixture at third base and a healthy Stargell was returning to left field to give Bob Robertson a chance to play first base and bounce back from his season-long slump in 1972. The pitching staff, with Blass and Giusti as its leaders, seemed to be a team strength, but they added more depth by acquiring spot starter and long reliever Jim Rooker from the Kansas City Royals.

On Opening Day, the Pirates, after a ceremony in which a tearful Vera Clemente accepted her husband's retired jersey, the Pirates, wearing Clemente's No. 21 on their sleeves, took the field at Three Rivers and went on to defeat the St. Louis Cardinals 7–5. The Pirates swept the Cardinals and, after splitting a doubleheader against the Cubs, stood at 8–2 near the end of April and seemed poised to make another run at the World Series. By the end of April, however, they were in the middle of a six-game losing streak. In May they went on another six-game losing streak. Then, in early

June, they went on a five-game losing streak, won one game, and proceeded to lose five more in a row. By the end of June, they were five games below .500 and struggling to stay out of last place.

• • •

Toward the beginning of "The Second Coming," one of the most famous poems of the great Irish poet William Butler Yeats, there is a line that reads: "Things fall apart; the centre cannot hold." That line is an apt description of what happened to the Pirates in the first half of the 1973 season. For all the talk in the press and among fans of a Pirates dynasty, the Pirates played poorly on the field. For all the praise about the team's diversity and unity, the Pirate clubhouse became a house of discord and division.

As good as his word, Stargell was there to listen to the most unhappy and frustrated of his teammates and offer advice, which usually reflected his philosophy of keeping calm and consistent in the best and the worst of times. He also set an example on the field by having one of the most productive years of his career. By mid-season, he was selected for the All-Star Game for the third consecutive year and the sixth time overall, and was hitting at such a remarkable pace that the talk around baseball circles was that he was headed for the National League MVP Award that had eluded him in 1971.

It became clear in the first half of the season, however, that the "Sanguillen experiment" had failed. Both Sanguillen and May were having subpar seasons at bat and on the field. Sanguillen was struggling in right field, but a bigger problem was the drop-off in the success of the Pirate pitching staff with the less experienced Milt May behind the plate. After 59 games, Sanguillen returned to his catcher position and a frustrated Gene Clines came off the bench to split time in right field with rookie Richie Zisk.

After leading the Pirates in hitting in 1972 with a .334 average, Clines felt that he should have been given the opportunity to start in right field after Clemente's death. He thought that the Pirates were going out of their way to appease their white working-class fan base by finding a place in the starting lineup for Milt May and Bob Robertson at the expense of Clines, who had to sit on the bench, and Al Oliver, who had to shift back and forth between center field and first base as Robertson struggled for the second straight season.

While Virdon made the necessary moves to stabilize his starting lineup, he was at a loss to fix the sudden collapse of Steve Blass, his most consistent and reliable pitcher. Dock Ellis, Bob Moose, and Luke Walker were having subpar years, but Steve Blass, after winning 19 games in 1972, completely unraveled. There was no sign of trouble in spring training, but once the season started Blass began to have trouble with his control. He managed to win a few games early in the season, but, on June 11, after lasting fewer than four innings in a loss against the Braves, Virdon sent Blass to the bullpen. In his first appearance in relief a few days later, he walked six Brave batters, threw three wild pitches (including one that went behind a batter) and gave up seven runs in less than two innings. Blass, pitching in relief and an occasional start, ended the season with a 3–9 record and a horrendous 9.85 ERA.

• • •

As dismal as the first half of the season was in 1973, Stargell did manage to provide one highlight that attracted national attention. On the night of May 8, a disappointed six-year-old Todd Shubin was walking with his father in the parking lot outside the right-field pavilion at Dodgers Stadium. They had to leave the Dodger game with the Pirates after the sixth inning because Todd's father had to go to work. Todd's biggest disappointment at the game was that he hadn't caught a foul ball, but his father, remembering that Willie Stargell had once hit a ball out of Dodger Stadium, told him not to give up.

At that moment, Todd and his father heard a baseball crashing onto the roof of a nearby bus. Todd chased down the ball, and Todd and his father took it to a security guard. The ball that Todd retrieved had left the bat of Willie Stargell in the top of the seventh inning on a pitch from the Dodgers' Andy Messersmith. The ball traveled an estimated 470 feet before landing on top of the bus. Stargell had been the only player to hit a ball out of Dodger Stadium and now he had done it twice.

The next morning the Dodgers called the Shubins and invited them to attend the game that night and meet Willie Stargell, so that he could autograph the ball for Todd. As Stargell was autographing the ball, Todd reached for Stargell's batting helmet and asked if he could have it. Stargell affectionally took off Todd's Dodger cap and gave him his batting helmet. That wasn't the only request that Stargell received that night. Dodger pitcher Andy Messersmith asked him for the home run bat as a souvenir. Stargell gave Messersmith the bat, but slyly told him he had four more just like it in case Messersmith had intended to bury or burn it.

• • •

The home run Stargell hit out of Dodger Stadium was one of 44 that he launched in what would become a record season. Three weeks later, against the Braves' Gary Gentry, he added his fourth upper-deck home run at Three Rivers. On July 11, he hit the 302nd home run of his career against the Padres' Steve Arlin, surpassing Ralph Kiner as the Pirates' all-time leader. On September 17, Stargell set another record when he hit a home run, triple, and two doubles against the Mets, and became the only player in National League history to have four extra-base hits in a game on four different occasions. By the end of the season he had 90 extra-base hits, three more than the record of 87 set by Kiki Cuyler in the Pirates' 1925 World Series–winning season.

In 1971, Willie Stargell had a great year and led the Pirates into the postseason; but in 1973 the best that he could do was to keep the team from falling completely out of the race for the division title. At one point in July, they fell seven games under .500 and were 10½ games out. Stargell, however, remained optimistic and declared, "This must be the best last-place club you have ever seen. Don't worry about us. We'll get along."

In mid-July, after signing former Cardinals and A's shortstop Dal Maxvill and replacing an injured Gene Clines on the roster by calling up Dave Parker from AAA Charleston, the Pirates went on a tear and, after a seven-game winning streak, were back at .500 by the end of the month. Fortunately for the Pirates, the Mets and the Cardinals, their chief rivals in the East Division, were barely playing above .500. The Pirates struggled in August and finished the month at .500, but they were only a game out of first place. On September 6, after the Pirates lost three out of four games to the Cardinals and fell to 67–69 on the season, Joe L. Brown decided that the team had reached the point where they "could not win in 1973" without a change in leadership. He fired Bill Virdon and convinced Danny Murtaugh to return, for the fourth time, as the Pirates manager. In making the announcement, Brown declared, "I hope we can still win with Murtaugh."

With Murtaugh back as manager, the Pirates, with Stargell on another home run streak, won seven of their next nine games and climbed into first place with a record of 74–71. They lost five of their next six games, however, and fell back into second place. They finished the season with an 80–82 record and ended up in third place, but only a game behind the second-place Cardinals and 2½ games behind the East Division–champion Mets.

• • •

After making the postseason for three straight years, winning a World Series in 1971, and barely missing another World Series appearance in 1972, the 1973 season was a bitter disappointment. The obvious reason for the team's slide was the loss of Roberto Clemente, but, with the exception of the home run heroics of Willie Stargell and the clutch performance of Al Oliver, who drove in a career-high 99 runs, the Pirate offense had a disappointing year. Rookie Richie Zisk, playing in 103 games, was the only Pirate to hit over .300.

After struggling early, Dave Giusti had another outstanding season out of the bullpen, but the Pirates' starting pitching could never make up for Steve Blass' disastrous collapse. After winning 19 games in 1972, Blass, while walking 84 batters in 88⅔ innings, finished with only three wins in 1973. Nellie Briles stepped in as the leader of the staff and newcomer Jim Rooker pitched well in relief and as a starter, but Ellis, Moose, and Walker had losing seasons, and Bruce Kison spent most of the season at AAA Charleston after struggling in spring training.

When Joe L. Brown sat down with Danny Murtaugh to decide on the changes the Pirates needed to make if they were going to return to the playoffs in 1974, they knew that, no matter what, they could count on Willie Stargell as the team leader. In a column for *The Sporting News*, Charley

Feeney wrote, "There are all kind of team leaders. There are the rah-rah guys...the chatter men in the clubhouse...the big hitters who produce in the clutch when the pressure is on." For Feeney, Stargell proved in 1973, more than in any other season, that he was a leader by example when he "lifted the club just when the Pirates were going to fade from the pennant picture in early September."

One measure of the respect that Stargell earned in 1973 was the admiration expressed by both Bill Virdon and Danny Murtaugh for what he had done to help them. In an interview before he was fired, Virdon said, "I think more of Willie than I do of anyone on the club.... Willie is as good a person as I've ever known.... He is considerate and goes out of his way to help me. He tries to lead the club by his performance and production." When Murtaugh replaced Virdon, he expressed the same view: "Willie has assumed the role as team leader. When the going gets rough, he is going to take over the responsibilities of winning the ballgame for you. In the clubhouse, if you are having a baseball problem...or problems with your wife and family, instead of going to the manager, you call this guy over and talk to him."

Jim Rooker, in his first year with the Pirates in 1973, noted that Stargell was as caring with the new players on the team as he was with those close to him. At clubhouse meetings, there were players who tried to preach to their teammates, but Stargell, by saying "a few simple things," would calm things down and remind them to have fun on the ballfield. Rooker, who had his best year in the majors in 1973, said that the most outstanding quality about Stargell was his ability "to make you feel good about yourself."

• • •

All that remained at the end of the 1973 season was to see if the baseball writers would recognize Stargell's outstanding performance and give him the National League MVP Award they had denied him in 1971. Remembering his disappointment in 1971, Stargell said, "I'll never get keyed up again for the MVP award. I refuse to after 1971. I should have had it 1971 and they gave it to Joe Torre, even though they said I carried the team." He tried to downplay the importance of the award, but admitted that, "If I get the award, it will probably be one of the greatest honors I've ever received. It would mean that everybody in the National League felt that I was the person responsible for so many things happening from a baseball standpoint."

Stargell received the Sultan of Swat award as the top slugger in baseball and the Mel Ott Award for leading the National League in home runs, but when the announcement came for the MVP award, Stargell learned that he'd finished second in the balloting to Pete Rose, who had led the National League in hitting with a .338 average. Stargell recognized that writers around the league admired Rose for his hustling play, but it was a bitter moment all over again to realize he had lost out to a player whose power numbers were far below his own, especially after slugger Reggie Jackson had been named the American League MVP.

A few months later, the Dapper Dan Club announced its winner of Pittsburgh's Sportsman of the Year Award. After the 1971 championship season, Stargell happily shared the honor with Danny Murtaugh and Roberto Clemente. This time, in a final touch of irony to the 1973 season, he finished second in the balloting to Pitt's new football coach, Johnny Majors, who had taken the Panthers from a 1–10 record to a winning season and an appearance in the Fiesta Bowl. Stargell was very gracious that night, but the selection of Majors was a bitter reminder from his adopted hometown that his great performance, during a season filled with adversity, had gone without recognition and honor.

Climbing Back to the Top

Joe L. Brown had never hesitated to make major changes when he felt the Pirates had failed to live up to expectations. He'd done it in the late 1950s and twice in the 1960s, and he was about to do it again. With Manny Sanguillen back at his catching position, Brown traded an expendable Milt May to the Houston Astros for a starting left-handed pitcher, Jerry Reuss. He acquired another talented left-handed starter, Ken Brett, from the Philadelphia Phillies for Dave Cash, who would be replaced at second base by Rennie Stennett. To make room for his new starters, he sold Luke Walker to the Detroit Tigers and traded Nellie Briles to the Kansas City Royals for two utility players, outfielder Ed Kirkpatrick and infielder Kurt Bevacqua.

After Gene Alley announced his retirement, Brown shipped weak-hitting Jackie Hernandez to the Phillies and gave the starting shortstop position to speedy rookie Frank Taveras. The departure of Alley meant that the last of the Pirate players from Stargell's rookie season in 1963 were gone. With Mazeroski deciding not to return as third-base coach, only Murtaugh and Stargell remained in uniform from that team.

When Stargell arrived at Bradenton for the start of spring training in 1974, he was 34 years old and about to enter his 12th full season in the major leagues. Though there was some speculation in the press that he was entering the final phase of his career, Stargell said that his knees felt great and that he was in good physical shape after working out at the University of Pittsburgh's field house all winter with trainer Tony Bartirome and several teammates, including Steve Blass. After hitting 44 home runs and driving in 119 runs in 1973, second only to his career-high 48 home runs and 125 RBIs in 1971, he was optimistic about his own prospects and the Pirates' chances, with their infusion of new talent, of returning to the postseason.

The only disturbing note at spring training was the continuing struggles of Steve Blass. After walking 25 batters in 14 innings, including eight in one inning, he remained at Pirate City when the ballclub headed north for Opening Day. He joined the ballclub after the first week of the season, but, after a disastrous outing against the Cubs at Wrigley Field, he agreed to go to AAA Charleston to see if he could recover his control. He'd never appear again in a major league game.

• • •

Steve Blass wasn't the only Pirate in trouble at the beginning of the 1974 season. The Pirates had sent engraved invitations to potential season ticket buyers from "Daniel E. Murtaugh" and "Wilver D. Stargell" to "share with them in the excitement and enjoyment of climbing back to the top." For all of the optimism about the team's new talent, however, the Pirates got off to a terrible start and quickly sank to the bottom of the division. After losing the opener to the St. Louis Cardinals, they went on to lose their first six games of the season. At one point, the team stood at 2–10 in April, finishing the month with a 6–12 record.

On May 1, the Pirates' frustrations reached a boiling point when Dock Ellis took the mound against the Cincinnati Reds. In spring training, Ellis vowed that he would hit the first five batters when he faced the Reds because he felt the Pirates had lost their aggressiveness ever since the painful loss to Cincinnati in the 1972 NLCS. He was also angry because, in the game before, a Houston relief pitcher had hit Willie Stargell in the head with a pitch. Instead of waiting for the next Houston series, he decided to take out his anger on the team that had made the Pirates "physically afraid."

He told Manny Sanguillen not to bother giving him signals because he was "going to mow the lineup down" and send a strong message to other teams that the Pirates were back.

While Ellis was warming up, he threw one of his pitches at Pete Rose, who was waiting in the on-deck circle. When Rose stepped into the batter's box, Ellis' first pitch sailed just over Rose's head. The second pitch hit the Reds MVP in the side. As Rose ran down to first base, he yelled at the next batter, Joe Morgan, not to worry because Ellis wasn't going to hit "a brother." Ellis' first pitch to Morgan nailed him in the kidney.

When Dan Driessen, another "brother," stepped up to the plate, Ellis hit him in the back with the first pitch. Recognizing that Ellis was "color-blind," the next batter, Tony Perez, managed to duck four pitches that had him skipping and jumping, and drew a walk. When the first two pitches to Johnny Bench just missed Bench's head, Murtaugh finally came out to remove Ellis. When a deadpan Murtaugh asked Ellis if he was having trouble finding the plate. Ellis, playing along, said, "I must have Blassitis."

• • •

Ellis hoped that his antics would snap the Pirates of their lethargy, but it didn't happen, at least not right away. Plagued by inconsistent hitting and pitching and poor defensive play, the Pirates continued their slide in May and ended the month 10 games under .500 at 17–27. Stargell got off to a decent start in April with four home runs and 15 RBIs, but he hit just two home runs in May. At one point in early June, he went hitless in 23 at-bats. He broke the skid with a two–home run game against the Giants at the beginning of June, but, by the end of the month, Stargell had only 12 home runs, and the Pirates were eight games under at 32–40.

In mid-July, with the All-Star Game only a little more than a week away, the Cincinnati Reds came to Pittsburgh for a five-game series. If Pirate fans expected an immediate explosion after the Dock Ellis incident, they were sadly disappointed. With Stargell nursing a sore knee and playing in only one game at first base, the Reds won the first four games of the series and, on July 14, seemed poised to sweep the series in the second game of a doubleheader. With the four losses to the Reds, the Pirates were at 37–49 for the season and on the verge of a major collapse.

The Pirate pitcher in the series finale was Bruce Kison, who, like Ellis, had a reputation for throwing at batters. Kison, who hit three Orioles in one game in the 1971 Series, kept throwing inside to the Reds batters, and, in the second inning, had Dave Concepcion hitting the dirt when a fastball came in at his head. When Kison batted in the bottom of the fourth, Reds pitcher Jack Billingham hit Kison in the left arm with a pitch, but when the ball bounced off his arm and knocked off Kison's helmet, it appeared that he'd been hit in the head.

Both teams charged out of the dugout, but nothing happened until the Pirates' Ed Kirkpatrick stepped on Sparky Anderson's foot. That, according to a delighted Ellis, was when "all hell broke loose." For the next 20 minutes, scrums broke out all over the ballfield, with Sanguillen, an amateur boxer in his youth, leading the way. Stargell tried to act as a peacemaker, though his one-sided tactic in breaking up a fight was to bend back the finger of any Red who had a headlock on one of his teammates. The most outrageous act came when the Reds' Pedro Borbon bit Pirate pitcher Daryl Patterson so severely that he had to get a tetanus shot. Borbon's nickname for the rest of his career was "Count Dracula."

The Pirates went on to win the game and felt they had won the fight. With what became known as the Bastille Day Brawl energizing the Pirates, they went on an eight-game winning streak that had them at 45–49 by the All-Star break. The All-Star Game, played at Three Rivers, was a disappointment for Stargell, who didn't make the National League squad after being selected for the past three years, but Pirate fans had something to cheer about when Ken Brett, the only Pirate representative, was the winning pitcher for the National League.

Unfortunately, after the All-Star Game, Brett developed a sore arm and had to go on the disabled list. Ellis then suffered a broken finger from a line drive, but the injuries didn't slow down the Pirates. They continued to play well, and in August had their best month of the season. On August 13, one month after the brawl, they pounded the Reds 14–3 and moved over .500 at 59–58. On August 21, they defeated the Giants and went on a six-game winning streak that had them in first place. After another six-game winning streak pushed them to a 76–63 record (38–14 since the brawl). The Pirates appeared to be cruising to the East Division title.

• • •

As the Pirates were streaking, there was one ugly moment in mid-August that threatened to disrupt their momentum and derail the season. In the August 10 *Post-Gazette*, Bill Christine reported that Willie Stargell's "long season" was stretched "considerably longer with the publication of a book that the Pirates outfielder thought was going to be bland, but instead qualifies as part of the Jim Bouton genre of sports literature." The book, *Out of Left Field,* by Bob Adelman and Susan Hall, was actually scheduled for publication at the end of August by Little, Brown, and Co., but review copies were already circulating.

With the permission of the Pirates organization, Adelman and Hall had access to the Pirates clubhouse during the 1973 season and had taped a number of conversations that Stargell and his teammates believed were off the record. Stargell thought that Adelman and Hall were writing a "feel good" book about the Pirates as they recovered from the loss of Clemente, but their book turned out to be a "tell-all" filled with the transcripts of players talking about Baseball Annies, drug use, and racial tension. The book was especially embarrassing for Stargell because of the intimate details of his womanizing that he and his wife, Dolores, had shared with Adelman and Hall.

Christine reported that Stargell's legal counsel, David Litman, upset with the "intimate conversations and activities" detailed in the book, had contacted Little, Brown to seek a delay in publication to give Stargell a chance to review the book and recommend some deletions and revisions. A few days later, Little, Brown recalled the review copies and stopped the distribution of the first printing of the book, which had been announced at 30,000 copies.

Under mounting pressure, Little, Brown dropped the book, though it did appear two years later in an amended version when Adelman and Hall found a different publisher. The reviewer for the *New York Times* described

Out of Left Field as a "good book," but it didn't have the impact or sales of Jim Bouton's controversial and best-selling "tell-all" *Ball Four*. It also did nothing to undermine Stargell's reputation with Pirate fans, though Stargell refused all offers from writers interested in his life story. Once his career was over, Stargell decided to write his autobiography with former Pirates publicist Tom Bird.

• • •

Stargell's advice to his teammates to remain calm and consistent in the face of adversity was severely tested when the news of the book broke in the papers, but he proved as good as his own words. He batted .332 in the second half of the season and, in a stretch of 52 games, hit .382. With Al Oliver having the best year of his career and Richie Zisk leading the Pirates with 100 RBIs, Stargell didn't have to carry the team, but he was an important contributor on the Pirates' stretch drive, after a miserable first half of the season.

The Pirates stumbled a bit in September and fell behind the Cardinals, but they bounced back and were in a position to capture the East Division for the third time in four years with a win over the Cubs in their final game of the season. The game was played on an early October night at Three Rivers when the temperature hovered near freezing. A photograph with the caption, "Chilly Willy," caught Stargell wearing a Steelers tassel cap before the start of the game.

The game proved as bizarre as the weather. With the Pirates trailing 4–2 in the bottom of the ninth, they rallied to pull within a run of the Cubs. With two outs and the tying run at third base, Bob Robertson struck out on a pitch that eluded the Cubs' catcher, Steve Swisher. As Robertson was lumbering to first base, Swisher's throw hit him in the back and allowed the tying run to score.

With the game tied in the bottom of the 10th, Al Oliver tripled with no one out. After the Cubs walked Willie Stargell and Gene Clines, Manny Sanguillen, swinging at the first pitch, hit a slow roller that Cubs third baseman Bill Madlock couldn't handle. When Oliver crossed home plate, the Pirates quickly headed for the clubhouse to douse themselves with champagne, though hot chocolate might have been more appropriate.

• • •

The Pirates expected to be playing the Cincinnati Reds in the NLCS, but the Los Angeles Dodgers, led by the strong pitching of 20-game winner Andy Messersmith and Don Sutton and the hitting of National League MVP Steve Garvey and Jimmy Wynn, won 102 games and beat out the Reds for the West Division title. With Ken Brett and Dock Ellis out with injuries, the Pirates were hard pressed to match the Dodgers' pitching, but they were confident that their offense, which led the National League in hitting, would give them an edge.

In the first game at Three Rivers in the best-of-five-series, the Pirates' 16-game winner, Jerry Reuss, gave up a run in the second inning, then matched the shutout pitching of Don Sutton. Dave Giusti, however, gave up two runs in the ninth, and the Pirates lost 3–0 to the Dodgers. The only encouraging sign in the game was Willie Stargell's two hits after going a combined 1-for-30 in the 1971 and 1972 NLCS.

In the second game, the Pirates went with another of their new left-handers, Jim Rooker, against Andy Messersmith. After giving up two early runs, Rooker kept the Pirates in the game until their offense finally broke through and scored twice in the bottom of the seventh to tie the score at 2–2. In the top of the eighth, Murtaugh brought in Giusti, who was ineffective in Game 1. He gave up hits to the first four batters, and, by the end of the inning, the Dodgers had a 5–2 lead. Mike Marshall, who'd set a major league record with 106 appearances, came in from the bullpen and pitched two perfect innings to preserve the victory.

The talk as the Pirates headed to Los Angeles was that the Pirates were flat after their exciting run to a division title. With his team a game away from elimination, Willie Stargell, as he had done so often in his career, lifted up his teammates, even if for only one game in the series. In the top of the first inning, with two men on base, he homered deep to right field off left-hander Doug Rau to give the Pirates a 3–0 lead. It was the first postseason home run of his career in 62 at-bats. After Hebner followed

Stargell's blast with a two-run homer, the Pirates took a 5–0 lead into the bottom of the first. Stargell reached on a fielder's choice in the third inning and scored on a Hebner hit as the Pirates continued to pad their lead. Kison shut out the Dodgers through 6⅔ innings, and Ramon Hernandez pitched 2⅔ scoreless innings for a 7–0 Pirate victory.

Any hope, however, that Stargell's home run had inspired a Pirates comeback in the series came to an early end in Game 4, when Jerry Reuss gave up three runs in the first three innings. Three Pirate relief pitchers surrendered eight more runs as the Dodgers, behind Don Sutton's pitching beat the Pirates 12–1 and ended the series. The only note of resistance for the Pirates came in the top of the seventh inning when Stargell homered for the only Pirate run. Pirate batters ended up hitting a dismal .194 for the series, but Stargell batted .400, with six hits and two home runs.

• • •

Since 1970, the Pirates had played in four NLCS, but won only once, in 1971. While disappointed in another lost opportunity to return to the World Series, Danny Murtaugh was so optimistic about the 1975 season, after his team's strong finish in 1974, that he agreed to return for another year as Pirate manager. Joe L. Brown shared Murtaugh's optimism and made only one significant deal during the off-season, acquiring Bill Robinson from the Philadelphia Phillies. Heralded as the next Mickey Mantle when he came up with the Yankees, Robinson had never lived up to his promise, but Brown felt that Robinson would provide some backup support in the outfield, where the Pirates were about to open a position for the player being anointed by Pittsburgh sportswriters as the next Willie Stargell.

When Stargell first saw Dave Parker, who stood at 6'5" and weighed 225 pounds, he described him as a "black Hercules." Like the Stargell of more than a decade ago, Parker had a powerful arm to go with his incredible strength as a hitter, but, unlike Stargell, he had two good knees. After two seasons of playing as a fourth outfielder behind Stargell, Oliver, and Zisk, Parker had an outstanding spring training and was ready to break into the starting lineup. That meant that the major question going into the

1975 season was the opening line in the old Bud Abbott and Lou Costello routine: "Who's on first?"

Just a little more than a week before Opening Day, Murtaugh announced that Willie Stargell would be moving from left field to first base, replacing Bob Robertson, who'd slumped badly the last few seasons. Murtaugh told the press, "It narrows down to the fact that I believe we have to play the nine men who can win the most games for us. And this is the lineup that can do it with Stargell at first base, Zisk in left field, Oliver in center, and Parker in right." He added that it was important to make the change now "to give Willie eight or nine days of work at first base so that he'll be ready for the opener."

Stargell publicly declared that he was willing to do anything to help the team, but he had mixed feelings about the move. He was 35 years old and about to play in his 13th season as a Pirate, so the move to first base would probably be easier on his aching knees and prolong his career. He was concerned, however, about the challenge of playing first base. He enjoyed the open spaces of left field and used the lull between plays to think about his hitting. He'd have no such luxury at first base, though he decided to have some fun tormenting base runners by blocking their path to second base with his "beer truck" body.

• • •

The Pirates began the 1975 season against the Cubs at Wrigley Field. Jerry Reuss had been the Opening Day pitcher in 1974 for the Pirates and was the team's biggest winner that season. Murtaugh, however, decided to reward Dock Ellis with the start, after Ellis had pitched so well in spring training.

The Pirates were scheduled to open the season on Tuesday, April 8, but they arrived in a still wintry Chicago. There was so much snow blowing around the Windy City that the Pirates and the Cubs didn't play their opener until Thursday. Ellis struggled with the cold weather and lasted less than five innings, but the Pirates, sparked by Stargell's four hits and two home runs, pounded out an 8–4 victory. They played their home opener the next day against the Mets and won 4–3. After a win in the second game of the short series, the Pirates stood at 3–0, in contrast to their 0–3 start in 1974.

Going into 1975, Stargell was optimistic after his strong finish in the second half of the 1974 season and his two home runs in the NLCS against the Dodgers. He'd also led the Pirates in home runs for the seventh straight year and batted over .300 for only the third time in his career. For the first time in four years, however, he'd failed to drive in a hundred runs, and his 25 home runs, down 19 from his 44 homers in 1973, were his lowest total since the Pirates moved to Three Rivers.

In the second half of the 1974 season, Stargell, recognizing pitchers were keeping the ball away from him, hit well over .300 by driving the ball to the opposite field. The strategy produced a higher batting average, but a lower home run total. He hoped his four hits and two home runs on Opening Day were an indication that, with a little more patience, he could wait for an occasional inside pitch and hit for power and average in 1975. He didn't have a record-breaking performance in April, but, by the end of the month, he had five home runs to go along with his .323 average.

• • •

After winning their first three games of the season, the Pirates lost their next four, but recovered in late April to finish the month with a 9–7 record. With Ken Brett and Dock Ellis out with injuries again and Stargell falling into a brief home run drought, the Pirates dropped to 18–18 with a loss on May 24. They ended the month on a six-game winning streak, however, and, on June 6, climbed into first place when Bruce Kison won a 7–2 decision over the San Francisco Giants.

With consistent starting pitching from Jerry Reuss, Jim Rooker, and Kison, and a strong bullpen led by Dave Giuisti and newcomer Kent Tekulve, the Pirates continued to surge in June and by the end of the month appeared to have a stranglehold on first place with a 45–29 record. With Manny Sanguillen having the best season of his career and Dave Parker hitting for power and average, the Pirates seemed to have a perfect balance of pitching and hitting. Even Stargell got into the fun by hitting five homers in June, while driving in 23 runs.

The Pirates gained some additional pitching strength in mid-July when they brought up John Candelaria from AAA Charleston after he posted an impressive 7–1 record with an ERA of 1.77. They had their fourth consecutive winning month above .500 and ended July with a won-lost record of 63–41. Helped by another 4-for-4 game at Wrigley Field, Stargell surged in July and raised his average well above .300. He also hit seven home runs and had 20 for the season, only five less than his entire total for 1974. With two months left in the season, there seemed to be nothing short of a major injury or some unforeseen disruption that could stop Stargell from another MVP season and the Pirates from another East Division title.

◆ ◆ ◆

On July 30, during a Pirates game against the Philadelphia Phillies, Willie Stargell, looking for an outside pitch from left-hander Joe Hoerner, took an inside fastball in the rib cage. Initial X-rays were negative, but, when the pain persisted, Stargell had to sit out several games with the injury. In a game against Houston, he fell after catching a pop fly. After the game, when he bent down to dry his legs after showering, he heard "something pop" in his side.

He was re-examined by Dr. Albert Ferguson, the team's orthopedic surgeon, who'd operated on Stargell's knees. When Ferguson looked more closely at the X-rays, he discovered that Hoerner's pitch had cracked Stargell's ninth rib. He recommended to the Pirates that Stargell sit out for at least the next two weeks.

With hitters like Parker, Zisk, Oliver, and Sanguillen, the Pirates had plenty of firepower, but Stargell was the heart of the lineup. During the period that he'd struggled to play with his injury, the Pirates had gone on a five-game losing streak. Without their emotional leader in the lineup, they went on a six-game losing streak. By August 18, they were only 12 games over .500 and had fallen into a tie for first place with the Philadelphia Phillies.

During that losing stretch, Danny Murtaugh decided to remove an inconsistent Dock Ellis from the starting rotation and put him in the bullpen; and at first Ellis refused to pitch in relief. However, when

Ellis asked for a clubhouse meeting, Murtaugh assumed he was going to apologize to everyone and accept the assignment. Instead, Ellis unleashed a tirade against Murtaugh for losing control of the team that so infuriated the Pirates manager that he had to be restrained from going after Ellis. Joe L. Brown's reaction to Ellis' outburst was to suspend him indefinitely. Brown reinstated the regretful Ellis two weeks later, but he pitched sparingly for the rest of the season.

Several days after the incident, the poet Donald Hall drove to Pittsburgh to visit Dock Ellis. He'd become fascinated with the controversial Ellis after participating, with several friends, including his literary agent, in the Pirates' 1973 spring training camp. They published their experiences a year later in a book called *Playing Around*. Hall, who would be named America's poet laureate in 2006, was in the process of writing a follow-up book about Ellis when he came to Pittsburgh. He wanted to get Ellis' side of what had happened in the clubhouse and interview several of his teammates for their views.

When the book, *Dock Ellis in the Country of Baseball*, was published in 1976, it contained an unflattering account of Hall's conversation with Willie Stargell. Disappointed that Stargell didn't defend or support Ellis, Hall wrote that "I have seen other Willie Stargells, the joking ballplayer, the kind giant among kids, the sleek and sophisticated bon vivant, dazzling in shades and a dark suit. Today I see the public Willie, team captain, talking for publication about his old roommate in trouble" and trying to see the clubhouse altercation as a misunderstanding between "good people."

According to Hall, Stargell's "take" on the incident was that a well-meaning, but "short-fused" Ellis, frustrated with his assignment to the bullpen, went too far when he tried to agitate his teammates out of their lethargy, just as he had done the year before. Instead of taking Ellis' side in the matter, however, Stargell went on to tell Hall that, for the good of the team, Ellis needed to admit he was wrong and that "maybe it would be best for the team if he didn't play for the Pirates any longer."

While Ellis was making the headlines in Pittsburgh and around the country, the Pirates, without Ellis in the clubhouse or Stargell in the lineup, went on a tear in which they won seven of their next eight games and moved three games ahead of the slumping Phillies. By the time Stargell returned to the lineup at the end of August, the Pirates were well on their way to the East Division title. They had a 17–11 mark in September, punctuated by a 22–0 thrashing of the Cubs, in which Rennie Stennett tied a major league record with seven base hits. They finished the season with a 92–69 record and ended up 6½ games ahead of the second-place Philadelphia Phillies.

Stargell hadn't hit a home run since his injury at the end of July, but, after his return, he homered twice in a series against the Expos in early September and finished the season with 22 home runs, three behind team leader Dave Parker. It was the first time since 1967 that Stargell had failed to lead the Pirates in home runs; but, out with a cracked rib and needing to rest his knees from time to time, he'd played in only 124 games, the fewest since 1964.

• • •

After winning their fifth East Division title in the last six years, the Pirates faced their playoff nemesis, the Cincinnati Reds, for the third time since 1970. While the Pirates, after struggling for a few weeks in August, won their division handily, the Reds, with 108 wins, completely dominated the West Division and finished 20 games ahead of the Dodgers. By the end of the season, baseball pundits were calling them "the Big Red Machine" and comparing the Reds with Babe Ruth's 1927 Yankees as the best team in baseball history.

Unfortunately for the Pirates, the 1975 NLCS lived up to all the press predictions that the series was a mismatch. In the opening game in Cincinnati, the Pirates took a 2–0 lead in the top of the second inning off the Reds' Don Gullett on hits by Hebner and Taveras. The Pirates' starter Jerry Reuss, however, gave up a run in the bottom of the inning, and three more in the bottom of the third, the last two coming on a Ken Griffey double. With the Pirates trailing 4–2, Murtaugh went to his bullpen, but in the bottom of the fifth, reliever Larry Demery gave up four runs, the last two on a Gullett home run. The Reds, behind Gullett, coasted the rest of the way for an 8–3 victory. Stargell went 0-for-4 in the game, and Dock Ellis pitched the last two innings in relief.

The second game in Cincinnati was another lopsided affair. The Reds took a 2–0 lead in the bottom of the first on a home run by Tony Perez and never fell behind. The Pirates cut the lead to 2–1 in the top of the fourth on a Stargell double and a Hebner RBI force-out, but Pirates starter Jim Rooker, with the Reds running wild on their way to stealing seven bases in the game, gave up two runs in the bottom of the inning. Trailing 4–1, Murtaugh, once again went to his bullpen, but Tekulve and Kison gave up two more runs and the Reds coasted behind Fred Norman to an easy 6–1 victory, and a 2–0 lead in the series.

When the Pirates returned home, Murtaugh decided to start rookie John Candelaria, who delivered a stunning record-breaking performance, striking out 14 Reds batters in 7⅔ innings. After giving up a home run to Concepcion in the second inning, Candelaria pitched brilliantly, but the Pirates couldn't break through against the Reds' Gary Nolan until Al Oliver's home run gave them a 2–1 lead in the bottom of the sixth. In the top of the eighth, however, Candelaria, surrendered a two-run homer to Pete Rose that put the Reds ahead 3–2. The Pirates, sparked by Willie Stargell's leadoff single, rallied in the bottom of the ninth and tied the score on a bases-loaded walk to pinch-hitter Duffy Dyer. In the top of the 10th, the Reds scored two runs on a sacrifice fly by Ed Armbrister and Joe Morgan RBI double. Pedro Borbon, the infamous "Count Dracula," closed out the game in the bottom of the 10th, giving the Reds a 5–3 victory and a three-game sweep in the series.

• • •

After struggling with a rib injury in August and September and going only 2–11 with no RBIs in the October playoff loss to the Reds, Stargell was frustrated and disappointed with the way his 1975 season ended. He'd already made it clear, however, in a late September interview with the *Post-Gazette*'s Charley Feeney, that he was returning to the Pirates for the 1976 season.

Four years ago, with more surgery scheduled for his damaged knees, Stargell had serious concerns about his career, but the surgery had gone so well that his knees still were feeling sound: "I'm always looking ahead now. It's a good feeling." He'd be 36 years old and about to enter his 14th season with the Pirates, so, as Feeney reported, Stargell "knows he can't allow himself to get out of shape. He has shown over the years that he is willing to pay the price."

Also returning to the Pirates in 1976, despite growing concerns about his health, was manager Danny Murtaugh. Frustrated by his talented team's failure to make it to the World Series the last two years, Murtaugh wanted one more chance to bring the Pirates a world championship. He told the *Post-Gazette*'s Al Abrams, "Yes, we can win the pennant this year if we perform in certain areas. We have as good, if not better, pitching than any other club. We can bomb away better than anybody. We'll have to cut down on the errors, and I think we're going to run a lot more."

Joe L. Brown was so confident in the Pirates' prospects for 1976 that he made only one deal during the off-season. During the December baseball meetings, he traded malcontent Dock Ellis with often-injured Ken Brett and highly regarded minor league prospect Willie Randolph to the New York Yankees for starting pitcher George "Doc" Medich, a native of Aliquippa, Pennsylvania, and a Pitt medical student in the off-season. Ellis, however, wasn't the only controversial voice silenced during the off-season In a stunning move, KDKA, with the approval of the Pirates, announced that it had fired longtime announcer Bob Prince and his broadcast partner and former Pirate pitcher Nellie King because of declining ratings.

Bob Prince had joined the popular Rosey Rowswell in the Pirates radio booth in 1948, and, after Rowswell's death in 1955, became the Pirates' lead broadcaster. Over the years, he'd become as colorful as the beloved Rowswell and far more opinionated. The *Post-Gazette*'s Bob Smizik once described him as "a flamboyant, hard-living, mammoth-hearted loudmouth who loved to have fun and loved to do good."

The firing outraged Pirate fans and devastated Bob Prince. Stargell, who regarded Prince as one of his closest friends, found it hard to accept the firing. His trip to Vietnam with Prince had been a turning point in his life. He'd spent the New Year's Day after Clemente's tragic death at Prince's home. In his autobiography, Stargell remembered that, "The only time [I] saw the Gunner depressed was when he was fired. To him, he'd just fallen from Heaven. He'd not only given his time to the job, he'd given his heart." Looming just ahead for the Pirates in 1976 was America's bicentennial year and the centennial year of the creation of the National League. Bob Prince, however, would not be a part of the excitement and celebration, at least not in Pittsburgh. Despite public protests and demonstrations that included both Pirate fans and players, including Willie Stargell, KDKA refused to back down from its decision. When the 1976 season opened, the person who had been the voice of the Pirates for over 20 years and the team's biggest fan, win or lose, was no longer in the broadcast booth to describe the season's first pitch.

Overcoming Adversity, While Displaying Character

Since the late 1950s, a change in the design of the Pirates' uniform heralded a World Series title. The Pirates weren't the first team to wear vest-like tops, but a year after they made the change in 1957, they had their first winning season in 10 years. Two years later, wearing those sleeveless jerseys, they defeated the pin-striped Yankees in the 1960 World Series. In 1970, at the inaugural game at Three Rivers, the Pirates became the first team to wear double-knit uniforms with form-fitting jerseys and pants. A year later they were wearing those uniforms in the 1971 World Series against the Baltimore Orioles.

In 1976, as part of America's bicentennial celebration and the commemoration of the National League's centennial, the League announced that the Pirates would be one of five teams wearing a throwback pillbox-shaped hat with three stripes around it. The Pirates cap, yellow with black stripes and a black bill, was so popular with Pittsburgh fans that the Pirates wore the caps for the rest of the decade. In 1977, they also dropped their traditional white and gray uniforms for a combination of white, gold, and black with pinstripes. In 1979, the Pirates switched the coloring of the caps from yellow to black and, adorned with Stargell Stars, wore them in the 1979 World Series against the Orioles.

• • •

At the beginning of spring training in 1976, the Pirates weren't just hoping that their new caps were the harbinger of another World Series title. They also had to hope they'd have a baseball season. During the off-season, the baseball owners lost an arbitration hearing that threatened to make every player a free agent in one year. Marvin Miller, the players union representative, had argued that the standard baseball contract, which gave the owners the right to renew a contract "for the period of one year on the same terms" if the player refused to sign, did not give the owners the right to renew the contract year after year.

Two pitchers, the Dodgers' Andy Messersmith and the Expos' Dave McNally, after playing the 1975 season without a contract, tested Miller's assertion by declaring themselves free agents for 1976. When the owners lost an arbitration hearing, they went to the United States Court of Appeals, but the Court of Appeals sided with Messersmith and McNally. In reaction, the owners locked the players out of spring training camps until baseball commissioner Bowie Kuhn ordered the camps open for the good of baseball.

Marvin Miller and the owners eventually worked out an agreement that would allow players to become free agents only after they played six years in the major leagues. It was the beginning of free agency in baseball and the beginning of the end of a time when ballplayers, like Roberto Clemente and Willie Stargell, played their entire careers with one team.

• • •

The Pirates opened the 1976 season with an exciting 5–4 victory over Philadelphia in 11 innings. The high point came three innings earlier, however, when Dave Parker barreled over Phillies catcher Johnny Oates to tie the game. They went on to win their first five games of the season, but they'd have trouble keeping pace with the talented Phillies after sweeping them in their two-game season-opening series.

As promised by Murtaugh, the Pirates, known as the Lumber Company because of their hitting, added speed to their lineup and became Lumber and Lightning in 1976. With veterans Stargell and Oliver and rising stars Parker and Zisk, the Pirates had a strong hitting attack but, with Taveras and Stennett, as well as Oliver and Parker, they also had speed in the lineup. With John Candelaria emerging as a star and Doc Medich joining Reuss, Kison, and Rooker, the Pirates had a solid starting rotation. Murtaugh though, was worried about his aging relievers and decided to send Bob Moose to the bullpen to support Giusti and Hernandez.

The Pirates biggest challenge in 1976 was the development of the Phillies from a last-place ballclub in the early 1970s into a legitimate contender. They had a powerful lineup with Dick Allen, Greg Luzinski, and emerging home run–king Mike Schmidt, as well as a solid defense up the middle with Larry Bowa at shortstop, former Pirate Dave Cash at second, and Gold Glove- winner Garry Maddox in center field. Their pitching staff, led by future Hall of Famer Steve Carlton, was loaded with veterans who had World Series experience, including starters Jim Lonborg and Jim Kaat, and closer Tug McGraw.

◆ ◆ ◆

On Opening Day, Willie Stargell looked fully recovered from his rib injury when he banged out three hits and drove in two runs in the 5–4 win against the Phillies. While the Pirates—after a season-opening five-game winning streak—went on a four-game losing streak and finished at 8–8 in April, Stargell had his best opening month since 1971. He had a 14-game hitting streak and finished April with an amazing .417 batting average. He hit only three home runs, but each one added to Stargell's reputation as one of baseball's all-time sluggers.

His first home run of the season, on April 15 against the Cardinals, was the 369th of his career and tied him with former Pirate Ralph Kiner for 23rd place on the major league's all-time home run list. Three days later, he hit his 370th home run, passing Kiner and moving into a tie for 22nd place with Gil Hodges. By the end of the season, after a grand slam against the Mets' Jon Matlack and a home run two days later, he moved passed Frank

Howard to move into 18th place on the all-time list. His 20 home runs in 1976 would give him 388 for his career.

Stargell cooled off in the first three weeks of May, but the Pirates, even though they were having trouble keeping pace with the Phillies, rode a six-game winning streak to a 25–19 record by the end of the month. Before May was over, however, a near tragedy struck Willie Stargell's family, sent him into an emotional tailspin, and all but eliminated any real chance of the Pirates catching the surging Phillies.

On Sunday, May 23, while Stargell and his wife, Dolores, were watching a late movie on television, she began to complain of a terrible headache. After the pain didn't ease off and actually seemed to increase during the night, Stargell decided to take his wife to the emergency room. After an examination found nothing serious, she was allowed to go home; but, as a nurse helped Stargell wheel his wife out of the hospital, she had a seizure.

While Dolores was going through extensive tests at Presbyterian Hospital, Stargell decided to play that night against the Montreal Expos. However, after a call from the hospital came to Three Rivers, he never played the game. In an interview a week later with Bob Smizik of the *Pittsburgh Press*, Stargell remembered being told on the phone that his wife had a blood clot on the brain: "They said they had to go in [operate] real quick or they might lose her. She could have gone like that. It was a battle for her life." The operation took two and a half hours, but for Stargell, it "seemed like a year. I sat there waiting and thinking of all the things we'd done and hadn't done. The mind plays all kinds of tricks on you at a time like that. You start thinking what if she pulls through and isn't all right."

By the time Smizik interviewed Stargell, Dolores was out of danger and recovering from her brain surgery. She still had some slight paralysis on her left side, but the prognosis was optimistic for a full recovery. Stargell, by then, had returned to the Pirates and was in New York for a series against the Mets. When he talked to his wife on the phone, she kept telling him "to make sure the kids eat their vegetables and to see that Kelli [his six-year-old daughter] gets to her tutor, and my son [eight-year-old Wilver Jr.] is at his Little League games." As for her husband, Dolores told him, "Just go out and play ball."

• • •

After being in and out of the lineup for two weeks, Stargell began to play regularly by early June, but he was clearly having trouble concentrating on the game. While the Pirates played well and ended the month with a 41–29 record, Stargell went into a tailspin and hit only .214 in June. When Stargell continued his struggles at the plate well into July, an old friend, now in Yankee pinstripes, tried to needle "Old Wil" out of his prolonged slump.

Dock Ellis asked a reporter, "How's Wil doin'? That man's carried the Pirates on his shoulders so long he ought to be bowlegged by now." When told that Stargell was struggling and the Pirates had fallen well behind the Phillies, he added, "He's not long for Pittsburgh.... Starg is tired, real tired about now." He thought Stargell would be better off leaving Pittsburgh and becoming a designated hitter in the American League where he wouldn't have to run or field as much. Stargell got a kick out of Ellis' ribbing, but responded, "It sounds good, but I always figured I'd end it all playing right here."

Ellis' effort to help Stargell with a little light-hearted kidding didn't have any effect on Stargell's performance in August. He hit only .189 for the month and saw his average, once .417 at the end of April, fall to a season low of .250. He hit only three home runs in August and had only 16 overall going into the final month of the season. The Pirates, on the other hand, finally made a move to catch the runaway Phillies. When John Candelaria pitched a no-hitter at Three Rivers on August 9th, they were 13½ games behind the Phillies. After a loss to the Padres on August 24, they fell 15½ games back; but the next night Bruce Kison shut out the Padres, and the Pirates went on a 10-game winning streak.

They played well in head-to-head games with the Phillies and managed to close to within three games of the lead in mid-September. The Phillies, however, won 12 of their last 14 games and finished with a record of 101–61, nine games ahead of the Pirates. The season was a major disappointment for the Pirates, though they'd won 92 games, the same as they had in 1975 when they won the division.

With his wife, Dolores, recovering from her brain surgery, Stargell hit four home runs in September, his best power output of the season. His total of 20 home runs, however, was good for only third on the team behind Richie Zisk and Bill Robinson. It also marked the third season in a row that his home run total had declined. Even more alarming was the drop in RBIs from 90 in 1975 to 65 in 1976. His 65 RBIs were his lowest total since his rookie season in 1963.

• • •

If Stargell's bad year, both professionally and personally, had him contemplating retirement, he was going to have to wait in line to make an announcement. On September 29, just before the last Pirates series of the season, Joe L. Brown unexpectedly announced he was stepping down as general manager. He'd been in the position since replacing Branch Rickey in 1956. Brown cited his desire to spend more time with his family as his reason for retiring, but it was far more likely that he knew that the dawn of free agency was going to change the financial structure of baseball and make it far more difficult for the Pirates organization to keep their players and remain competitive.

Two days later, an exhausted and ailing Danny Murtaugh made the more expected announcement that he was retiring as Pirates manager, but not before he had some parting fun with the press. He told reporters, "I'm here to announce that I'll be back for two more years. I signed a contact with Joe this morning." After reporters realized Murtaugh was joking, he told them, "I think this year was one of the worst years I've had in the last three as far as my health is concerned. I was ill a few more times than anybody realized.... I think that I've been around long enough."

With the Pirates organization reeling from the dual retirements, the most shocking and tragic news was still to come. On October 9, barely a week after the announcements by Brown and Murtaugh, Bob Moose died in a car crash on his way to a party celebrating his 29th birthday. In his autobiography, Stargell remembered sitting in a hotel room when he heard the news on television: "I saw Bob's picture appear on the screen. At first

I thought, 'What has this crazy guy done now?' Then I heard the news. I couldn't believe it."

Less than two months later, the Pirates had to cope with yet another devastating death in the family. On November 30, after Danny Murtaugh returned to his home after a morning visit to his doctor, he suffered what a hospital spokesman described as a "serious stroke." On December 2, Murtaugh, known as a battler throughout his baseball career, opened his eyes, looked at his son, squeezed his hand, and died just two months after his 59th birthday. Murtaugh's death was hard on everyone in the Pirates organization, but no one took it harder than Joe L. Brown. He told reporters, Murtaugh "was like my brother. I loved him." Remembering the brother he lost in World War II, he added, "I feel I've lost a second brother."

• • •

The retirement of Brown and the deaths of Moose and Murtaugh, coupled with his wife Dolores' near fatal stroke and slow recovery from brain surgery, had Stargell giving serious thought to his own retirement from the game. He was now approaching his 37th birthday and had played 14 full seasons, many of them on bad knees. But Stargell knew that in many ways baseball was his life, and he was not ready to give it up. He also felt that, with so many losses, the Pirates would be going through a difficult transition and, with his experience, he was in a position to help the team, especially its new general manager, manager, and younger players.

When Joe L. Brown stepped down, the Pirates, as they had done in replacing Branch Rickey, stayed within the organization by naming Harding "Pete" Peterson as the new general manager. After a brief playing career in the 1950s as a catcher with the Pirates, Peterson had worked his way through the organization and, by the late 1960s, had become the Pirates' minor league director and head of scouting.

As soon as Peterson stepped into the position, he tackled his most challenging job in the postseason, finding the right manager to replace Danny Murtaugh. At the top of his list was Oakland A's manager Chuck Tanner, a native of New Castle, located about 45 miles north of Pittsburgh. Before taking the job with the A's for the 1976 season, Tanner had managed the Chicago White Sox for five seasons and was named American League Manager of the Year in 1972. To get Tanner, Peterson had to trade the popular Manny Sanguillen and pay $100,000 to the A's. It was a highly controversial move, but it turned out to be one of the most important deals in Pirates history. With his infectious optimism, Tanner had an uncanny ability to draw the best out of his players.

With Chuck Tanner in place, Peterson then moved to shore up an aging and depleted bullpen. At Tanner's recommendation, Peterson traded Richie Zisk to the Chicago White Sox for left-hander Terry Forster and right-hander Rich "Goose" Gossage. He also acquired Grant Jackson from the Seattle Mariners. Forster and Gossage had struggled as starting pitchers with the White Sox, but Tanner believed that they'd excel as relievers, especially Gossage with his blazing fastball.

Peterson hoped that the Pirates had the young players to fill in at third base when Richie Hebner signed a free agent contract with the Phillies, but, when no one stepped up in spring training, he followed Tanner's advice once more and traded Dave Giusti, Doc Medich, and four prospects to the Oakland A's for Phil Garner, a hard-nosed player who'd earned the nickname "Scrap Iron" for his aggressive play. Garner was a significant defensive improvement at third base over the error-prone Hebner, and promised to be a spark plug and clutch performer on offense.

◆ ◆ ◆

When Willie Stargell learned that Chuck Tanner was the Pirates' new manager, he was delighted with the hiring. In his autobiography, he described himself as happy "as a pig in slop." Stargell loved Tanner's enthusiasm for the game and his reputation for honesty in dealing with his players. According to Stargell, the word around baseball was that, "If you can't play for Tanner you can't play for anybody." Tanner believed that playing baseball should be fun, and, injuries and all, no one had more fun than Willie Stargell when it came to playing baseball.

Stargell was so excited when he arrived at spring training that, when told that Tanner liked to play an aggressive, running game, he gleefully proclaimed that he'd likely steal at least 10 bases now that he finally had a manager willing to turn him loose on the base paths. Pirate catcher Steve Nicosia, a rookie at the time trying to make the team as a backup to Ed Ott, remembered Stargell deciding to demonstrate his speed by challenging Miguel Dilone, the fastest runner in camp, to a 100-yard dash. In front of the entire squad, he told Dilone that he'd race him for $500.

After taking one look at Stargell's oversized body, Dilone told his challenger he didn't have a prayer, but Stargell insisted that he'd race him for $500. So Stargell and Dilone headed out to center field and, with Tanner and the rest of the Pirates gleefully watching, Dilone finished 50 yards ahead of the lumbering Stargell. When Stargell finally finished the race, he huffed and puffed his way to Dilone and asked for his $500. When a flabbergasted Dilone said that he'd won the race, Stargell impishly replied, "I told you I'd race you for $500. I didn't say I'd beat you."

• • •

When the 1977 season started, Willie Stargell, despite his "challenge" to play a speed position, like center field, was still at first base. The only change for Stargell on Opening Day was that Tanner had dropped him to fifth in the batting order, behind Dave Parker and Al Oliver in the third and fourth spots. It was a decision that Stargell graciously accepted because he thought he'd be in a position to protect Parker and Oliver. The Pirates stumbled at the beginning of the season, losing their first three games, but they won the next four. After losing another three games in a row, they went on a five-game winning streak and finished the month at 10–7.

After the first three games, Stargell had to sit down for a few games with a pulled leg muscle. Shortly after he returned to the lineup, Stargell complained of feeling "woozy and dizzy," and had to be admitted to Pittsburgh's Eye and Ear Hospital for tests. Eventually he had to go on the 15-day disabled list with what was diagnosed as a "middle-ear problem." There were also indications that Stargell had suffered warning symptoms of the high blood pressure that would eventually kill him. After he came out of the hospital, he told Charley Feeney, in an interview published in *The Sporting News*, "I've been put on a diet. No caffeine. I can live without coffee. No alcohol. I really like a good glass of wine. The doctors told me to quit. I miss a good glass of wine with my meal.... But I'll adjust."

• • •

Stargell didn't hit his first home run of the season until the last day of April, but May was a different story. Stargell caught fire on May 1, as the Pirates went on an 11-game winning streak. In the first week of May, Stargell went 10-for-22, hit five home runs, and was named co-winner, with the Cubs' Manny Trillo, of the National League Player of the Week Award. He finished May with seven home runs for the month and a season batting average of .302.

By the end of the month, the Pirates were battling the Phillies for first place, but dropped off the pace after a seven-game losing streak in mid-June. They bounced back with a six-game winning streak, but lost eight of nine at the end of the month and were struggling to stay above .500. After his sensational May, Stargell also fell into a slump. He hit only four home runs in June and ended the month with a .272 average.

The Pirates came roaring back in July with five-game and eight-game winning streaks and, by the end of the month, they were back in contention with the Phillies for the East Division title. This time, however, they'd have to catch the Phillies without Willie Stargell. With the tension mounting between the Pirates and the Phillies, the teams met for a three-game series beginning on July 8. In the first game, the Pirates sent Bruce Kison to the mound to face the Phillies. The aggressive Kison kept pitching inside to Phillie batters until he hit Mike Schmidt with a pitch.

Schmidt charged the mound and, within seconds, the Pirates and the Phillies were entangled in a major brawl. Since no one wanted to challenge Willie Stargell, he went around from scrum to scrum, pulling Phillie bodies off his teammates. Unfortunately for Stargell, there were some heavyweights, like Greg "Bull" Luzinski, on the Phillies team and he felt something pop in his left elbow. Stargell tried to play with the pain for the next few weeks, but he finally had to go on the disabled list, effective August 4.

When doctors discovered a pinched nerve in Stargell's elbow, he had to undergo surgery to repair and relocate the damaged nerve. Stargell had to sit out the rest of the season, while his replacement at first base, Bill Robinson, led the Pirates with 26 home runs, and his young protege, Dave Parker, led the National League in hitting with a .338 average.

With Robinson and Parker leading the way on offense, Candelaria winning 20 games, and Gossage becoming a dominant closer, the Pirates stayed close to the Phillies, but could never catch up. They finished five games behind the Phillies, but their record of 96–66 was their best since their division-winning season in 1972. With their infusion of new talent and their success on the field, the Pirates had every reason to be optimistic about next season; but Stargell, who appeared in the fewest games, at 63, and had his fewest at-bats, at 186, of any of his years as a Pirate, had every reason to consider retirement.

• • •

While rumors swirled in the press about his retirement, Stargell had already made up his mind that he was returning to the Pirates for the 1978 season. He liked to describe himself as a tall oak with roots in Pittsburgh. There was no place that Stargell was more of a towering presence than in the Pirates clubhouse. He enjoyed the ribbing and the horseplay, but he was also there as a calming and reassuring influence on his teammates. Phil Garner said that every season Stargell seemed to grow taller and taller.

Proud of his accomplishments, Stargell was not willing to let an injury determine when he would stop playing baseball. He told reporters he'd know when it was time to retire, but he felt that he still had a few more good seasons left in him. And, of course, there was that dream that had haunted him since childhood. He played on a World Series championship team, but the heroics of Bill Mazeroski and Roberto Clemente had eluded him. He thought the current Pirates team had the talent and the drive to play its way into the World Series, and Stargell wanted not just to be a part of it, but to lead the way.

• • •

At the recommendation of Phil Garner, Stargell began an extensive off-season program at Steel City Nautilus to restore the strength in his damaged left elbow. Biz Stark, the top Nautilus trainer in Pittsburgh, told the *Post-Gazette*'s Charley Feeney that Stargell had trouble lifting 20 pounds with his left elbow when he began the training program in October, but, by January, he was "moving nearly 130 pounds." Stargell believed that his elbow had more strength and flexibility in it than it had in the "last six years." He was so encouraged that he'd already talked to Chuck Tanner about his role in the 1978 season. They'd agreed that, with an occasional day off, there was no reason Stargell couldn't return to his position in the starting lineup.

Pirate general manager Pete Peterson was so pleased with Stargell's progress that he decided to roll the dice and trade Al Oliver to make room in the outfield for Bill Robinson now that Stargell appeared healthy enough to return to first base and play on a regular basis. He thought the team needed a dominant starting pitcher, like the Phillies' Steve Carlton, so he traded Oliver to the Texas Rangers for All-Star right-hander Bert Blyleven. The Pirates also received hard-hitting John Milner in that four-team trade from the New York Mets as insurance in case Stargell faltered during the season. The rap against John Milner was that he had one of the worst temperaments in baseball, but Peterson was confident—as it turned out, with good reason—that Stargell would be a positive influence on Milner in the clubhouse.

Peterson had his pitching ace to join Candelaria, Rooker, and Reuss in the starting rotation, but he'd lost Gossage and Forster in the off-season to free agency. He felt confident that the Pirates had a strong rookie candidate for the starting rotation in right-hander Don Robinson, and that Kent Tekulve was ready to step up as the Pirates' closer out of the bullpen. To give Tanner some more flexibility with his pitching staff, however, Peterson signed his own free agent in veteran right-hander Jim Bibby, who could fill in as a starter or in relief.

With Bill Robinson moving out to left field, Peterson felt that Robinson's bat would compensate for the loss of Al Oliver, but he was worried about Rennie Stennett's return from the broken leg that he had suffered in mid-August. He was also concerned about finding an adequate

Willie Stargell played brilliantly in the 1979 National League playoffs and World Series and had good reason for jumping with joy during the postseason.

Willie Stargell hits the 1979 World Series–winning home run against the Baltimore Orioles in the seventh and deciding game. (AP Images)

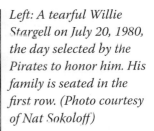

Left: A tearful Willie Stargell on July 20, 1980, the day selected by the Pirates to honor him. His family is seated in the first row. (Photo courtesy of Nat Sokoloff)

Below: Willie Stargell breaks down as he hugs his father, William, now confined to a wheelchair. The Pirates surprised "Pops" by bringing his parents to Willie Stargell Day. (Photo courtesy of Nat Sokoloff)

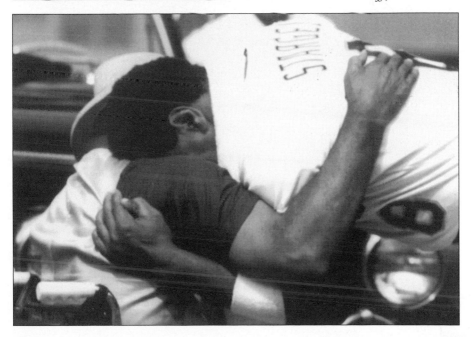

Pirate broadcaster Bob Prince was one of Stargell's dearest friends. The baseball patches on Prince's coat enclose his most famous lines, like "Kiss it goodbye," when Stargell hit a home run.

Chuck Tanner hugs Willie Stargell at Stargell's final game on October 3, 1982.

A beaming Willie Stargell with two of his daughters at the pre-induction news conference at the Baseball Hall of Fame in 1987.

Willie Stargell delivering his induction speech at the Baseball Hall of Fame ceremonies in 1987.

A visibly ailing Willie Stargell looks down at the model of the statue to be built in his honor at a pregame ceremony in 2000. The statue was unveiled on April 7, 2001, two days before Stargell's death.

Stargell's statue stands coiled and ready to crush another ball into the seats. (AP Images)

backup to catcher Ed Ott, who had a solid season in 1977, but needed to sit out a game from time to time. Peterson felt that rookie Dale Berra, the son of the Yankee-great Yogi Berra, was ready to fill in if Stennett wasn't ready to play, but to get another catcher, Peterson redeemed himself with Pirate fans by trading Miguel Dilone, Elias Sosa, and a minor leaguer to the Oakland A's for Manny Sanguillen.

• • •

The Pirates looked loaded and ready to challenge the Phillies after a 1–0 Opening Day victory over the Cubs at Three Rivers, behind the strong pitching of John Candelaria. But after bouncing back and forth between winning and losing streaks they finished April at only 10–9. They suffered through a series of three-game losing streaks in May, and finished the month with a disappointing 22–25 record.

There were a number of reasons for the Pirates' slow start, including a wave of minor injuries and inconsistent pitching, but the focus for the criticism of fans and the press was Willie Stargell's poor start. He hit only two home runs with three RBIs in April and finished the month with an anemic .195 average. He didn't hit his third home run of the season until May 15, then homered again the next day. His two home runs against the Expos a week later got him to four for the month, but he ended May with only a .214 average.

While Tanner remained optimistic that the Pirates and Stargell would pull out of their slumps, many fans were unhappy with the team and thought the 38-year-old Stargell should not have tried to come back from his elbow injury. The criticism increased as the Pirates continued to play under .500 in June, while Stargell fell into another home run drought.

In the last few weeks of June, however, Stargell finally recaptured his swing. He hit five home runs over a span of three weeks, ended up with a .390 average for the month, and was batting .278 on the season. After he banged out three hits, including a home run and double, against the Mets on June 29, Bob Smizik, in the *Pittsburgh Press*, happily declared, "The old man is back" and hoped the Pirates "would soon do as well as Willie Stargell."

The Pirates, however, continued to play inconsistent baseball despite Stargell's best effort to carry them as he had in the past. To make matters worse, Dave Parker fractured his cheekbone in a collision at home plate in a game against the Mets on the last day in June. He wore a batting helmet with a special face mask and stayed in the lineup; but Parker's determination failed to inspire the Pirates. They went on a seven-game losing streak after the All-Star break and finished July with a 48–52 record. With the Pirates continuing to lose, the only good news for Stargell came when he was named as Dave Parker's replacement for the All-Star Game, after Parker bowed out of the game. It was Stargell's seventh selection, but his first since 1973.

• • •

It took until mid-August, but the Pirates finally caught fire. On August 12, after a stretch in which they lost five out of six games to the Phillies, they fell to 51-61, 11½ games behind the division leaders. On August 16, however, they started a 10-game winning streak and, by the end of August, were finally over .500 at 66–64.

Stargell continued his hot hitting in August, but on August 6, after homering earlier in the game against the Phillies' Dick Ruthven, he achieved a dubious distinction when he struck out against Ruthven in the bottom of the ninth. The strikeout was the 1,711th of Stargell's career and broke the all-time strikeout record held by the Yankees' Mickey Mantle. Stargell's only comment after the game was typically low-keyed: "I didn't go up to the plate today with intentions of striking out. I never do."

With the all-time strikeout record behind him, Stargell ended up hitting five home runs in August for a total of 20 heading into the last month of the season. He also drove in 20 runs in August, his best RBI month so far in 1978, and raised his season's batting average to .286. The best, however, was yet to come for the Pirates and for Stargell. On August 27, the Pirates began one of the most remarkable stretch runs in the team's history when they went on an 11-game winning streak. They followed that streak with seven straight wins in mid-September and five straight wins after sweeping a doubleheader at Three Rivers against the Phillies on September 29.

The Pirates' doubleheader victory came at the beginning of a four-game series with the division-leading Phillies that would bring the 1978 regular season to an end. When the Pirates took the field at Three Rivers the next day, they trailed the Phillies by a game and a half. A win by the Pirates would move them within a half-game of first place, and another win Sunday would put them up by a half-game, forcing them to play a makeup game against Cincinnati that would determine if they won the division title or had to play a tiebreaker game with the Phillies. For the Phillies to win the division, all they had to do was win one of their last two games against the Pirates.

After the doubleheader win, Chuck Tanner sent out rookie Don Robinson to pitch against the Phillies. Robinson, a leading candidate for the National League Rookie of the Year Award, had 14 wins on the season, tying him with Bert Blyleven for the team lead. In the bottom of the first, Willie Stargell gave Robinson a 4–0 lead when he hit a grand slam off Phillies left-hander Barry Lerch. It was Stargell's 28th home run of the season and his 11th career grand slam, tying him with Ralph Kiner for the team record.

Pittsburgh, however, couldn't hold the lead, and, going into the bottom of the ninth, the Pirates trailed the Phillies 10–4. The Pirates had battled back all season and, after rallying for four runs, appeared to have one more miracle left in their bats. With the score 10–8 and Bill Robinson at first base with one out, Stargell came to the plate representing the tying run.

In his autobiography, Stargell remembered the moment as "the type of situation I'd dreamed of as a boy." The hard reality, however, was that he was facing Ron Reed's "blazing fastball" not "a bottle cap tossed lightly into the air." He went to the plate "thinking only one thing—home run." With two strikes, he swung as hard as he could, but "guessed wrong and struck out."

When Phil Garner grounded out to Larry Bowa, the Phillies won the game and clinched their third straight East Division title. When Stargell singled after Chuck Tanner batted him in the leadoff spot in the meaningless final game of the season, speculation immediately began that, after his outstanding season, Stargell had taken his last at-bat for the Pirates. Many fans and writers assumed that, after proving himself once again—his 28 home runs and 97 RBIs were his best since 1973—Stargell, at the age of 38, would want to end his career at the top of his game.

• • •

On November 1, Stargell put an end to the speculation when he signed a two-year contract with the Pirates for $500,000. Shortly after signing the contract, United Press International and *The Sporting News* named him the Comeback Player of the Year. At the end of the month, major league sportswriters and broadcasters voted Stargell, who had fought back from injury, the winner of the prestigious Fred Hutchinson Award. Named after the former Cincinnati Reds manager who'd died in 1964 after a courageous battle with cancer, the award went each year to honor a player for "overcoming some form of adversity while displaying the competitive instincts and character of Fred Hutchinson."

With Stargell safely under contract, the Pirates turned their attention to Dave Parker, who'd been named the 1978 National League Most Valuable Player, an honor that had eluded Stargell throughout the 1970s. With Parker a year away from free agency, the Pirates gave serious thought to trading him during the off-season, but, instead, they found the money to sign Parker to a five-year, $7 million contract, the biggest in baseball at that time.

Pete Peterson still had some tinkering to do with the Pirates bench, but, after the sensational comebacks of Stargell and the Pirates in 1978, there was no question in the minds of Peterson and Tanner that their talented Pirates were in a position to dethrone the Phillies after their three-year reign in the East Division and make it back to the World Series for the first time since 1971. For Stargell, as disappointed as he was in falling short of his dream at the end of the 1978 season, he believed more than ever that the elusive dream of his childhood was still within his grasp.

CHAPTER **11**

We Are Family

On March 6, 1979, Willie Stargell celebrated his 39th birthday at the Pirates' spring training camp in Bradenton. Two generations of teammates had passed since he'd driven from Columbus to Pittsburgh with Bob Veale to begin his major league career. Those who were with Stargell in his rookie season in 1963—Bill Mazeroski, Vern Law, Bob Bailey, Bill Virdon—were long gone from the Pirates' clubhouse. Two of those closest to him, Roberto Clemente and Danny Murtaugh, were dead.

Of the Pirates who were part of the 1971 World Series championship team, only Manny Sanguillen, Bruce Kison, and Rennie Stennett were still with the team, though 1979 would be the last year for Kison and Stennett in a Pirates uniform. Dock Ellis, Al Oliver, Dave Giusti, and so many of his favorite teammates had been traded away and were finishing out their careers with other teams. Bob Moose had died in a car crash, and Steve Blass had to leave the game after he lost the ability to throw strikes.

The 1979 Pirates, however, had a host of characters as diverse and colorful as any that Stargell had the good fortune of calling teammates in the past. In 1971, the Pirates were pioneers when they fielded an all-black team, but, in 1979, no one seemed to notice that minorities were still in the majority in the Pirates' starting lineup. There was no Dock Ellis to agitate his teammates, but the outspoken Dave Parker had become a lightning rod for controversy. There was no clubhouse clown to match Steve Blass' antics, but Phil Garner had his own way of bedeviling his teammates, especially

Parker. He had an ongoing bet with Parker that, if he ever outhit him in a season, Parker would shut up for the next 10 years.

In 1979, the Pirates had a cast of characters with nicknames right out of a Stephen King plot. They had Scrap Iron (Garner), Troll (Ed Ott), Hit Man (Mike Easler), Hammer (John Milner), and Cobra (Parker). In April they added a Crazy Horse (Tim Foli), and by mid-season, a Mad Dog (Bill Madlock). In 1971, the Pirates had the aloof "Great One," who, with his pride and passion, drove the Pirates to a World Series victory. In 1979, they had a great one in Pops, who had a more embracing way of bringing out the best in his teammates.

. . .

If there was any doubt of Stargell's greatness, all one had to do was look at his record of accomplishments heading into the 1979 season His 28 home runs in his comeback season of 1978 gave him 429 for his career. Not only had he shattered Ralph Kiner's all-time Pirates career home run record of 301, he'd become only the 17th player in major league history to reach the 400 home run mark. As he entered the 1979 season, he needed only 46 more home runs to tie the 475 career home runs hit by his idol, Stan Musial.

At the end of the 1978 season, Stargell had reached 2,026 hits for his career, a total that put him ahead of Bill Mazeroski into seventh place on the Pirates all-time list. The six Pirate greats ahead of him, including Roberto Clemente, who topped the list with 3,000 hits, were members of the Baseball Hall of Fame. His 1,394 RBIs had moved him past Roberto Clemente into second place on the Pirates all-time list. He needed only 82 more to pass Honus Wagner and become the all-time RBI leader. The National League MVP Award may have eluded him, but there was little doubt that he was playing his way into the Baseball Hall of Fame.

. . .

Barring a major injury, Stargell was in a position in 1979 to move even higher on the Pirates all-time lists and add to his reputation as one of the greatest home run hitters in baseball history. The only goal, however, that really mattered to him was returning to the World Series. He wanted one last chance to fulfill his boyhood dream and join his former teammates Bill Mazeroski and Roberto Clemente as World Series heroes. To do that, he'd have to lead the Pirates on the field, while giving them confidence in the clubhouse that 1979 was their year to become champions.

When the Pirate players had closed-door meetings, they had their share of clubhouse lawyers and preachers. Stargell would usually listen, calm things down with a few words, and offer his standard advice on having fun and playing together as a team. Though his teammates, like Rooker and Garner, couldn't remember Stargell saying all that much that was memorable or inspirational at the meetings, they were ready to run through flames when he finished because his presence seemed to dominate the room.

Early in the 1979 season, Stargell decided that another way of encouraging his teammates was to give them small felt stars to stick on their caps when they did something well. He came up with the idea while visiting a friend and seeing a packet of stickers in the shape of a rose. When the friend told him that he used the stickers as rewards for good deeds, Stargell had hundreds of gold stars made up and started handing them out as rewards for his teammates' good plays. At first the idea seemed corny, but they were Stargell Stars. They soon became such prized possessions that Stargell designated Ed Ott, a former high school wrestler, as their guardian. In a few cases, the stars became a little too coveted. Phil Garner said that Kent Tekulve had so many stars that he aroused suspicions among his teammates that he was stealing them when Ott wasn't looking. Tekulve was having a great season as the Pirates' closer, but, according to Garner, the number of stars on his always immaculate cap seemed to far exceed his accomplishments.

In addition to handing out gold stars to reward his teammates for playing well, Stargell came up with another idea to bring the Pirates closer together. During a long rain delay in late June at Three Rivers, the loudspeakers were blaring out the top disco hits of the day. One song that caught Stargell's attention was Sister Sledge's summer hit, "We Are Family."

Remembering that Joe L. Brown had talked about the Pirates organization as a family as far back as the 1960s, Stargell decided that the

Sisters Sledge song should become the Pirates' anthem. Kent Tekulve, who was sitting beside Pops in the dugout, remembered Stargell picking up the dugout phone, calling upstairs to the Pirates publicity director and telling him he wanted the song played in the bottom of the seventh inning at every Pirates game.

For the Pirates and their fans, 1979 became the season of Stargell Stars and "We Are Family." It also, however, became the season when the player they called "Wil" in the 1960s, and "Starg" in the 1970s had become the head of the Pirates' family. For the rest of his career and for the rest of his life, he'd be celebrated as "Pops," the name that Dave Parker had first started using to express his affection for Stargell and to rib him a bit about his age.

• • •

It took a while for Stargell's magic to take hold and for the Pirates to play like champions in 1979. They lost their season opener at Three Rivers to the Montreal Expos and struggled for the rest of the month. After losing four of their first five games, they won three games in a row; then went on a six-game losing streak. They finished April with a 7–11 record. While the Pirates struggled, Stargell, back in his clean-up spot in the starting lineup after his comeback season, got off to a fast start. For the month, he hit four home runs, drove in 14 runs, and batted .327.

When the season opened, the Pirates fully expected the Philadelphia Phillies to be their major rival once again. The Phillies, after winning three straight East Division titles, appeared to be even stronger in 1979 when they signed Pete Rose as a free agent. The dark horse out of the gate in 1979, however, was the Montreal Expos. With a powerful lineup, led by future Hall of Famers Gary Carter, Andre Dawson, and former Reds nemesis Tony Perez, the Expos jumped off to a 14–5 record in April and took an early 6½-game lead over the Pirates.

General manager Pete Peterson's main concern going into the 1979 season was his middle infield. The Pirates' Opening Day lineup had Frank Taveras at shortstop and Rennie Stennett at second base. Taveras gave the Pirates a premier base-stealer at the top of the batting order, but he was inconsistent at shortstop. Rennie Stennett's range at second base had become a concern ever since he'd broken his leg during the 1977 season. He was also going to be a free agent after the 1979 season.

On April 19, Peterson made the first of two significant moves during the 1979 season when he traded Taveras to the New York Mets for Tim Foli. The Pirates were giving up speed, but, with Foli, the Pirates now had a solid defensive shortstop with a reputation as a clutch hitter. The Pirates also entertained the idea of moving Phil Garner to second base, but didn't have any options at third base beyond an inexperienced Dale Berra.

With Stargell out of the lineup with a bruised hip for the first two weeks of May, the Pirates dropped to 12–18, but, when he returned, the Pirates went on a six-game winning streak to get back to .500. During that stretch, Stargell hit four home runs in three games shortly after returning to the lineup. With the help of a five-game winning streak at the end of the month, the Pirates finished May at 23–21. Though Stargell missed 10 games in May, he hit six home runs, drove in 14 runs for the month, and was batting a lofty .339 on the season.

• • •

A five-game losing streak in early June had the Pirates back at .500 by mid-June, but they bounced back with a six-game streak to climb six games over .500. On June 28, with the Pirates fighting to stay in contention, Pete Peterson made his second significant move of the 1979 season. He traded three players, including pitchers Al Holland and Ed Whitson, to the San Francisco Giants for infielder Lenny Randle, pitcher Dave Roberts, and third baseman Bill Madlock. A two-time National League batting champion, Madlock was the key to the deal because it allowed Chuck Tanner to move Phil Garner to second base.

With Madlock in the lineup, the Pirates surged in July, at one point winning 13 out of 14 games. They finished the month at 57–45 and were back in striking distance of a first-place Montreal team that had continued to play well after their early season surge. After a subpar June in which he hit two home runs and drove in only five runs, Stargell exploded in July with nine home runs and 17 RBIs. He was not selected to the All-Star

Game, but Dave Parker, the Pirates' lone representative, stole the show with two spectacular throws that earned him the MVP Award.

At the end of July, Stargell was among the National League leaders with 21 home runs and a batting average of .317. While he slowed down in August, hit only three home runs, and saw his batting average slip under .300, the Pirates continued to play well. They had winning streaks of five and six games and, at the end of the month were 24 games over .500 at 78–54. Going into the final month of the season, they'd moved ahead of the Expos by three games.

The Pirates had plenty of heroes in September, but none shone brighter than Willie Stargell. He started the month by hitting two home runs against the Giants on his way to hitting eight for the month. The Pirates were also helped by the return of Jim Rooker from the disabled list. Rooker won the 100th game of his career on Labor Day and kept the Pirates ahead of the streaking Expos.

With Candelaria and Robinson also struggling with injuries, Peterson decided to purchase Dock Ellis from the New York Mets. After Pops Stargell embraced his exiled son, Dock Ellis proclaimed, "I'll die a Pirate." With a bolstered pitching staff, the Pirates began a four-game series with the Montreal Expos on September 24. It was the last head-to-head series between the two teams and came with the Pirates now trailing the Expos by half a game.

After splitting a doubleheader, the Pirates hammered the Expos in the third game behind Willie Stargell's two home runs in his first two times at bat to move back into first place. After Bruce Kison's complete game gave the Pirates a victory in the series' finale, the Pirates were in first place by 1½ games.

• • •

On September 30, the Pirates played their last game of the season. It was against the Chicago Cubs at Three Rivers. The Pirates had a one-game lead on the Expos, but the teams were tied in the loss column. If the Pirates lost to the Cubs and the Expos won their last three games, including two makeup games, the Expos would end the season as East Division champions. The only way the Pirates could win the East Division on the last day of the season was with a win against the Cubs and an Expos loss to the Phillies. If the Pirates and Expos won out, they'd meet in a playoff to decide the division winner.

Chuck Tanner's choice in the critical final game against the Cubs was Bruce Kison. He'd pitched a complete game in his last start and was undefeated in September. After Kison retired the Cubs in the top of the first, Willie Stargell drove home the first run of the game in the bottom half of the inning with a sacrifice fly. With the Pirates ahead 2–0 in the bottom of the fifth, Stargell hit his 32nd home run of the season to give the Pirates a 3–0 lead. He received a standing ovation from the sell-out crowd and had to come out of the dugout and tip his cap before the cheering died down.

With the Pirates ahead 3–1 in the top of the seventh, Tanner decided to bring in Kent Tekulve. With the score 3–2 in the bottom of the seventh, the crowd roared when the scoreboard flashed the news that the Phillies' Steve Carlton had shut out the Expos 2–0. Knowing that a win would clinch the East Division title, the Pirates added two runs on a Bill Robinson base hit. When Tekulve retired the Cubs in the last two innings, the season was over. For the first time since 1975, the Pirates were division winners and returning to the National League Championship Series.

• • •

There were plenty of star-studded heroes on the 1979 Pirates team. While enduring fan animosity over his multi-million dollar contract, Dave Parker had another strong year and led the team with 94 RBIs. Platooning in left field, Bill Robinson and John Milner were long-ball threats and contributed a number of clutch hits. The equally feisty Tim Foli and Phil Garner were solid up the middle, and Bill Madlock, after the mid-season trade, led the Pirates in hitting with a .328 average. Catcher Ed Ott had his best season as a Pirate, and his backup, Steve Nicosia, had a solid rookie season. Omar Moreno stole 77 bases and played a great center field.

With Jim Rooker in and out with injuries, John Candelaria, Bert Blyleven, Jim Bibby, Bruce Kison, and Don Robinson gave the Pirates consistent starting pitching. With Grant Jackson and Enrique Romo coming out of the bullpen to set things up for Kent Tekulve, the Pirates had one of the best bullpens in baseball. Between them, Jackson and Romo won 18 games and had 19 saves. There may have been some suspicions about the number of Tekulve's Stargell Stars, but he certainly earned his fair share by appearing in 94 games and finishing the season with 10 wins and 31 saves.

Pete Peterson and Chuck Tanner were also in line for Stargell Stars. During the off-season, Peterson signed former Dodger Lee Lacy as a free agent to strengthen the Pirates' bench and traded a handful of minor leaguers to Seattle for veteran reliever Enrique Romo to bolster his bullpen. During the season, he made two remarkable trades for Tim Foli and Bill Madlock that were critical to the Pirates' success. Without Foli and Madlock, it's difficult to imagine the Pirates winning a division title.

The Pirates' eternal optimist, Chuck Tanner, was also something of a maverick and gambler. On occasion, he'd do something so against conventional baseball strategy that he stupefied his players, outraged the fans, and had Pittsburgh sports reporters scratching their heads.

On August 5, in a dramatic game against the Phillies, Steve Nicosia had gone 3-for-3, including a home run, against Steve Carlton, one of the toughest left-handers in baseball. In the bottom of the ninth, with another tough left-hander, Tug McGraw, pitching and the scored tied 8–8 with the bases loaded, Tanner sent John Milner to bat for Nicosia despite Nicosia's four hits. Tanner claimed that even his wife booed the move. Milner made Tanner look like a genius by driving McGraw's first pitch into the right-field stands for a grand slam. When he reached home plate he was mobbed by his teammates and and carried off the field on their shoulders.

On August 11, in another game against the Phillies, the Pirates were losing 8–0 when Stargell reminded his teammates that the game was on national television. When he urged them to show baseball fans around the country "what the Pirates are made of," the team rallied and took a 9–8 lead late in the game with the bases loaded and Ed Ott, a left-hand batter, coming up against the left-handed Tug McGraw.

Ott looked to the dugout for a right-handed hitter to bat for him, but all he saw was a smiling Chuck Tanner cheering him on. Thinking his manager was crazy for letting him bat against McGraw, Ott took a pitch right down the middle, then launched the next pitch into the right-field stands for a grand slam. The Pirates ended up winning the game 14–11. Those improbable Milner and Ott grand slams knocked the Phillies out of contention and, for many Pirates fans, became the most memorable moments in the 1979 season.

• • •

For all the heroics and wild finishes, the key to winning the division title in 1979 was Willie Stargell. Not only was his quiet confidence and stately presence in the clubhouse critical to the team's morale and unity, his performance on the field, at the age of 39, was astounding.

Playing in 126 games, his most since 1974, Stargell led the Pirates in home runs with 32, his highest total since 1973, and his .997 fielding percentage was the best in the National League for first basemen. He was second on the team with 13 game-winning hits, and, in the stretch drive of September, he had five game winning RBIs, including four by home runs. He was clearly the Pirates' most valuable player. The only question was whether or not baseball writers would finally recognize his greatness and select him as the National League's Most Valuable Player.

Winning the National League MVP Award, however, was the last thing on Stargell's mind at the end of the season. The Pirates were headed to the NLCS for the sixth time in the 1970s, and their opponent, for the fourth time, was the Cincinnati Reds. No longer the Big Red Machine, the Reds had barely nipped Bill Virdon's Houston Astros for the West Division title. They'd lost key players, like Pete Rose, Tony Perez, and Don Gullett, but they still had Johnny Bench, Joe Morgan, and pitching ace Tom Seaver. The Pirates had lost all three of their previous NLCS matchups against the Reds, and Stargell had struggled. Going into the playoffs, no player had more incentive than Willie Stargell.

• • •

For the opening playoff game at Cincinnati's Riverfront Stadium in the best-of-five series, Chuck Tanner selected John Candelaria as his starting pitcher. Candelaria had been bothered by a bad back during the season, but he'd led the Pirate starters with 14 wins. Reds manager John McNamara countered with Tom Seaver, who had led the Reds pitching staff with 16 wins.

The game started well for the Pirates when Phil Garner homered in the top of the third, and, later in the inning, Tim Foli drove home Omar Moreno with a sacrifice fly for a 2–0 lead. The Reds, however, tied the score in the bottom of the fourth on George's Foster's two-run homer. Both teams missed scoring opportunities, and, going into the 11th inning, the teams remained in a 2–2 tie.

In the top of the 11th, Tim Foli led off with a single, and after Matt Alexander went in to run for him, Dave Parker singled Alexander to second base. As Willie Stargell stepped into the batter's box, he'd been experiencing his typical playoff game. He'd struck out against Seaver in his first at-bat, and had nothing but a walk to show for his four trips to the plate.

This at-bat, however, was different. Stargell lined a Tom Hume pitch deep into right-center field that cleared the fence and gave the Pirates a 5–2 lead. It wasn't the World Series, but it was the first time that Stargell had hit a dramatic home run in the postseason. When Don Robinson struck out Ray Knight with the bases loaded in the bottom of the 11th inning, the Pirates had a 1–0 lead in the NLCS.

In the second game, the veteran Jim Bibby faced rookie Frank Pastore, a surprise choice by McNamara, who was expected to go with 14-game winner Mike LaCoss. The Reds jumped ahead 1–0 in the bottom of the second, but, after tying the score in the top of the fourth, the Pirates went ahead 2–1 in the fifth on a Tim Foli double. The lead held up until the bottom of the ninth when Kent Tekulve gave up a game-tying double to Dave Collins.

For the second game in a row, the Pirates and the Reds headed into extra innings. In the top of the 10th, a Pirates slugger, once again, won the game in dramatic fashion, but this time it was Dave Parker. While Pops watched from the on-deck circle, Parker singled home Omar Moreno to give the Pirates a 3–2 lead. After Parker's hit, the Reds walked Stargell intentionally, his second walk of the game to go along with his two hits. The Pirates failed to score, but the one run lead held up in the bottom of the 10th when Don Robinson retired the Reds to give the Pirates a commanding 2–0 lead as the teams headed to Pittsburgh for the rest of the series.

• • •

A heavy rainstorm delayed the start of the third game of the series, but the Pirates wasted no time in taking control once things got underway. They scored a run in each of the first two innings on sacrifice flies and had a 2–0 lead going into the bottom of the third against Mike LaCoss. Reds manager McNamara brought in left-hander Fred Norman to pitch to Willie Stargell, who promptly lined a Norman pitch into the right-field stands. Bill Madlock followed Stargell's blast with another home run for a 4–0 Pirates lead. In the bottom of the fourth, Stargell doubled home two more runs off Norman, and the Pirates, comfortably ahead 6–0, were well on their way to the National League pennant.

For the third game in the series, Chuck Tanner had selected Bert Blyleven as his starting pitcher. Since coming to the Pirates in 1978, Blyleven had pitched well, but never at the All-Star level that Pete Peterson had anticipated when he traded for him. On this day, however, Blyleven was that dominant pitcher. With the exception of a Johnny Bench home run, Blyleven, who possessed one of the best curveballs in baseball, completely shut down the Reds. Going into the bottom of the seventh, the Pirates, behind Blyleven's pitching and Stargell's hitting, led 6–1.

Since that night in June when Stargell decreed Sister Sledge's "We Are Family" as the Pirates anthem, the loudspeakers at Three Rivers blasted out the song during the seventh-inning stretch. This time, when "We Are Family" started playing, something spontaneous and remarkable took place just behind the home-plate screen. Roger Angell, covering the game for *The New Yorker*, described what happened next: "The wives of Pirate players suddenly moved forward from their seats, just behind the screen, and clambered up onto a low, curving shelf that rims the field behind home plate. At first, there were only a few of them, but more and more of the young women ran down the aisles and were pulled onto the sudden stage, and then they were all dancing together there, arm in arm, jiving and boogieing, and high-kicking in rhythm, in their slacks and black-and-gold scarves, and long ballplayer-wife's fur coats, all waving and laughing and hugging and shaking their banners in time to the music. It was terrific."

After the Pirates added a run in the bottom of the eighth for a 7–1 lead, all that remained was for Blyleven to retire the Reds in the ninth inning, and he did it in a spectacular fashion befitting the day. With two outs and Cesar Geronimo at the plate, Blyleven snapped off a curve that buckled Geronimo's knees and broke over the plate for a called strike three.

After the Pirates mobbed Bert Blyleven, they headed for the champagne waiting for them in the clubhouse as National League champions. Willie Stargell, who'd struggled so mightily in the postseason, was named the MVP of the 1979 NLCS after hitting two home runs, driving in six runs, and batting .455. After so many frustrations and disappointments, it was a dream come true for Pops, but, more than that, he had one more chance to play in a World Series and fulfill his ultimate dream.

• • •

In the words of Yogi Berra, the 1979 World Series was "déjà vu, all over again." The Pirates opponent, as in 1971, was Earl Weaver's Baltimore Orioles. While pitcher Jim Palmer and shortstop Mark Belanger were the only remaining Orioles who played in the 1971 World Series, the team had basically the same look because of Weaver's managerial philosophy.

The Orioles manager believed in strong pitching and the three-run homer, so he stacked his teams with talented arms and long-ball hitters. The powerful Orioles lineup was led by Kenny Singleton, with 35 home runs and 111 RBIs, but it also had future Hall of Famer Eddie Murray, who homered 25 times and drove in 99 runs, along with home run–threats Gary Roenicke, Lee May, and Doug DeCinces. Jim Palmer was the only remaining starter from the four 20-game winners who pitched against the Pirates in the 1971 World Series, but Weaver had 23-game-winner Mike Flanagan, Dennis Martinez, Steve Stone, and Scott McGregor to throw at the Pirates. Unfortunately for Willie Stargell, Flanagan and McGregor were left-handed.

• • •

The first game in Baltimore had to be canceled because of a combination of rain and snow. The next evening, with temperatures headed into the lower 30s, baseball commissioner Bowie Kuhn decided that field conditions were playable and ordered the teams to open the World Series. It was a decision with immediate disastrous consequences for the Pirates.

In the bottom of the first inning with the bases loaded and one out, Phil Garner fielded a perfect double-play ball, but the ball was so slippery that Garner threw what felt like "a bar of soap" over Tim Foli's head. With the Orioles ahead 2–0, Pirates starter Bruce Kison unleashed a wild pitch that scored another run, then surrendered a two-run homer to Doug DeCinces. With the score 5–0, Tanner removed Kison from the game. Kison had been the Pirates' best pitcher during their September stretch drive, but on a cold, clammy night he'd lost the feeling in his pitching hand and would not be able to pitch for the rest of the World Series.

The only good thing to come out of the Pirates' terrible first inning was the stellar performance of their relief pitching and the tenacity of their hitters. While four Pirate relievers held the Orioles scoreless, the Pirates mounted a comeback against Mike Flanagan that just fell short. They cut the lead to 5–1 in the fourth on a Stargell RBI ground-out, and narrowed it to 5–3 in the sixth on a Garner two-run base hit. In the eighth inning, Stargell, who was batting fifth in the lineup, hit his first World Series home run off Mike Flanagan, one of the best left-handers in baseball, to make the score 5–4. In the top of the ninth, Parker singled with one out and worked his way around to third base with Stargell coming to bat with two outs. This time, however, Stargell was no match for Flanagan and struck out.

After the loss, Parker noticed that his teammates seemed demoralized. He stepped forward and delivered a profanity-laced tirade. He reminded them that Tanner said before the World Series that the Orioles had great players, but the Pirates had the best team. He reminded them that they had spotted one of the best pitchers in baseball five runs and nearly beat him. So they needed to get their heads up and go out the next night and "kick some Oriole butt." When he finished, his teammates, including Pops, gave him a standing ovation.

• • •

For Game 2, Tanner decided to pitch Bert Blyleven against the Orioles' Jim Palmer. With no score after the first inning, Stargell led off the top of the second with a single and came around to score on base hits by Milner and Madlock. Ed Ott then hit a sacrifice fly to score Milner and give the Pirates a 2–0 lead. Eddie Murray's home run in the bottom of the second narrowed the lead to 2–1, and his double tied the game at 2–2 in the bottom of the sixth. Only a brilliant throw from Dave Parker to cut down Murray trying to score on a fly ball kept the Orioles from taking the lead.

Both teams blew chances to score in the seventh, and Baltimore left a runner at third in the eighth, but in the top of the ninth, the Pirates recaptured the lead. Bill Robinson led off the inning with a single, but pinch runner Matt Alexander was thrown out trying to steal second base. With two outs, Ott singled, and Oriole reliever Don Stanhouse walked Garner. Tanner, on yet another hunch, sent up seldom-used Manny Sanguillen to pinch hit. Sanguillen, who later admitted he was "tight" from the cold, served Stanhouse's 1–2 pitch into right field for a base hit. Ott, one of the slower runners on the Pirates, chugged his way around third and barely beat the throw to home plate.

In the bottom of the ninth, Tekulve protected the Pirates 3–2 lead by striking out the first two Oriole batters and getting the the third out on a ground ball. After their dismal loss in the first game, the Pirates had tied the World Series at a game apiece and were headed back to Pittsburgh with renewed confidence that they were the best team. As for Sanguillen, he dedicated his winning hit to Roberto Clemente.

• • •

For Game 3, Chuck Tanner had John Candelaria ready to take the mound at Three Rivers. After Candelaria retired the Orioles in the first, the Pirates took a 1–0 lead in the bottom of the inning on a Parker sacrifice fly. In the bottom of the second, Stargell, batting fifth in the order against left-hander

Scott McGregor, singled to lead off the inning. After a Nicosia single, Garner drove in both runners for a 3–0 lead, but the lead didn't hold up.

After Benny Alaya's two-run homer in the third cut the lead to 3–2, the game was delayed by rain for an hour. When play resumed, things unraveled for the Pirates. In the top of the fourth, the Orioles loaded the bases on two hits and a Foli error, then Kiko Garcia unloaded the bases with a three-run triple. By the time the inning was over, the Orioles had scored two more runs off Candelaria and Romo and taken a 7–3 lead. Stargell's double in the sixth and Madlock's RBI single made the score 7–4, but Garcia's single in the top of the seventh increased the Oriole lead to 8–4. The Pirates couldn't do anything the rest of the way against McGregor, who retired the last 11 Pirate hitters.

After the frustrating 8–4 loss at home, the Pirates trailed the Orioles two games to one, but they were still confident that they were the best team. They'd fought back in the first game, won the second game in dramatic fashion, and led in the third game until the rain delay. They were disappointed that they'd have to return to Baltimore even if they won the next two games in Pittsburgh, but saw no reason why they couldn't win those games and take command of the World Series going back to Baltimore.

• • •

In Game 4, the Pirates, once again, took an early lead when Stargell led off the bottom of the second inning with a home run against Dennis Martinez to give the Pirates a 1–0 lead. When Ott doubled home two more runs and Moreno singled in Garner, the Orioles took out Martinez, but only after the Pirates had taken a 4–0 lead. A Madlock error helped the Orioles score three runs in the top of the third, but Bibby didn't give up another run for the next three innings as the Pirates increased their lead on RBI doubles by Milner and Parker to 6–3.

Grant Jackson helped Bibby out of a jam in the seventh, but in the top of the eighth things fell apart for the Pirates for the second game in a row. Pitching in relief of Grant, Don Robinson loaded the bases with one out. Tanner brought Kent Tekulve into the game, but, for one of the few times in the 1979 season, Tekulve couldn't hold the lead. He gave up a two-run double to pinch-hitter John Lowenstein, and after an intentional walk loaded the bases again, surrendered another two-run double to another pinch-hitter, Terry Crowley. He then gave up a run-scoring single to Tim Stoddard, the Orioles' pitcher. He finally got the second out of the inning on an Al Bumbry ground out, but another run scored on the play, the sixth for the Orioles in the inning.

Going into the bottom of the eighth, the demoralized Pirates trailed 9–6 after leading 6–3 going into the top of the inning. After going out easily in the eighth, they tried to mount a rally in the bottom of the ninth to come from behind as they had so many times during the season. After Stargell and Madlock singled, Ed Ott came to the plate with two outs. He missed tying the game with a long drive into the right-field stands that barely curved foul, then struck out on the next pitch to end the game.

In the clubhouse, Tekulve was devastated by the loss and felt that he had "messed up" and let the team down. Tanner, however, told his players to relax and turn the music on because they were going to win the next three games. A more somber Stargell wasn't as optimistic. He'd told his teammates they were probably not going to win the World Series, but he asked them to go out the next day and "show the world how the Pirates play baseball."

• • •

On the Sunday morning before Game 5, Chuck Tanner called the hospital to talk with his ailing mother. The nurse at the reception area didn't know who was on the phone and told the caller Mrs. Tanner had died. Tanner's father confirmed what had happened, but told his son that his mother would want Tanner to manage Sunday's game. When Tanner arrived at the clubhouse, he told his players that his mother had decided that the Pirates needed some divine help, so she went to heaven to plea their case.

The Pirates decided to play the game for Tanner's mother, but they had additional motivation going into the game. In the Sunday morning *Baltimore Sun*, the city's mayor gave out the parade route for the World

Series celebration. Stargell told his teammates, "We're going to cancel that parade."

Tanner seemed to be playing another of his hunches when he named Jim Rooker to oppose Mike Flanagan, who would be named the AL Cy Young Award winner a few weeks after the World Series ended. Struggling with injuries, Rooker had posted a 4–7 record during the season, but Tanner remembered that Rooker had pitched well in relief in Game 1. Rooker made Tanner look like a genius, once again, when he held the Orioles hitless through the first four innings, though the Pirates couldn't score against Flanagan.

In the top of the fifth, the Orioles scored the first run of the game on a double play after the first two batters doubled and singled. When the Pirates failed to score in the bottom of the fifth, Tanner brought in Bert Blyleven. After Blyleven held the Orioles scoreless in the top of the sixth, the Pirates finally broke through against Flanagan. Foli led off with a walk, Parker singled, and Robinson moved them into scoring position with a sacrifice bunt. Weaver played the odds by letting the left-handed Flanagan pitch to Stargell with first base open, but Stargell managed to hit a sacrifice fly to tie the score. When Madlock singled home Parker, the Pirates had a 2–1 lead.

The Orioles couldn't do anything with Blyleven for the rest of the game, but the Pirates weren't finished. They added two more runs in the bottom of the seventh on a Foli RBI triple and a Parker double, and, after Stargell led off the bottom of the eighth with a single, scored three more runs, two of them coming home on another key hit from Tim Foli. After Blyleven retired the last Oriole batter in the ninth to preserve a 7–1 victory, the Pirates packed their bags for Baltimore, where its mayor was busy delaying the Orioles victory parade.

• • •

Before the start of Game 6, Stargell told his teammates that even though they were still trailing 3–2, they had the better team and the World Series "was in the bag." All they had to do was "jump on my back and ride me." Once the game started, however, it was John Candelaria's back that they rode for the first six innings, though Stargell played a role in motivating his pitcher. He had Grant Jackson write and post an anonymous note on the bulletin board claiming Candelaria, who pitched badly in Game 3, would choke again. It was an angry Candelaria who took the mound for Game 6.

After threatening in the bottom of the first inning and failing to score, the Orioles could do nothing against Candelaria, but Palmer pitched just as well and kept the game scoreless through six. In the top of the seventh, the Pirates finally broke the scoreless tie on consecutive singles by Moreno, Foli, and Parker. When Stargell lifted a sacrifice to deep left field, the Pirates had a 2–0 lead.

Tanner, who'd pinch hit for Candelaria in the top of the seventh, decided to bring Kent Tekulve into the game, even though Tekulve had surrendered a three-run lead in the Pirates' loss in Game 4. Once again, Tanner had made the perfect move. Tekulve dominated the Oriole hitters, allowing only a base hit and striking out four Orioles over the last three innings. For good measure, the Pirates added two runs on a Robinson sacrifice fly and a Moreno base hit and coasted to a 4–0 victory and a 3–3 tie in the World Series.

• • •

Sanguillen had a premonition about the outcome of the 1979 World Series. He remembered Roberto Clemente telling him, as they drove to Baltimore's Memorial Stadium for Game 7 of the 1971 World Series, that he shouldn't worry because Clemente was going to hit a home run. When Sanguillen got to the clubhouse, there was Willie Stargell calmly telling his teammates not to worry because he was going to carry them to a World Series championship.

Stargell had scored the winning run in the 1971 World Series, but felt he had let his teammates down with his poor overall performance. For the second time in a decade, he had a chance to play the hero, but this time there was no Clemente in the clubhouse to set the standard and lead the way if he failed. He was "Pops," the team patriarch, the one they'd counted on all season in clutch situations. This was his team, his moment, and he felt confident that, this time, after 17 years in a Pirates uniform, he'd fulfill the dream he'd been pursuing since his project days in Alameda.

• • •

For the seventh and deciding game, Chuck Tanner selected the veteran Jim Bibby, who'd pitched so well in his previous two postseason starts. Bibby would go against the Orioles' left-hander Scott McGregor, the winning pitcher in Game 3. Though Stargell had hit well against Oriole left-handers and homered in the first game off Mike Flanagan, Tanner decided to keep Stargell fifth in the batting order behind Bill Robinson. He also decided to get an extra right-handed bat in the lineup by starting rookie Steve Nicosia instead of Ed Ott, even though Nicosia had only one hit in the World Series and was batting under .100 against Oriole left-handers.

After a scoreless first inning, Stargell opened the top of the second with a single to left field and went to second on an outfield bobble. The Pirates, however, were unable to bring Stargell home. In the bottom of the third, Bibby made his one mistake of the game and gave up a leadoff home run to second baseman Rich Dauer. In the top of the fourth, with the Pirates trailing 1–0, Stargell gave the Pirates another chance to score when he doubled off McGregor, but the Pirates, once again, stranded Stargell on base.

After pinch hitting for Bibby in the top of the fifth, Tanner brought in Don Robinson to pitch in the bottom of the fifth. After Robinson walked McGregor to put runners at first and second with two outs, Tanner, for once, played the percentages and brought in lefty Grant Jackson to pitch to left-hand-hitting Al Bumbry. Jackson kept throwing breaking balls away from Bumbry until he reached out and popped up to third base.

With one out in the top of the sixth, the shoddy field conditions proved costly to the Orioles when Bill Robinson bounced a bad hop single through the left side of the infield. In his first two times at bat, Willie Stargell had followed Harry Walker's old advice about hitting left-handers by taking Scott McGregor's breaking pitches to the opposite field. The result had been a single and a double in his first two at-bats. He thought, however, if he waited on McGregor's curveball long enough he could get the good part of the bat on the pitch and pull the ball into right field. To help slow down his swing, he went to the plate with Manny Sanguillen's heavier bat.

When McGregor threw a breaking ball, Stargell waited on it and drove it to right field. He thought he'd swung too early and didn't get all his power into the swing, but the ball rocketed deep into the night. The Oriole right fielder, Ken Singleton, drifted back to the fence and leaped in the air. The ball, however, sailed just inches over his glove and landed in the Pirates bullpen for a two-run homer.

Pirate fans had witnessed a jubilant Mazeroski wheeling his cap as he romped around the bases in the 1960 World Series. In the 1971 World Series, they watched a stately Clemente jog around the bases. This time, however, they watched the massive Pops as he seemed to jog on air around the bases.

Stargell, however, had little time to savor the moment. When he reached the dugout, he encountered pandemonium. He was pounded by his teammates, who felt that their Pops, as he'd promised, had just won the World Series for them. Mike Easler, who loved to talk about hitting, kept hugging him and asking him how he had done it. Stargell, however, tried to calm things down because he knew that it was only the top of the sixth inning. He'd hit the home run he'd dreamed about, but the Pirates still had to hold a narrow 2–1 lead against a hard-hitting Orioles team for four more innings to win the World Series.

• • •

After pitching out of a jam in the bottom of the fifth, Grant Jackson easily retired the Orioles in the sixth and seventh innings. In the top of the eighth, Stargell extended his remarkable night by banging out a double, his fourth straight hit, but the Pirates couldn't bring him home. After Jackson got the first out in the bottom of the eighth, he tired and walked the next two batters. Tanner summoned Tekulve from the bullpen to hold the Pirates lead.

Exhausted after pitching three innings the night before, Tekulve struggled to throw strikes, but he managed to retire pinch-hitter Terry Crowley on a ground ball that advanced the runners. With the tying and go-ahead runs in scoring position, Tanner now had the choice of pitching to the Orioles' best hitter, Ken Singleton, or walking him to face Eddie Murray, who'd been struggling ever since Game 2. Tanner ordered Tekulve to walk Singleton.

As Murray came to the plate, Willie Stargell called time and walked to the mound to talk with Kent Tekulve. He offered Tekulve his first baseman's glove, and told him, "If you can't do this, go play first base and I'll pitch." Tekulve declined the offer, but, for one heart-stopping moment, he may have wished he'd taken Stargell's mitt and headed for first base. Eddie Murray lined a 2–2 pitch deep to right field. Parker drifted back on the ball, but slipped on the wet outfield grass. He managed to recover just in time to reach up and catch Murray's long drive.

After their scare in the bottom of the eighth, the Pirates managed to scrap together two more runs in the top of the ninth against four Baltimore pitchers. After hitting a double, Garner came home on a Moreno single. After Foli singled and Parker was hit by a pitch, Bill Robinson came up with the bases loaded. The first pitch appeared to hit Robinson in the hand, though later he admitted it probably hit the knob of his bat. Before the home plate umpire could change his mind, trainer Tony Bartirome came out to check Robinson's "injury" When Robinson said he was all right, Bartirome told him to let him spray his hand because he wanted to get some TV time.

After Stargell hit into an anticlimactic double play to end the inning, the Pirates had a 4–1 lead heading into the bottom of the ninth inning. Tekulve started the ninth by throwing seven straight pitches out of the strike zone. The first two Oriole hitters only took one ball between them, both anxiously striking out swinging. When Tekulve finally threw a strike to pinch-hitter Pat Kelly, he lofted a fly ball into left-center field that Moreno settled under, squeezed into his glove, then leaped high into the air. The Pirates were World Series champions.

As the Pirates rushed out of the dugout and bullpen to join those already mobbing Tekulve on the mound, a photographer snapped a picture of Stargell's reaction at the moment of victory. He was caught in mid-leap, arms outspread, with a look of absolute joy on his face. He looked like a child who'd just taken his first bounce on a trampoline. There's no photograph that better captures the boyish spirit of the Pirate who, over the years, kept reminding his teammates that it's "play ball" not "work ball."

In the clubhouse, while his delirious teammates sprayed themselves with champagne, a weary Stargell took a bottle of his favorite chardonnay and tried to celebrate more privately. There was no way, however, that the player just declared the World Series MVP after a record-breaking performance could escape being the center of attention. After answering a barrage of questions at his locker, he finally agreed to come to the interview room.

While Stargell was politely responding to more questions, he saw his half-sister, Sandrus, sitting among the crowd of reporters. He stopped suddenly and said, "That's my sister out there." When he beckoned to her, she ran up on the platform and embraced the brother she always called, "Bubba." At that moment, Stargell was no longer the calm and stately "Pops." Tears poured down his face, as he held the person who had known and loved him since she "was a little girl."

Of all the memories of childhood that must have been rushing through his mind at that moment, there was probably none more relevant to this moment than the one that he had reminded Sandrus of the night before Game 7: "Remember when we lived in the projects in Alameda?.... I couldn't have been more than 14, and what I'd do was find me a wooden stick somewhere, go down to the vacant lot near the railroad tracks and practice hitting those rocks with that stick." That boy, now 39 years old, had just hit a dramatic home run in the deciding game of the World Series and joined the company of Honus Wagner, Bill Mazeroski, and Roberto Clemente.

CHAPTER 12

I'm Now Alongside of Roberto

If Hollywood ever decided to make a movie of Willie Stargell's baseball life and wanted it to be another *Field of Dreams* or *The Natural*, they couldn't ask for a more emotional and inspirational closing scene than a tearful Stargell embracing his half-sister, Sandrus, moments after winning the World Series with his dramatic home run. After overcoming childhood adversity, racial hatred, and physical injuries, he'd reached the heroic heights he could only dream of when he was a boy hitting rocks with a stick.

Stargell's life, however, wasn't a movie. After the thrill of seeing his dream come true, his life became a whirlwind of honors and activities that at first seemed to extend the dream, but eventually turned nightmarish. At first, there were all those awards—NLCS and World Series MVPs, co-winner of the National League MVP, *The Sporting News* Major League Player of the Year, co-winner of the *Sports Illustrated* Man of the Year with Terry Bradshaw, the Dapper Dan Sportsman of the Year. There were also all those banquets and personal appearances, many of them impossible to turn down because they often benefitted the Willie Stargell Foundation and its campaign against sickle cell anemia.

Life became so hectic that the baseball hero celebrated as "Pops" had little time for his own family. From the end of the World Series in October until mid-February when Stargell took time out for a brief vacation in Hawaii, his wife, Dolores, estimated she'd spent 12 days with her husband. In an interview for an article by Ron Cook in the *Beaver Valley Times*, she admitted their marriage was under a strain: "She'd like to forget the past winter. It was the most trying four months of the Stargell's 13-year marriage." She was hopeful their marriage would survive, but they separated during the 1980 season. Not long after, the marriage ended in divorce.

Another problem for Stargell during the off-season was finding time for his physical conditioning. He had so many commitments, traveled so often, that he was unable to follow the training schedule that had kept him in shape for the past few seasons. After all those banquets, keeping his weight down had also become a problem. All the running around had put a strain on surgically repaired knees that were beginning to become arthritic.

After spending long hours during the past two off-seasons working out under the watchful eye of Tony Bartirome, Stargell had outstanding seasons in 1978 and 1979. In late February, when he headed to Bradenton to get ready for the 1980 season, he was simply not in the same physical shape he'd been when he arrived at his last two spring training camps.

• • •

When the Pirates published their first official Spring Training Roster booklet in 1964, the thumbnail sketch for Willie Stargell listed his birth date as March 6, 1941. Each subsequent booklet through the rest of Stargell's career listed the same birth date. In Stargell's autobiography, published in 1984, two years after his retirement, he also gave his birth date as March 6, 1941. When reporters mentioned Stargell's age in the articles they wrote about him over the years, they used the official birth date listed by the Pirates.

The only problem with the March 6, 1941, birth date was that Stargell signed his first professional contract with the Pirates in 1958. He was 18 years old at that time and had just graduated from high school. That would make Stargell's birth date March 6, 1940. That's the date of birth listed in his Baseball Hall of Fame and Society of Baseball Research biographies and in his entry in *The Pittsburgh Pirates Encyclopedia*. It's also the birth date given in his obituaries in the *New York Times* and the *Pittsburgh Post-Gazette*.

When Stargell celebrated his birthday at Bradenton in 1980, he was more likely 40 years old, not 39. His teammates decided to honor the occasion with a birthday cake that had a suspiciously large amount of whipped cream topping. Jim Rooker and Phil Garner presented the cake to Stargell in appreciation for all that he had done for them last year, then launched the cake into his face. Stargell loved pranks and practical jokes, even when the joke was on him. He licked the icing approvingly, while shouting, "I'll get even. I'm going to Baltimore."

• • •

One of the witnesses to the birthday cake caper was Marvin Miller, the Players Association executive director. He was in the Bradenton clubhouse to update the players on stalled labor negotiations and the possibility of a baseball strike. When negotiations continued to go nowhere, the players staged a walkout that forced the cancelation of the last week of exhibition games. They agreed to open the season on time, but set a May 23 strike deadline for a new contract.

The Pirates lost their opener to the Cardinals in St. Louis, but they were an optimistic ballclub at the beginning of the season. They'd lost Bruce Kison and Rennie Stennett to free agency, but they planned to move Don Robinson into the starting rotation and still had their starting infield in place from their 1979 championship team. Willie Stargell and Bill Robinson would need more days off, but Chuck Tanner had John Milner and a rising star in Mike Easler to fill in for them.

After their Opening Day loss, the Pirates won their next three games in St. Louis and headed to Pittsburgh for their home opener. The pregame ceremonies at Three Rivers were a festive celebration and reminder of the 1979 World Series triumph. Sister Sledge sang the national anthem, then rocked the sell-out crowd with "We Are Family."

Before the game began, Willie Stargell received his National League MVP honor from the Baseball Writers of America Association and the Roberto

Clemente Memorial Award from the Pittsburgh chapter of the BWAA. Kent Tekulve and the members of the Pirates' bullpen accepted *The Sporting News* Rolaids Relief Team Award, and Pirates president John Galbreath helped with the unfurling of the Pirates' official World Series banner.

The moment that everyone at Three Rivers had been waiting for came when National League president Chub Feeney presented World Series rings to the Pirates. With Kison and Stennett gone, the only Pirates in attendance from the 1971 championship team to receive a second World Series ring were Stargell and Sanguillen. Afterward, Bill Robinson said, "Everybody wanted that ring. It's almost as exciting as winning the World Series. It's a topping to the World Series." In an AP photo showing Stargell pushing his ring onto his finger, the caption described "his diamond-like smile."

Rain threatened to delay the game, but it held off until the third inning. There were four rain delays totaling two hours and 14 minutes during the game, but Bill Robinson gave the hardy fans who were still at Three Rivers a thrill when he homered in the bottom of the 10th for a 5–4 victory over the Cubs. It was the Pirates' fourth win in a row and a hopeful sign that they would be contenders for another World Series title. They continued to play well and finished April with an 11–5 record.

• • •

The only ominous sign in April was the absence of Willie Stargell from the starting lineup for almost half of the Pirates games. He suffered a bruised thumb in the Pirates' home opener and missed the next seven games of the season. By the end of April, he'd hit only one home run and driven in just four runs.

Missing only a few more games to rest, Stargell remained relatively healthy in May and bounced back to hit four home runs with 17 RBIs for the month. Sparked by the outstanding pitching of Jim Bibby and the hot hitting of Mike Easler, the Pirates played steady baseball in May and kept pace with the Expos and Phillies in a tight early race for first place.

The biggest threat to the Pirates in May was the looming deadline for a players strike. On May 23, just 10 hours before the strike deadline, the owners and players reached a deal on all issues except for free-agent compensation. In a decision that would have dire consequences for the 1981 season, they agreed to table their discussion of free agency until the 1980 season was over.

The Pirates celebrated the settlement by announcing that Willie Stargell had signed an extension to his contract through 1982. His old contract would have expired at the end of the season. They also announced they were scheduling a Willie Stargell Day between games of a doubleheader against the Dodgers on Sunday, July 20, to honor "his accomplishments the previous 19 years." Among the many gifts Stargell would receive "was an oil portrait of himself painted by the world renowned sports artist LeRoy Neimann."

Stargell celebrated in his own way by hitting over .300 for the rest of the month. He also hit well for the first few weeks of June, and had his finest game of the season on June 13 when he went 4-for-4 against the Astros with two home runs. Unfortunately, he pulled his hamstring a week later and was restricted to pinch-hitting until he was finally placed on the disabled list in early July. With Stargell leading the way, the Pirates had surged into first place in early June, but they slumped after his injury. They finished the month only four games over .500 at 38–34 and in third place behind the Phillies and the first-place Expos.

• • •

July 20 was a blistering hot day in Pittsburgh. By the time the Pirates' first game against the Dodgers ended, the temperature had reached 98 degrees. With the sun baking the artificial turf at Three Rivers, the temperature on the field had soared to well over 100 degrees. The heat, however, didn't stop a crowd of 43,194 fans from coming to Three Rivers to receive a Stargell Star and honor, with several standing ovations, their beloved Pops.

Willie Stargell received many elaborate gifts that day, some of them outrageous, like a mink cowboy hat. Others were more appropriate to the occasion, like his 1979 World Series glove plated in sterling silver and a solid gold Stargell star. The Pirates organization presented Stargell with a $10,000 check for the Willie Stargell Foundation and its battle against sickle cell anemia.

The most emotional moment came at the end of the program. As a surprise, the Pirates organization flew Stargell's mother, father, and step-father in for his special day. Stargell had started to tear up when he embraced Roberto Clemente's widow, Vera, but, when he saw his parents, he completely broke down.

Embracing his mother with one arm and holding the microphone with the other, he told the crowd, "The one thing I always wanted to do was play the game of baseball. I had the love and inner strength of my parents, and particularly my mother, who was such a forceful individual in our family." He added, "I knew that with her love and guidance I would one day make her proud." With that, he burst into tears. When he recovered, he told the adoring crowd, "I'm not going to stand here and complicate words with feelings because it's all very difficult for me.... I just want to say thanks to each and every one of you."

· · ·

When the Pirates honored Willie Stargell on July 20, he was still on the disabled list and wouldn't be activated until August 1. A week after Stargell returned to the lineup, the Pirates went on an eight-game winning streak that had them back in contention for the division title. Their last win in the streak, however, came with a heavy cost when Stargell injured his left knee diving for a ground ball against the Mets. Over the next few days, he tried to play with the pain, but, on August 21, he went back on the disabled list. He remained there for the rest of the season.

Because of their deteriorating condition, any injury to Stargell's knees was career threatening. In his autobiography, he described how bad they were going into the 1980 season: "My knees had gotten progressively worse. After all the operations they'd undergone, all the material between their bones had been extracted. I had a bone-on-bone situation, no cartilage, no ligaments, nothing. My bones scrapped against each other with every step I took. They'd also become arthritic and they stiffened up immediately if they weren't kept in constant motion or out of cold weather."

Stargell underwent arthroscopic surgery in late August, but hoped to return to the Pirates lineup no later than the second week in September.

With Stargell out and Parker playing on a bad knee that would also require surgery, the Pirates struggled in August, but managed to stay close in the division race. After splitting a doubleheader with the Astros on September 1, they sat in a three-way first-place tie with the Phillies and Expos, but then went on a five-game losing streak.

Any hope of one last surge received a major blow when Stargell's surgeon, after examining his knee, ruled him out for the rest of the season. At a players-only meeting on September 10, Bill Robinson delivered the bad news to his teammates. No one said much at the meeting. Afterward, Bill Madlock told Ron Cook, "I think we all knew he wasn't coming back. We'd have been more surprised if they told us he was.... They're better off letting him take the rest of the year off to get ready for next year."

Pirate players said all the right things after the news broke about Stargell. They were going to give "101 percent instead of 100 percent." They couldn't use Stargell's absence "as an excuse for playing badly." The heart, however, had gone out of the ballclub. They played losing baseball for the rest of the season and finished in third place, eight games behind the Phillies, who would go on to win the World Series.

His surgeon's decision was a major disappointment for Stargell, but it wasn't devastating. He'd learned that his knee was slowly improving and, with proper exercise, he could return to the Pirates for the 1981 season. That was enough to convince Stargell that he'd be back in the Pirates' lineup by Opening Day. He'd be 41 years old and in his 19th full season, but he still loved playing baseball and wasn't ready to retire.

• • •

In an article written for *The Sporting News* just as the Pirates were arriving for spring training in 1981, Charley Feeney announced, "Happy days are here again for Willie Stargell." Feeney reported that Stargell wasn't worried about his knee any longer: "The doctor took a lot of garbage out of my knee. That's behind me. I expect big things out of myself.... I'm not thinking anything but good things. Spring is near. Man, it's a wonderful feeling." Not surprisingly, the ever upbeat Chuck Tanner shared Stargell's optimism. He told Feeney that he was counting on Stargell "to play 100 games for us in 1981."

The Pirates were going to need all the help Stargell could give them in 1981. They were a different ballclub going into the 1981 season, and not for the better. During the off-season, they traded away Bert Blyleven, who'd become unhappy with Tanner's five-man pitching rotation and his heavy reliance on the bullpen. The Pirates also lost Jim Rooker, who'd retired after struggling with injuries the last two seasons, and were worried about injuries to Don Robinson and John Candelaria. They were also concerned about Kent Tekulve, who'd dropped off significantly in 1980 after his sensational relief pitching in 1979.

Besides their pitching woes, the Pirates also had major problems with their starting lineup. Willie Stargell wasn't the only position player trying to overcome an injury. Like Stargell, Parker was coming back from knee surgery, and Phil Garner had recurring shoulder pain. The popular Ed Ott was gone in a trade with the Angels for first baseman Jason Thompson. The deal irked Willie Stargell, but general manager Pete Peterson, not quite as optimistic as Tanner, wanted a backup plan for first base if Stargell was unable to play.

Peterson's caution turned out to be well founded. A week before the start of the season, Tanner optimistically declared that Stargell was ready to play and wouldn't be placed on the disabled list. He qualified his statement, however, by saying that he'd likely be used only as a pinch-hitter: "It would take a miracle for him to do more in the first week or two of the season." That unusually cautious comment from Tanner turned out to be realistic. Stargell appeared in only five games for the entire month of April, all as a pinch hitter. He managed to start three games in May, but he appeared in nine others only as a pinch hitter.

During that stretch the Pirates, after losing four of their first five games against the Expos and the Phillies, improved their record to 7–6 by the end of April. At the end of May, they were only 20–20, but they started to play better in the first week in June when Stargell finally returned to the starting lineup. Stargell hit well once he was back in the lineup. He started five games and went 7–19 with three doubles. The timing of his return, however, couldn't have been worse. On June 10, after months of futile negotiations between the owners and the Players Association over free agency compensation, Marvin Miller declared, "We have accomplished nothing. The strike is on."

• • •

The 1981 baseball strike was long and bitter. When it finally ended on July 31 and play resumed, 38 percent of the season was gone. With 706 games lost to the strike, Commissioner Bowie Kuhn decided to divide the season into two halves, with the division winners of each half meeting in a postseason playoff. His decision gave first-place Philadelphia a postseason playoff spot. The Pirates, at 25–23, finished in fourth place, 5½ games behind the Phillies.

During the strike, Stargell used the time off to rest his aching knees, but he also took advantage of his celebrity status. On July 14, he met with President Reagan to discuss proposed cuts in federal funding for his foundation. The Stargell Foundation had been struggling financially and was facing a major audit from Pennsylvania's Commission on Charitable Organizations. He then flew to New York to join Sister Sledge for a taping of NBC's *Tomorrow* show. The taping went well, but the Stargell Foundation soon received an order from the Commonwealth of Pennsylvania to stop soliciting funds because of its internal financial problems.

When the season resumed on August 10, Stargell was in the starting lineup for the Pirates. In his second at-bat, however, when he started to run out of the batter's box on a routine ground ball, he heard something pop in his heel. He finished the game, but the heel swelled up so badly that he wasn't able to play again for the next few weeks. When he did return, he appeared only as a pinch-hitter for the rest of the season.

At season's end, Stargell had appeared in only 38 games and, in 29 of those games, only as a pinch hitter. He still had his swing and batted .308 as a pinch hitter, but, with his bad knees, the power was gone. He had no home runs and only four doubles in 60 official plate appearances. He drove in a just nine runs, with two of those coming on his last hit of the 1981 season.

While Stargell watched from the bench in the second half of the season, the Pirates completely fell apart. After several key players, including Jim Bibby and Dave Parker, followed Stargell to the bench with injuries, the Pirates went on an extended losing streak and never bounced back. They finished the second half of the season in last place with a dismal 21–33 record.

Recognizing that the team was aging and slowing down, general manager Pete Peterson began to trade his veteran players for young prospects. In one of his key moves during the season, he traded Phil Garner to Houston for second baseman Johnny Ray. During the off-season, he traded Phil Garner's double-play partner, Tim Foli, to the Angels for catcher-outfielder Brian Harper, who'd led the Pacific Coast League in hitting. With so many of Stargell's teammates from the 1979 World Series traded or sold to make room for younger players, the biggest question going into the 1982 season was whether or not Willie Stargell would return for the last year of his contract or announce his retirement.

• • •

Willie Stargell knew that his days of playing regularly were probably over. His knees were so bad that, if he returned in 1982, Tanner would have to use him almost solely as a pinch hitter. He loved playing the game, and he was still a young boy in spirit, but he had an old man's arthritic knees.

In his autobiography, Stargell claimed that he decided not to retire because Dave Parker urged him to come back. Stargell's reasons for returning, however, went far beyond Parker. He loved the camaraderie of the clubhouse as much as he loved the game. With the Pirates in the middle of a youth movement, he couldn't resist playing Pops one more time. He was also unhappy with the way his season ended in 1981. He loved the spotlight and wasn't about to fade away. Before he retired, he wanted to finish his career on his own terms.

• • •

At Bradenton, Stargell began spring training the way he'd been doing it since Danny Murtaugh named him team captain after Roberto Clemente's death. Every spring, according to the *Post-Gazette*'s Charley Feeney, he'd walk to the rookies' corner of the clubhouse and tell them, "I'm Willie Stargell. Welcome to the Pirates. Let's have some fun."

He thought that the 1982 edition of the Pirates were a bit more subdued than the wild bunches he presided over in the past, but that didn't prevent his current teammates, with a little agitating from veterans John Candelaria and Bill Robinson, from delivering a birthday cake to Pops in a way that had become a tradition in the clubhouse. He celebrated his birthday, once again, with cake on his face.

At the age of 42 and with arthritic knees, Stargell was of minimal help in a season in which the Pirates, after a miserable 18–27 start in April and May, finally started turning things around in June. They managed to play above .500 for the rest of the season and finished in fourth place, eight games behind the East Division–champion St. Louis Cardinals, with a record of 84–78.

Coming out of spring training, Stargell thought his knees had improved, but any hope of extending his career beyond the 1982 season faded when the team started playing in cold weather, and his knees starting aching. Realizing that he was running the risk of crippling himself, he made the official announcement that this would be his last season. He made eight appearances in April, but had only one hit. He did manage to make two starts in May, but went 0-for-7. By the end of the month, he was batting only .125 with no home runs and no RBIs.

With the weather warming in June, Stargell had his most productive month of the season. He made no starts, but he did go 4-for-9 as a pinch hitter and drove in seven runs. The highlight of the month came in the Pirates' last game in June when he hit a three-run pinch-hit home run at Wrigley Field against the Cubs' Dick Tidrow. It was his first home run since he connected off the Phillies' Dick Ruthven in a game at Three Rivers on August 8, 1980.

In games on July 8 and 21, he hit pinch-hit home runs against the Cincinnati Reds. His homer on July 21 off the Reds' Tom Hume was the 475th of his career and tied him with Stan Musial for 16th place on the all-time list. It was also the last home run of his career. As he rounded the bases for the last of his home run trots, the crowd at Riverfront Stadium gave him a standing ovation that continued until he came out of the dugout and lifted his cap to the cheering crowd.

The standing ovation for Willie Stargell became a common event around National League ballparks during the summer. Every time the Pirates played their last series at a major league ballpark, Stargell was showered with cheers and gifts. A photography buff, he received camera equipment from the Dodgers. A wine connoisseur, he received a case of his favorite chardonnay from the Giants. The New York Mets gave him a trophy with Stargell's career home runs, runs-batted-in, and total-base records against the Mets inscribed in it. In collaboration with the Fels Planetarium in Philadelphia, the Phillies had a distant star named after the player who gave so many stars to teammates and friends over the last few years. Perhaps the most touching tribute to Stargell came at Busch Stadium in St. Louis. On that night, Stan Musial, Stargell's idol when he was growing up, greeted him at home plate before a roaring Cardinals crowd.

• • •

The Pirates selected Labor Day, September 6, 1982, for its own Willie Stargell Day. Before the event, they printed a commemorative program with his year-by-year highlights, Pirate and major league records, and home run milestones. The program also included a "From Those Who Know Him Best" section with quotations from "Current and Former Teammates" and a "From Those Who Fought the Fight" section with quotations from "Opposing Players."

The former teammates praising Stargell ranged from those who were with him at the very beginning of his career with the Pirates, like Bill Virdon, Gene Alley, and Bill Mazeroski, to current players, like Johnny Ray and Tony Pena. There were also, however, fond words from old friends and favorites from the 1971 and 1979 World Series championship teams.

Steve Blass expressed his admiration for the way Stargell loved to play the game: "Even if he hadn't set all those records, the people in Pittsburgh would still love Willie Stargell just because he portrayed to them the fun of the game and the fun he had playing it." Bill Madlock remembered that "Will came up during the old school days when all the negatives and problems that blacks had to face were very strong. He turned the negatives around to positives. Will has always been respected by white and blacks." Grant Jackson simply stated, "A good friend—one of my brothers."

Many of the "opposing players" tributes to Stargell came from his old rivals on the Cincinnati Reds, including Joe Morgan, a friend since their Oakland-area days together. Morgan's tribute was one of the most eloquent in the program: "As a kid I had idols like Jackie Robinson and Nellie Fox. But, as an adult, my only idol has been Willie Stargell, both as a player and a friend. He's just special people. If you took a poll of all 650 major league players, there wouldn't be a guy who wouldn't like him. He is caring and understanding, both as a player and as a friend. 'Pops' is a fitting nickname because he's like a father to so many."

• • •

Back in 1980, on the first special day honoring him, Stargell draped a towel around his neck to wipe away his tears. On his second Willie Stargell Day, he would need the towel more than ever. Covering the event for the *Post-Gazette*, Bill Stieg wrote, "By the time Stargell was halfway through his hugs and handshakes with the Pirates, the tears were falling faster than he could wipe them off." As for the more than 38,000 fans who attended the game, Stieg added, "All and all, it was a mushy, sentimental, nostalgic, corny, and thoroughly enjoyable afternoon."

The cheering began when Stargell emerged out of the dugout, then rode around Three Rivers in Dave Parker's convertible. When he arrived back at home plate, both the Pirates and Mets players were waiting in line to embrace him. Once the ceremony began, the speakers and presenters ranged from Kent Tekulve, who represented his teammates, to President Reagan, whose telephone call from the White House was piped in through the loudspeakers. The fan favorites, however, were one of Stargell's oldest teammates, Bill Mazeroski, and one of his oldest and dearest friends, Bob Prince. They also rose to their feet to cheer Roberto Clemente Jr., who presented a statue of his father to Stargell.

Among the gifts the wine-loving Stargell received was a trip to France from his teammates. To make sure that he had the proper vessel in which to savor his wine, the Baseball Writers Association of America gave Stargell engraved pewter wine goblets. The Pirate management presented Stargell with a $10,000 check for his "favorite charity," and, saying that the Pirates also wanted to leave Stargell with "a piece of Pittsburgh," President John Galbreath gave him $15,000 in stock from Pittsburgh's Fortune 500 companies.

After the Pirates officially retired Stargell's No. 8 and Franco Harris and Lynn Swann presented him with a Steelers No. 8 jersey, Pops finally had his opportunity to speak to the adoring crowd. Never a great orator, Stargell always managed to find just the right words when he spoke on public occasions. He thanked the Pirates, not only for their generosity, but for turning the event into a fund-raising effort for unemployed steelworkers by asking fans to bring cans of food to Three Rivers: "During these trying times economically, there are a lot of people who would like to work and can't."

Stargell thanked his Pirates family and his own family, then broke down in tears. When he recovered, he looked into the crowd and spoke to them, not as fans, but as friends. Searching into the deepest recesses of the stands, he concluded his remarks by addressing those who were facing the same challenges that he had endured and overcome during his career: "If there's anyone in the projects sitting up there, here's living proof.... with hard work, determination, and dedication, you can make a great indentation."

With Stargell unable to start at first base because of his bad knees, the Pirates-Mets game seemed anticlimactic, but Pops had one more thrill to give Pirate fans. With the Pirates ahead 6–1 in the bottom of the eighth, the crowd started chanting, "We want Willie! We want Willie!" With two outs, Tanner pushed Stargell out of the dugout and sent him up to home plate to pinch hit for Tony Pena.

The crowd's roar at the sight of Stargell pinwheeling his bat turned into boos when the Mets' Doug Sisk threw his first two pitches outside the strike zone. Aware of the crowd's reaction, Sisk then threw his next pitch down the middle of the plate. Stargell's knees were bad, but he still had his swing. He lined the pitch into right-center field, hobbled his way down to first, and, after having a little fun and faking a dash for second base, returned to first base. When Tanner sent out Rafael Belliard to run for him, Stargell lifted his batting helmet high in the air to his cheering "friends," then slowly and graciously made his way back to the dugout, where he was hugged by Chuck Tanner and mobbed by his teammates.

• • •

On Sunday, October 3, Pirate fans had one more chance to say goodbye to Willie Stargell. Only 14,948 fans paid their way into Three Rivers for the Pirates last game of the season, but they were witness to one more vintage moment from Stargell's career. For what Paul Smith of the *Pittsburgh Press* described as "Willie's Last Hurrah," Chuck Tanner decided to start Stargell at first base and bat him in the leadoff spot, thereby adding "the slowest leadoff hitter in Pirates history" to Stargell's various titles and records.

In the bottom of the first inning, Stargell came to bat against the Expos' Steve Rogers and bounced a pitch back to the mound for what appeared to be a routine out. Normally a good fielder, Rogers reached out for the ball, but it deflected off his glove and rolled behind the mound. When Rogers, shortstop Chris Speier, and second baseman Doug Flynn did their best imitation of the old baseball "I've got it, no you take it" routine, Stargell lumbered to first base for what generously was ruled a base hit.

Wanting to join in on the fun, Stargell, bad knees and all, took off for second base with Omar Moreno at the plate, but Moreno fouled the pitch back into the stands. On Rogers' next pitch, Stargell took off again, but this time Moreno lined the ball to left field for a base hit. Stargell kept on running and made it into third base when the Expos' left fielder mercifully threw the ball into second.

Fearing that Stargell might be on the verge of ending his career with a heart attack, Tanner sent out Doug Frobel to run for him. For one last time as an active player, Pops waved to the crowd to acknowledge yet another standing ovation. As the Pirates' organist played "Pomp and Circumstance," Stargell strolled to the dugout and headed into the clubhouse.

A few hours later, he departed, leaving behind the remnants of his brilliant career. As Paul Smith reported, "In front of No. 8 [locker] was a rocking chair. Empty. Inside was a uniform that would never be worn again by an active Pirate, No. 8, next to which hung a black hat with gold pipe-stemming and gold stars. Its occupant was gone forever."

• • •

When Stargell left the field for the last time as an active player, there was little doubt that the baseball journey he began on the dirt fields of the Alameda projects would end at the Hall of Fame podium in Cooperstown. In his 20 full seasons in the major leagues, he'd become one of the greatest home run hitters in baseball history. After moving from mammoth Forbes Field to the friendlier confines of Three Rivers in 1970, he'd hit more home runs in the 1970s than any other player in the major leagues. His 475 career home runs tied him with Stan Musial for 16th place on the all-time list.

Playing most of his career on surgically repaired knees, he was named to the National League All-Star squad seven times. His teams played in six National League Championship Series and won two World Series. He carried the Pirates to the 1971 World Series with a career-high and league-leading 48 home runs. In 1979, at the age of 39, he dominated the NLCS and the World Series. After being selected as the MVP in both postseason series, he was named the co-winner of the National MVP Award.

When asked what he thought of Willie Stargell belonging in the Baseball Hall of Fame, Chuck Tanner replied, "The Hall of Fame was made for players like Willie Stargell. It couldn't be a Hall of Fame without Willie Stargell." The only question was whether the Baseball Writers Association of America would vote Stargell, after his five-year waiting period, into the Hall of Fame in his first year of eligibility.

The baseball writers had not treated Stargell kindly in the past. They'd passed over him in 1971 and 1973 when he was the clear favorite to win the National League MVP Award. In 1979, even though he received the most first-place votes, he had to share the National League MVP award with Cardinal Keith Hernandez when four writers inexplicably left him off their ballots. Had one of them placed Stargell even 10th on his ballot, Pops would have won the award by one vote. The baseball writers had snubbed Joe DiMaggio, Rogers Hornsby, Dizzy Dean, and the Pirates' Pie Traynor in their first year of eligibility, and, considering their past voting record on Willie Stargell, it seemed unlikely they would vote him into the Hall of Fame when he became eligible for the first time.

• • •

For years, when a player was elected to the Hall of Fame, he received a phone call from Jack Lang, the secretary-treasurer of the Baseball Writers Association of America. On January 12, 1987, shortly before 9:00 PM, the phone rang at Stargell's home in Stone Mountain, Georgia. When he picked up the phone, he heard the voice of Jack Lang telling him that he'd been elected to the Baseball Hall of Fame.

He was so overcome by the news that all he could tell Lang was "I'll be forever in your debt," before breaking down. After hanging up, he hugged his son, Willie Jr., and told him, "I just wanted to play. I didn't go out there to be considered great."

Needing 75 percent of the ballots, Stargell had received 352 of the 427 votes cast by the baseball writers, good for 82.4 percent. He'd become the 200th player voted into the Baseball Hall of Fame and only the 17th to make it to Cooperstown the first time on the ballot. The first two had been Jackie Robinson and Bob Feller. The last before Stargell's election was his home run–hitting rival, Willie McCovey.

In the long history of the Pirates franchise, 10 players who'd spent all or most of their careers in Pittsburgh had preceded Stargell into the Hall of Fame. Along with baseball legends Babe Ruth, Ty Cobb, and Cy Young, Honus Wagner was inducted at Cooperstown in 1939, after being selected as one of the Hall of Fame's first members three years earlier. When Lloyd Waner was inducted in 1967, he joined his brother Paul, who'd been elected in 1952. The Pirates' first great slugger, Ralph Kiner, was inducted into the Hall of Fame in 1975 in his last year of eligibility. Two years earlier, in 1973, the baseball writers removed the five-year waiting period to elect Robert Clemente after his tragic death.

• • •

On July 31, 1988, under a blazing summer sun, Willie Stargell sat on a platform in an unshaded field near the National Baseball Hall of Fame Library and listened to Commissioner Peter Ueberroth introduce him to an overflow crowd that including a contingent of fans from Pittsburgh and many of his old friends and teammates. Stargell was the only player to be inducted that day, though there were 25 members of the Hall of Fame seated on the platform with him, including Ted Williams, Ernie Banks, Stan Musial, and Willie McCovey.

Just before he left his room at the Otesaga Hotel, he wadded up the sheets of paper containing his acceptance speech and tossed them away. He told his son, "I'm going to wing it. I'm going to stand up and talk from my heart." When the moment came for Stargell to deliver his speech, he thanked Commissioner Ueberroth, then, as he had done so often in his career, spoke briefly but managed to touch on just the right things.

Stargell started off by saying that "you're looking at one proud individual," then asked the members of his family to stand up as he called their names. His mother, Gladys, was there with his step-father, Percy, as was his half-sister, Sandrus. He then acknowledged all five of his children: Wendy, Precious, Dawn, Willie Jr., and Kelli. The night before they'd doused their Pops with champagne.

He went on to talk about his baseball family, not only his many teammates over the years, but "the clubhouse guys, the bat boys, the ground crews, the announcers, the media...so fair with me throughout my career." Of the managers he played for during his career, Stargell gave special thanks to the late Danny Murtaugh, whose family had come to Cooperstown for the induction ceremony, and his favorite cheerleader, Chuck Tanner. He also gave special thanks to Joe L. Brown, his first general manager, and Bob Zuk, the scout who had signed him to his first contract.

Stargell, however, saved his highest praise and his fondest words for the two greatest honors in his baseball life leading up to his induction into the Hall of Fame. Though he'd moved just outside Atlanta when he joined Chuck Tanner's Braves coaching staff in 1986, his baseball home would always be the city of Pittsburgh. When he first arrived in Pittsburgh, the city "didn't know an awful lot about me, but I certainly knew an awful lot about Pittsburgh. I knew there was a tradition, a very proud tradition. It wasn't a fancy place because the people are real. If you went out and did what people expected of you, you could win the admiration of that city."

Besides recognizing the honor of playing in Pittsburgh, Stargell wanted to "single out" the one teammate he most respected in his 20 years in a Pirates uniform: "He kinda shined a little brighter and stood a little taller than most men.... I'm talking about a player who has a very special place in my heart and always will, Roberto Clemente." There was no player who taught him more about playing the game with passion and the will to win: "It makes it such a real honor to be here because I'm now alongside of Roberto."

Until this moment in his speech, he'd expressed his gratitude to those he most loved, honored, and respected during his life in baseball, but now he turned to "the young people" just beginning to pursue their dreams. Remembering the projects kid who lived to play baseball, the undernourished teenager in his first uniform, the gangly high-schooler trying to impress baseball scouts, the insecure minor leaguer battling racial hatred, he wanted the next generation to know that he was proof that dreams do become reality.

It was a long journey from Alameda to Cooperstown, but Willie Stargell believed that he'd been born to play baseball. He'd suffered debilitating injuries and humiliating losses, but he never lost his love for the game. He played with and against some of the greatest players in baseball history and knew the joy of winning championships. Today he was being honored as a baseball immortal, but, in his heart, he knew that if someone offered to let him take a few swings at a baseball one more time, he'd ask the commissioner to hold his plaque, roll up his sleeves, and head for a Cooperstown cow pasture to play ball.

Acknowledgments

I have so many people to thank for their help and support, but I'd like to begin with Sally O'Leary. From her earliest days as Bob Prince's secretary through her current role as Alumni Liaison to the Pittsburgh Pirates Alumni Association, she has been the Pirates' guardian angel. Sally supported my work on the book from the beginning and contacted Willie Stargell's teammates on my behalf. She also read each chapter of the book in draft form and, always very gently, corrected my errors and suggested improvements. I don't see how I could have written this book without Sally's help.

I also owe a great debt to Laurie Graham, author of *Singing the City* and a longtime editor at Scribner's. As she was reading through the chapters, Laurie was unrelenting in pointing out the need for clarification and explanation when my poor prose meandered into vague passages. I'm just grateful that Laurie, a die-hard Pirates fan, showed me the same patience and support that she's needed in rooting for her favorite, but often woeful, baseball team.

My Pittsburgh Marathon mentor and baseball buddy, Joe Shuta, was immensely helpful in reading through the chapters. The sports talk show host for *Leading Off* out of Altoona, Pennsylvania, Joe also set up interviews for me with former teammates of Stargell that he'd had on his program and introduced me to longtime sportswriters Paul Meyer and John Mehno, who were very generous in sharing their knowledge of the Pirates and their insights into the team's history.

Of Stargell's teammates and friends, I owe a special debt to Bill Mazeroski for his generosity. I also wish to expressed my deep gratitude, for sharing their memories and stories, to Gene Alley, Tony Bartirome, Mike Easler, Phil Garner, Dave Giusti, Mudcat Grant, Vance and Vernon Law, Steve Nicosia, Al Oliver, Harding "Pete" Peterson, Jerry Reuss, Jim Rooker, Zane Smith, Bob Veale, and Bill Virdon. Willie Stargell's longtime friend and attorney Nat Sokoloff was also very helpful and gave me permission to use his wonderful photographs from the 1980 Willie Stargell Day.

As I was doing my research on Willie Stargell, I had the opportunity to visit old friends again and make several new friends. I'd like to thank Dave Hart, Patti Mistick, Jim Tridinich, and Terry Rodgers for making the articles and photographs in the archives at PNC Park available to me. I'm also grateful to Tim Wiles of the National Baseball Hall of Fame and Cassidy Lent, his research intern, for sending me a complete copy of their research file on Willie Stargell.

During my visit to the archives at the Heinz History Center, I had great help from Art Louderback, Bob Stakeley, and Jennifer Kissel. Gil Pietrzak at the Pennsylvania Room of the Carnegie Library was also very helpful in identifying valuable material. I owe a debt of gratitude to Bob Spoule of Pittsburgh's Forbes Field chapter of the Society for American Baseball Research and for the response of chapter members, especially Paul Adomites, Jim Haller, and Bob Trumpbour. I'd also like to give my special thanks to my favorite broadcaster and good friend, Rob King, who provided me with the DVDs for television specials he had narrated for *Roots Sports* on the 1971 and 1979 World Series and on Willie Stargell.

No writer could ask for a better editor than Triumph Book's Don Gulbrandsen. I first met Don when we worked together on the *50 Great Moments in Pittsburgh Sports* book that I edited with the *Pittsburgh Post-Gazette*'s David Shribman. I'll always be grateful to Don for inviting me to write a book on Willie Stargell, and for his generosity and openness to my ideas and patient, caring, and perceptive editing of my work.

I also wish to thank Jesse Jordan for his diligent and knowledgeable editing in preparing the final manuscript. Jesse turned a normally arduous task into a rewarding experience with his upbeat and caring attitude.

Don, Jesse, and the others at Triumph, especially marketing coordinator Andrea Pelose, made me feel that I was part of a family and deserve Stargell Stars.

My wife, Anita, has been there for me from the very beginning. She traveled with me on my research trips and helped with the selection and gathering of materials for the book. She listened with infinite patience to my stories about Willie Stargell and encouraged me when I became frustrated with my work on the book. When Anita agreed to marry me, I considered myself the luckiest man on the face of the earth. She's been the perfect companion ever since and has even forgiven me for raising our three kids, Anne, Amy, and Stephen, as Pirates fan.

Notes

Chapter One: Why Won't Time Stand Still

All-Star catcher Jason Kendall: Editorial, "The Spirit of Stargell," *Pittsburgh Post-Gazette*, April 10, 2001.

Moved almost to tears: Charles Sheehan, "Pirates Unveil Statue of Stargell," *USA TODAY*, April 9, 2001.

By the end of the 1985 season: David Nightingale, "The Pirate Problem," *The Sporting News*, September 9, 1985.

McClatchy, regarded as an outsider: Bob Smizik, "Pops Is Home" *Pittsburgh Post-Gazette*, February 12, 1997.

That phone call led: Mike Dodd, "Stargell Returns to Pirates As Assistant to GM," *USA TODAY*, February 12, 1997.

When Stargell first received: "Pops Is Home."

In his dedication to Jim Rooker: Interview with Jim Rooker.

In his dedication to Sally O'Leary: Interview with Sally O'Leary.

Stargell admitted at the news conference: Mark Stacy, "Stargell Returns; All's Well," Stargell archives, PNC Park, March 8, 1983.

At spring training in Bradenton: Bob Hertzel, "Stargell Is Still Throwing His Weight Around in Pirates Camp," *Pittsburgh Press*, February 26, 1984.

But Stargell was eager: Mickey Fufari, "Stargell Back to Coach Bucs," *Dominion Post*, June 15, 1985.

Tanner told his players: Dejan Kovacevic, "Chuck Tanner, Popular Pirates Manager, Dies at 82," *Pittsburgh Post-Gazette*, May 29, 2012.

As a player, he said he'd never manage: "Stargell Wants to Manage," *Albany Times Union*, July 25, 1985.

Stories began circulating: James Forr, "Willie Stargell," SABR Bio Project (online), pp. 1-8.

Chuck Tanner was so upset: Forr, "Willie Stargell."

Besides the booing incident: Forr, "Willie Stargell."

Just before the Pirates home opener: Bob Smizik, "Give Him a Break, Don't Boo Bonds," *Pittsburgh Post-Gazette*, April 4, 1991.

Hall of Fame pitcher: Forr, "Willie Stargell."

Shortening the distance: A Night 4 Kiner, September 19, 1987.

McClatchy remembered: Ron Cook, "Blass Delivers a Final Pitch to Stargell," *Pittsburgh Post-Gazette*, April 15, 2001.

He wept at the Friday: Robert Dvorchak, "Stargell Statue to Grace PNC Park," *Pittsburgh Post-Gazette*, September 30, 2000.

He said that, even after a game: "Stargell Statue to Grace PNC Park."

That night he told the crowd: "Blass Delivers a Final Pitch to Stargell."

Paul Meyer, who was covering: Correspondence with Paul Meyer.

Steve Blass, who just months ago: Gene Collier, "Let's Not Forget Stargell," *Pittsburgh Post-Gazette*, April 7, 2001.

Tim Foli, Stargell's teammate: Alan Robinson, "PNC Park Opens on a Sad Note," *USA TODAY*, April 10, 2001.

The *Post-Gazette's* Gene Collier: "Let's Not Forget Stargell."

When he wandered: "Let's Not Forget Stargell."

One sign read: "PNC Park Opens on a Sad Note."

In a prepared statement: Rob Biertempfel, "Stargell's Death Hits Home in Pirates Organization," *Tribune-Review*, April 10, 2001.

Baseball commissioner Bud Selig: "Stargell's Career Touched so Many," *Tribune-Review*, April 10, 2001.

He was so grief-stricken: Ron Cook, "Stargell Touches 'em All Again," *Pittsburgh Post-Gazette*, April 15, 2001.

National Baseball Hall of Fame: "Stargell Touches 'em All Again."

Joe Morgan, both a longtime friend: "Stargell Touches 'em All Again."

After the service was over: Bill Modoono, "Goodbye, Willie," *Tribune-Review*, April 15, 2001.

Ellis, in an earlier tribute: Willie Stargell Day program, September 6, 1982.

He reminded his teammates: "Goodbye, Willie."

But it was Joe Morgan: "Goodbye, Willie."

A few days later: Johnna A. Pro, "A Stellar Tribute," *Pittsburgh Post-Gazette*, April 18, 2001.

McClatchy called Stargell: "A Stellar Tribute."

Al Oliver simply talked: "A Stellar Tribute."

But the most touching words: "A Stellar Tribute."

Chapter Two: I Felt at Home

Baseball Hall of Fame: Frederick G. Lieb, *The Pittsburgh Pirates*, New York: Putnam, 1948, p. 54.

His most memorable moment: John P. Carmichael, *My Greatest Day in Baseball*, Lincoln: Univ. of Nebraska, 1996, p. 23.

August Wilson wrote: August Wilson, *Fences,* New York: Penguin, 1986, xvii.

Matson, at one point: *Fences,* p. 33.

His wife Christine remembered: Andrew O'Toole, "The Forgotten Pirate Pioneer," Pittsburgh History, Summer 1997, p. 80.

He was so electrifying: Richard "Pete" Peterson, "Growing Up With Clemente," *Pittsburgh Post-Gazette,* April 17, 2005.

When Les Biederman: "Growing Up With Clemente."

When Clemente, at the age: "Growing Up With Clemente."

He remembered that: Luis Rodriguez-Mayoral, "Willie Stargell," typed manuscript in Stargell holdings at PNC Park.

Stargell told the crowd: Bob Smizik, "A Day for Roberto," *Pittsburgh Post-Gazette,* July 9, 1994.

Instead of addressing the crowd: "A Day for Roberto."

Clemente played a pivotal role: "Growing Up With Clemente."

He didn't experience: Bob Adelman and Susan Hall, eds., *Out of Left Field,* New York: Two Continents, 1976, p. 20.

It was an area: Willie Stargell and Tom Bird, *Willie Stargell: An Autobiography,* New York: Harper & Row, 1984, p. 62.

In his autobiography: Willie Stargell, p. 65.

In an interview: Eliot Asinof, "Where I Come From, Where I'm Going," *Sport,* April 1980, pp. 29-36.

Sanguillen spoke for: "How Sweet It Is," Root Sports documentary.

Around the third: Bruce Markensen, *The Team That Changed Baseball,* Yardley, PA: Westholme, 2006, p. 110.

Dick Young, writing for: "Young Ideas," April 24, 1971.

Like Clemente in 1960: *Out of Left Field,* p. 216.

Stargell preferred: Willie Stargell: *Willie Stargell: An Autobiography,* p. 154.

He told Les Biederman: "Ghetto Work Intrigues Willie Stargell," p. 16.

Two weeks after: Randy Roberts, *Pittsburgh Sports,* p. 150.

The flamboyant Pirate: Michelle Pilecki, "Go Spread Some Chicken on the Hill," *Pittsburgh Post-Gazette,* July 6, 1973.

Mudcat Grant remembered: Dick Young, "Young Ideas," *New York Daily News,* June 24, 1971.

In Dock Ellis: "Doing Time," p. 169.

In an interview: Lacy Banks, "Big Man, Big Heart, Big Man," p. 134.

At the end: Charley Feeney, "Clemente Award Given to His Ex-Mate Willie," *The Sporting News,* April 27, 1974.

Stargell told Pittsburgh: "Stargell Secure on First Base in the Game of Life," *Pittsburgh Press,* January 21, 1977.

Four of the Writers: "Stargell, Hernandez, in a Surprise Vote, Share the M.V.P.," *New York Times,* November 11, 1979.

Lowell Ridenbaugh: "Stargell No. 1 in '79," *The Sporting News*, January 12, 1979, p. 3.

The cover of: "Two Champs From the City of Pittsburgh," *Sports Illustrated*, December 24, 1979.

Stargell, who wore: "Dr. Willie," *Beaver County Times*, April 16, 1980.

When asked to narrate: Eastman School of Music public relations release, August 11, 1982.

After the premiere: "Stargell Hits Homer As Narrator for King," January 19, 1983.

After a minute: John Perrotto, "The Reluctant Hero," in *The Pirates Reader*, ed. Richard Peterson, *The Pirates Reader*, Pittsburgh: Univ. of Pittsburgh, 2003, p. 320.

When Mazeroski: Bill Mazeroski Statue Dedication, YouTube, September 5, 2010.

In 1971, Mazeroski: "My Sixteen Years with Roberto Clemente," *Sports*, November, 1971, p. 61.

When Stargell joined: *Willie Stargell: An Autobiography*, pp. 99-100.

Chapter Three: A Tall, Skinny Kid

Of Earlsboro's history: Oklahoma Historical Society digital library.

In his autobiography: *Willie Stargell: An Autobiography*, p. 5. Stargell also links himself with Thorpe by claiming in the opening pages of his autobiography that his "great-grandmother was a Seminole squaw." p. 4.

In his autobiography: *Willie Stargell: An Autobiography*, p. 6.

Paul and Lloyd: Lawrence Ritter, *Glory of Their Times*, New York: William Morrow, 1984, p. 332.

That Lucy didn't: *Willie Stargell: An Autobiography*, p. 13.

While his Encinal: *Willie Stargell: An Autobiography*, p. 42.

With his long: "Stargell," *Roots Sports* documentary.

He described himself: Charley Feeney column, *Pittsburgh Post-Gazette*, 1971.

Stargell loved socializing: *Willie Stargell: An Autobiography*, p. 49.

Years later, Bartirome: Interview with Tony Bartirome.

The air inside: *Willie Stargell: An Autobiography*, p. 63.

Another future major leaguer: Interview with Gene Alley. See also Willie Stargell Day, September 6, 1982, program.

Pirates manager: Bill Ballew, *Baseball in Asheville*, Charleston SC: Arcadia, 2003, p. 51.

When Dick Groat: Willie Stargell Day, September 6, 1982, program.

Bill Mazeroski remembered: "Stargell," *Roots Sports* documentary.

Bill Virdon: Interview with Bill Virdon.

In his October 1964 book: *October 1964*, New York: Random House, 1995, p. 115.

He remembered waiting: *Willie Stargell: An Autobiography*, p. 83.
Believing that the demotion: Interview with Bob Veale.
Ron Brand, Stargell's: Willie Stargell Day, September 6, 1982, program.
The caption read: See photo section.
Once Stargell: *Willie Stargell: An Autobiography*, p. 89.

Chapter Four: Now Batting for Pittsburgh

He was so lacking: "Stu Miller," *Baseball: The Biographical Encyclopedia*, New York: Total/ *Sports Illustrated*, 2000, p. 784-785.
In his autobiography: *Willie Stargell: An Autobiography*, p. 93.
On April 23, brief article in *The Sporting News*, PNC archives.
In an interview: *The Sporting News*, July 4, 1964.
In his autobiography: *Willie Stargell: An Autobiography*, p. 106.
Writing in the: Colleen Hroncich, *The Whistling Irishman*, Philadelphia: Sports Challenge, 2010, p. 162.
After the game: "Willie's Three Homers, Cardwell's Pitching Spark Rout, 13–3," *Pittsburgh Press*, June 25, 1965, p. 27.
He'd watched Stargell: Interview with Vernon Law.
He thought that: Les Biederman, "Surgeons Give Willie Stargell 'New Knee,'" *Pittsburgh Post-Gazette*, November 13, 1965.
He claimed that: "Surgeons Give Willie Stargell 'New Knee.'"
After his struggles: Joe Helling, "Stargell Learned to Go With Pitch," *Houston Post*, July 24, 1966.
Stargell said he swung: "Stargell Not Upset by Failure to Set League Hit Record," *Los Angeles Herald Examiner*, July 8, 1966.
Later, he expressed: Les Biederman, "Stargell Humbled by His Own Success," *The Sporting News*, September 17, 1966, p. 3.

Chapter Five: You Have to Fail

The team had been bothered: *The Whistling Irishman*, p. 164.
When Murtaugh took over: "Roamin' Around," September 12, 1967.
Brown was also: "How Sweet It Is! '71 Pirates," *Roots Sports* documentary.
Near the end: "Roamin' Around," September 12, 1967.
Just before Brown: Les Biederman undated article in PNC archives.
Stargell felt: Les Biederman, "Stargell Raps for Attention with Three-Homer Salute," *The Sporting News*, June 8, 1968.
That Stargell was: "Ghetto Work Intrigues Willie Stargell," August 10, 1968, p. 16.
The quality that: Interview with Al Oliver.
He recalled that: *The Whistling Irishman*, p. 167.

He told Pittsburgh: "Stargell Will Enjoy Happy Hunting Ground," article in PNC Park archives.

After writing his: Bill Christine, "Willie's Will," *Pittsburgh Post-Gazette*, January, 1970.

Chapter Six: Going for All the Marbles

Mazeroski told reporters: Charley Feeney, "Stargell Team Outsmarts Maz," *Pittsburgh Post-Gazette*, March 2, 1970.

As for Dave: Daniel Malloy, "Obituary: Dave Ricketts/ Former Catcher, Coach for Pirates, Cardinals," *Pittsburgh Post-Gazette*, July 15, 2008.

When the Tour ended: Dick Young, "How Stargell's Saigon Visit Made Him a Better Hitter," *New York Daily News*, April 6, 1971.

Even Bob Prince: Jim O'Brien, "Willie at the Front," April 26, 1971, PNC archives.

Once he was home: Charley Feeney, "Graveyard Strolls Keep Slugger Stargell Slim." *The Sporting News*, April 22, 1971. See also "How Stargell's Visit Made Him a Better Hitter,."

To stay in shape: "Graveyard Strolls Keep Slugger Stargell Slim."

He said that after: "Graveyard Strolls Keep Slugger Stargell Slim."

When Murtaugh saw: "How Stargell's Saigon Visit Made Him a Better Hitter."

After a few weeks: *The Whistling Irishman*, p. 174.

In 1970, Oliver: Bruce Markusen, *The Team That Changed Baseball*, Yardley, PA: Westholme, 2006, p. 17.

Brown went so far: *The Team That Changed Baseball*, p. 23.

During the off-season: "Graveyard Strolls Keep Slugger Stargell Slim."

Chapter Seven: If He's Going to Be a Man

He told Phil: "Pirate Loss to Dodgers Dims Stargell's Feat," April 28, 1971, p. 76.

During his two-week: Colleen Hroncich, *The Whistling Irishman*, p. 176.

Two months after: "Stargell: You Can't Think Homers," *The Star-Ledger*, July 13, 1971.

Phillies Shortstop: Frank Fitzpatrick, "Blast from the Past," *Pittsburgh Post-Gazette*, June 30, 2003, p. c-6.

Hobbling, twitching: "On the Lam with the Three Rivers Gang," *Sports Illustrated*, August 2, 1971, p. 17.

Years later: *A Pirate for Life*, p. 126.

For all the humor: "On the Lam with the Three Rivers Gang," pp. 14-17.

Now at their lowest: *The Team That Changed Baseball*, p. 101.

Grant was one: Interview with Mudcat Grant.

In an interview: "Stargell: You Can't Think Homers," July 17, 1971.

In the clubhouse: *The Team That Changed Baseball*, p. 116.

His locker was: Interview with Dave Giusti.

Blass was excited: Steve Blass, *A Pirate for Life*, Chicago: Triumph, 2012, p. 133.

Later, when a reporter: "Stargell Still Cool Despite Slump," October 11, 1971, PNC archives.

Dock Ellis Remembered: "How Sweet It Is! '71 Pirates," *Roots Sports* documentary.

He could very: *Willie Stargell: An Autobiography*, p. 148.

A chorus of: *A Pirate for Life*, p. 136.

An article in: *The Whistling Irishman*, p. 181-182.

After the game: "How Sweet It Is, '71 Pirates,"

A headline in: *The Team That Changed Baseball*.

He told a doubting: *The Whistling Irishman*, p. 186.

In his autobiography: *Willie Stargell: An Autobiography*, p. 149.

When Stargell greeted: *The Team That Changed Baseball*, p. 148.

Murtaugh, however: *The Team That Changed Baseball*, p. 160.

It was fitting: *The Team That Changed Baseball*, p. 160.

When asked by: "Clemente Drives Pirates to Title," *Pittsburgh Press*, October 18, 1971.

In a telling: Roger Angell, "Wilver's Way," *New Yorker*, October, 1979.

Chapter Eight: Adios, Amigo Roberto

On November 23: *The Whistling Irishman*, p. 199.

Dr. Joseph Finegold: "Sidelights on Sports," February 14, 1972.

Willie Stargell was: "Playing Games," April 12, 1972.

After telling them: David Maraniss, *Clemente*, New York: Simon & Shuster, 2006, p. 284.

He told Blass: *A Pirate for Life*, p. 105.

He told reporters: Maraniss, *Clemente*, p. 348.

In his biography: *Clemente*, p. 349.

Stargell then spoke: *Clemente*, p. 349.

Brown believed that: "Stargell Could Be Buc Leader," January 24, 1973.

Bob Smizik, in: "Stargell Lacks Finishing Touch," March 11, 1973.

Murtaugh responded: *Willie Stargell: An Autobiography*, p. 159.

Stargell, however, remained: *Out of Left Field*, p. 100.

On September 6: *Out of Left Field*, p. 164.

In a column: "Bucs' Leader? Stargell Fills Role by Example," October 6, 1973.

In an interview: *Out of Left Field*, p. 124.

When Murtaugh replaced: *Out of Left Field*, p. 170.

At clubhouse meetings: Interview with Jim Rooker.

Remembering his disappointment: "Stargell Hoping for '73 M.V.P. Award," *New York Times*, October 14, 1973.

Chapter Nine: Climbing Back to the Top

The Pirates had: Dave Finoli and Bill Ranier, eds., *The Pittsburgh Pirates Encyclopedia*, Champaign, IL: Sports Publishing, 2003, p. 174.

Instead of waiting: Donald Hall, *Dock Ellis in the Country of Baseball*, New York; Simon & Shuster, 1989, pp. 35-37.

In the August 6: "Stargell's 'Bland' Book Turns Out to Be a Sizzler," p. 6.

The book was especially: Stargell, at one point, talks about getting "two women pregnant in 1962" and marrying the one he'd "known the longest," p. 53. Later in the book, his wife Delores says, "I was just another one of Willie's victims. I got pregnant, too." p. 58.

The reviewer for: John Leonard, *New York Times Book Review*, October 17, 1976.

A Photograph with: "Pirates Clinch Pennant; The Night Chicago Died," *Tribune Review*, October 3, 1974.

When Stargell first: *Willie Stargell: An Autobiography*, p. 162.

Murtaugh told the press: Luke Quay, "Who's on First?—Stargell, That's Who," March 28, 1975, PNC archives.

Disappointed that Stargell: Donald Hall, *Dock Ellis in the Country of Baseball*, p. 295-296.

He'd already made it: "Bucs' Stargell Feels Frisky at Age 35," *The Sporting News*, November 22, 1975.

He told the: *The Whistling Irishman*, p. 225.

The Post-Gazette's: "The Prince of Pittsburgh," June 9, 1995.

In his autobiography: *Willie Stargell: An Autobiography*, p. 163.

Chapter Ten: Overcoming Adversity, While Displaying Character

In an interview: "The Long Week of Torture for Willie Stargell," June 2, 1976.

Dock Ellis asked: Norm Vargo, "Ellis Claims Vet Stargell Would Be Great AL 'DH'," July 21, 1976, PNC archives.

He told reporters: *The Whistling Irishman*, p. 228.

In his autobiography: *Willie Stargell: An Autobiography*, p. 177.

On November 30: *The Whistling Irishman*, pp. 229-231.

He told reporters: *The Whistling Irishman*, p. 237.

In his autobiography: *Willie Stargell: An Autobiography*, p. 139.

Pirate catcher Steve: Interview with Steve Nicosia.

After he came out: "Aging Stargell Still a Buc Dynamiter," May 21, 1977.

Biz Stark, the top: "Body Shop Repairs Stargell's Elbow," PNC Park archives.

After he banged: "Rebuttal with a Bat," June 30, 1978.

Stargell's only comment: "Hero Stargell Breaks 'K' Mark," August 8, 1978, PNC Park archives.

In his autobiography: *Willie Stargell: An Autobiography*, p. 188.

Named after: "Stargell Honored with Baseball's Hutch Award," November 22, 1978.

Chapter 11: We Are Family

In 1979, the Pirates, "The 1979 Pirates: A Family Affair," *Roots Sports* documentary.

Though his teammates: Interviews with Jim Rooker and Phil Garner.

Phil Garner said: Interview with Phil Garner.

Kent Tekulve, who: "The 1979 Pirates: A Family Affair."

For the rest of: *Willie Stargell: An Autobiography*, p. 203.

After Pops embraced: *The Pittsburgh Pirates Encyclopedia,* p. 189.

On August 11: "The 1979 Pirates: A Family Affair."

Roger Angell, covering: "Wilver's Way," October. 1979.

In the bottom: "The 1979 Pirates: A Family Affair."

So they needed: "The 1979 Pirates: A Family Affair."

Sanguillen, who later: "The 1979 Pirates: A Family Affair."

He told his teammates: "The 1979 Pirates: A Family Affair."

In the Sunday morning: "The 1979 Pirates: A Family Affair."

Before the start: "The 1979 Pirates: A Family Affair."

He offered Tekulve: "The 1979 Pirates: A Family Affair"

When Robinson said: "The 1979 Pirates: A Family Affair."

He stopped suddenly: Milton Richman, "Stargell Personifies Pirate Tradition," October 18, 1979, PNC archives.

Chapter 12: I'm Now Alongside of Roberto

In an interview: "Mrs. Willie Stargell Deserves Gold Star," March 30, 1980.
In January 1993, Stargell married Margaret Weller. She was the executive director of the Crisis Line-Open House, a youth and rape counseling center in Wilmington, N.C. It was his third marriage.

He licked the icing: "Cake in the Face for Cap'n Willie," March 7, 1980, PNC Park archives.

Afterwards, Bill Robinson: Bob Osbourne, "Festive, for a While," April 15, 1980.

They also announced: "Special Announcement Concerning Willie Stargell Day," Publicity Department release, July 8, 1980.

Among the many: Publicity Department release, July 8, 1980.

Embracing his mother: "His 'Day' Brings Tears to Willie," *Tribune Review,* July 21, 1980.

In his autobiography: *Willie Stargell: An Autobiography*, p. 228.

Afterward, Bill Madlock, ".... Minus Willie," *Beaver County (Pa.)Times,* September 12, 1980.

They were going: "....Minus Willie."

In an article: "Perennial Kid Stargell (40) Getting the Old Spring Itch," February 14, 1981.

He qualified his: Ron Cook, "Stargell Forecast a Bit Brighter," *Beaver County (Pa) Times,* April 1, 1981.

On June 10: Burt Solomon, ed., *The Baseball Timeline,* New York: DK, 2001, p. 843.

The Stargell Foundation: A year later the Commonwealth of Pennsylvania ordered the Stargell Foundation to stop soliciting funds. In 1984, the foundation sold off its remaining assets and closed its doors after 20 years of operation. In 1985, Stargell faced another threat to his reputation when Dale Berra accused him of passing out amphetamines in the clubhouse. After denying the charge, Stargell was exonerated by Commissioner Peter Uberroth, who thought the charge was ridiculous.

In his autobiography: *Willie Stargell: An Autobiography*, p. 239.

The program also: "Willie Stargell Day, September 6, 1982."

Steve Blass expressed: "Willie Stargell Day."

Bill Madlock remembered: "Willie Stargell Day."

Grant Jackson simply: "Willie Stargell Day."

Morgan's tribute was: "Willie Stargell Day."

Covering the event: "Love Feast: Pirate Players, Fans, Pay Stargell Tribute," September 7, 1982.

The Pirate management: Dan Donovan, "Stargell Act Tough One to Follow," *Pittsburgh Post-Gazette*, September 7, 1982.

He thanked the: "Stargell Act Tough One to Follow."

With the Pirates: "Love Feast."

For what Paul Smith: "Stargell: Someone Special," October 4, 1982.

As Paul Smith: "Stargell: Someone Special."

When asked what: Alan Robinson, "Tanner: Hall of Fame Made for Players Like Stargell," January 13, 1988, PNC Park archives.

He was so overcome: Bob Hertzel, "Hall of Fame Stirring Hit for Stargell," *Pittsburgh Post-Gazette*, January 13, 1988.

He told his son: Hal Bodley, "Honored Stargell Prepared to Give Back to Baseball," *USA TODAY*, August 1, 1988.

Stargell started off: "Wilver Dornel Stargell—Induction Speech," July 31, 1988.

He went on to: "Wilver Dornel Stargell—Induction Speech."

When he first arrived: "Wilver Dornel Stargell—Induction Speech."

Besides recognizing the: "Wilver Dornel Stargell—Induction Speech."

Until this moment: "Wilver Dornel Stargell—Induction Speech."

Selected Bibliography

Books

Adelman, Bob and Susan Hall. *Out of Left Field: Willie Stargell and the Pittsburgh Pirates.* New York: Two Continents Publishing, 1976.

Ballew, Bill. *Baseball in Asheville.* Charleston, SC: Arcadia, 2003.

Blass, Steve, with Erik Sherman. *A Pirate for Life.* Chicago: Triumph Books, 2012.

Carmichael, John. *My Greatest Day in Baseball.* Reprint, Lincoln: University of Nebraska Press, 1973.

Finoli, David and Bill Ranier, eds. *The Pittsburgh Pirates Encyclopedia.* Champaign: Sports Publishing, 2003.

Halberstam, David. *October 1964.* New York: Random House, 1995.

Hall, Donald, with Dock Ellis. *Dock Ellis in the Country of Baseball.* New York: Simon & Shuster, 1989.

Honig, Donald. *The October Heroes.* Lincoln: University of Nebraska Press, 1979.

Hroncich, Colleen. *The Whistling Irishman: Danny Murtaugh Remembered.* Philadelphia: Sports Challenge, 2010.

Lieb, Frederick. *The Pittsburgh Pirates.* New York: G. P. Putnam, 1947.

Lorant, Stephan. *Pittsburgh: The Story of an American City.* Lenox, MA: Authors Edition, 1975.

Maraniss, David. *Clemente: The Passion and Grace of Baseball's Last Hero.* New York: Simon & Shuster, 2006.

Markusen, Bruce. *The Team That Changed Baseball: Roberto Clemente and the 1971 Pirates.* Yardley, PA: Westholme, 2006.

McCollister, John. *The Bucs: The Story of the Pittsburgh Pirates.* Kansas City, MO: Addax, 1998.

O'Brien, Jim and Marty Wolfson, eds. *Pittsburgh: The Story of the City of Champions.* Pittsburgh: Wolfson, 1980.

Peterson, Richard, ed. *The Pirates Reader.* Pittsburgh: University of Pittsburgh Press, 2003.

Ritter, Lawrence. *The Glory of Their Times.* New York: William Morrow, 1984.

Roberts, Randy. *Pittsburgh Sports: Stories from the Steel City.* Pittsburgh: University of Pittsburgh Press, 2000.

Sahadi, Lou. *The Pirates: "We Are Family."* New York: Times, 1980.

Stargell, Willie, and Tom Bird. *Willie Stargell: An Autobiography.* New York: Harper & Row, 1984.

Wilson, August. *Fences.* New York: Penguin, 1986.

Magazine Articles

Angell, Roger, "Wilver's Way," *The New Yorker,* October, 1979, reprinted in *Late Innings: A Baseball Companion,* New York: Ballantine, 1982, pp. 191-226.

Asinof, Eliot, "Where I Come From, Where I'm Going," *Sport,* pp. 29-32.

Banks, Lacy. "Big Man, Big Bat, Big Heart," *Ebony,* October 1971, pp. 133-137.

Blount, Roy. "On the Lam with the Three Rivers Gang," *Sports Illustrated,* August 2, 1971, pp. 12-17.

Fimrite, Ron, "Two Champs From the City of Pittsburgh," *Sports Illustrated,* December 24, 1979 (see the online *SI* Vault).

Mazeroski, Bill, as told to Phil Musick, "My Sixteen Years with Roberto Clemente," *Sport,* November, 1971, pp. 61-63, 110-111.

O'Toole, Andrew, "The Forgotten Pirate Pioneer," *Pittsburgh History,* Summer 1997, pp. 77-81.

Nightingale, Bob, "The Pirate Problem," *The Sporting News,* September 9, 1985, pp. 2-3, 25.

Other Sources

Baseball Almanac (online).

Baseball Reference (online).

A Night 4 Kiner (souvenir program), September 19, 1987.

Pittsburgh Pirates 1963 Yearbook.

Pittsburgh Pirates Spring Training Roster (booklet) 1964–1982.

Pittsburgh Pirates Media Guide (reference), 2007.

SABR Bio Project (online).

Willie Stargell Day (souvenir program), September 6, 1982.

The Baseball Encyclopedia. Ninth Edition. New York: Macmillan, 1993.

The Baseball Timeline. New York: DK, 2001.

The Sports Encyclopedia: Baseball, eds. David Neft et al. New York: Grosset & Dunlap, 1974.

Baseball: The Biographical Encyclopedia. New York: Total/*Sports Illustrated,* 2000.

Roots Sports (TV documentaries), "How Sweet It Is! '71 Pirates," "Inside Pirates Baeball: Stargell," and "The 1979 Pirates: A Family Affair."

Career Statistics

Lifetime Records

Year	G	AB	R	H	2B	3B	HR	RBI	BB	SO	BA
1962	10	31	1	9	3	1	0	4	3	10	.290
1963	108	304	34	74	11	6	11	47	19	85	.243
1964	117	421	53	115	19	7	21	78	17	92	.273
1965	144	533	68	145	25	8	27	107	39	127	.272
1966	140	485	84	153	30	0	33	102	48	109	.315
1967	134	462	54	125	18	6	20	73	67	103	.271
1968	128	435	57	103	15	1	24	67	47	105	.237
1969	145	522	89	160	31	6	29	92	61	120	.307
1970	136	474	70	125	18	3	31	85	44	119	.264
1971	141	511	104	151	26	0	48*	125	83	154*	.295
1972	138	495	75	145	28	2	33	112	65	129	.293
1973	148	522	106	156	43*	3	44*	119*	80	129	.299
1974	140	508	90	153	37	4	25	96	87	106	.301
1975	124	461	71	136	32	2	22	90	58	109	.295
1976	117	428	54	110	20	3	20	65	50	101	.257
1977	63	186	29	51	12	0	13	35	31	55	.274
1978	122	390	60	115	18	2	28	97	50	93	.295
1979	126	424	60	119	19	0	32	82	47	105	.281
1980	67	202	28	53	10	1	11	38	26	52	.262
1981	38	60	2	17	4	0	0	9	5	9	.283
1982	74	73	6	17	4	0	3	17	10	24	.233
Career	2360	7927	1195	2232	423	55	475	1540	937	1936	.282

(*) Denotes League Leader

Championship Series

Year	G	AB	R	H	2B	3B	HR	RBI	BB	SO	BA
1970	3	12	0	6	1	0	0	1	1	1	.500
1971	4	14	1	0	0	0	0	0	2	6	.000
1972	5	16	1	1	1	0	0	1	2	5	.063
1974	4	15	3	6	0	0	2	4	1	2	.400
1975	3	11	1	2	1	0	0	0	1	3	.182
1979	3	11	2	5	2	0	2	6	3	2	.455

World Series

Year	G	AB	R	H	2B	3B	HR	RBI	BB	SO	BA
1971	7	24	3	5	1	0	0	1	7	9	.208
1979	7	30	7	12	4	0	3	7	0	6	.400